UNLOCK

BASIC LITERACY

Emma and Gary Pathare

CAMBRIDGE UNIVERSITY PRESS

CAMBRIDGE
UNIVERSITY PRESS

University Printing House, Cambridge CB2 8BS, United Kingdom

One Liberty Plaza, 20th Floor, New York, NY 10006, USA

477 Williamstown Road, Port Melbourne, VIC 3207, Australia

4843/24, 2nd Floor, Ansari Road, Daryaganj, Delhi – 110002, India

79 Anson Road, #06–04/06, Singapore 079906

Cambridge University Press is part of the University of Cambridge.

It furthers the University's mission by disseminating knowledge in the pursuit of education, learning and research at the highest international levels of excellence.

www.cambridge.org
Information on this title: www.cambridge.org/9781316636497

© Cambridge University Press 2017

This publication is in copyright. Subject to statutory exception and to the provisions of relevant collective licensing agreements, no reproduction of any part may take place without the written permission of Cambridge University Press.

First published 2017

20 19 18 17 16 15 14 13 12 11 10 9 8 7 6 5 4 3 2 1

Printed in the United Kingdom by Latimer Trend

A catalogue record for this publication is available from the British Library

ISBN 978-1-316-63649-7 Unlock Basic Literacy Teacher's Book with Downloadable Audio
ISBN 978-1-316-63648-0 Unlock Basic Skills Teacher's Book with Downloadable Audio and Video
ISBN 978-1-316-63646-6 Unlock Basic Literacy Student's Book with Downloadable Audio
ISBN 978-1-316-63645-9 Unlock Basic Skills Student's Book with Downloadable Audio and Video

Cambridge University Press has no responsibility for the persistence or accuracy of URLs for external or third-party internet websites referred to in this publication, and does not guarantee that any content on such websites is, or will remain, accurate or appropriate. Information regarding prices, travel timetables, and other factual information given in this work is correct at the time of first printing but Cambridge University Press does not guarantee the accuracy of such information thereafter.

CONTENTS

Your guide to *Unlock Basic Literacy*		4
Helping Arabic speakers develop literacy in English		6
Teaching tips		13
STARTER UNIT	The basics	26
UNIT 1	Meeting people	35
UNIT 2	People and things	46
UNIT 3	University life	57
UNIT 4	Different countries	69
UNIT 5	Work	79
UNIT 6	Food and health	90
UNIT 7	Places	100
UNIT 8	Spending	111
UNIT 9	Technology	121
UNIT 10	Free time and fashion	132
Wordlists		142
Acknowledgements		144

YOUR GUIDE TO UNLOCK BASIC LITERACY

UNLOCK BASIC LITERACY

Unlock Basic Literacy is tailor-made for Arabic speakers and provides your students with extra support in:
- left-to-right reading and writing that recycles the language from *Unlock Basic Skills*
- handwriting with tracing exercises, writing lines and extra space to write
- sound and spelling informed by research into learner errors
- key words for literacy informed by research into the academic language students use

UNLOCK BASIC LITERACY UNIT STRUCTURE

The units in *Unlock Basic Literacy* are carefully scaffolded so that students build the skills and language they need throughout the unit in order to cope successfully with the final listening and writing tasks.

LISTENING AND READING 1
LISTENING AND READING 2
LISTENING AND READING 3

Provides information about the topic, introduces new vocabulary in context and focuses on the handwriting of these words. It practises listening and reading skills. Where relevant, this lesson also includes a focus on Sound and Spelling, which will further enhance literacy skills and listening and speaking comprehension. It contains Writing challenge sections and a Spelling challenge section.

LANGUAGE FOCUS

Practises the vocabulary and grammar from Listening and Reading 1–3, focuses on functional language and pre-teaches the vocabulary and grammar needed for the final listening and writing tasks. This lesson also includes a full-page Sound and Spelling section.

LISTENING FOCUS

Features a listening text in an academic context that practises listening skills. It uses the language learned over the course of the unit.

KEY WORDS FOR LITERACY

Features a list of carefully selected, high-frequency and often problematic words. It provides students with an opportunity to practise these in detail with the aim of achieving automatic recognition.

READING AND WRITING

Features a reading text in an academic context that practises reading skills and acts as a model for the final writing task that uses the skills and language learned over the course of the unit.

INTRODUCTION UNLOCK

UNLOCK RESEARCH

UNLOCK BASIC ADVISORY PANEL

Unlock Basic has been developed in collaboration with the *Unlock Basic* Advisory Panel, expert teachers experienced in teaching pre-A1 level EAP students, so we can be sure the course meets your students' needs.

THE CAMBRIDGE CORPUS

Unique research using the **Cambridge English Corpus, the Cambridge Learner Corpus and English Profile** has been carried out to ensure the language provided is the right level and relevant to learners' studies. Our exclusive insights into official Cambridge English exam papers enable us to identify the most common errors that Arabic learners make and provide focussed practice material to give them support where they need it most.

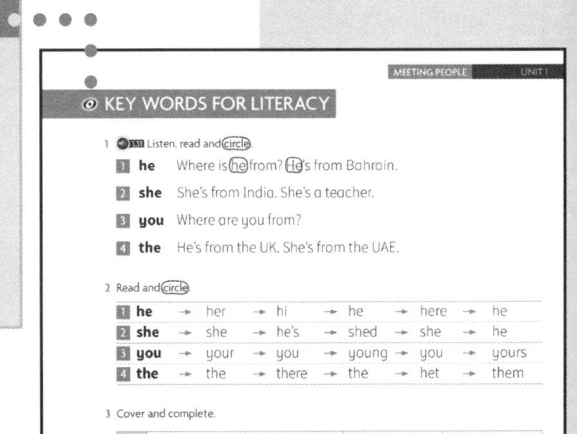

UNLOCK BASIC

COURSE COMPONENTS

- *Unlock Basic* consists of two Student's Books: *Unlock Basic Skills* and *Unlock Basic Literacy*. There is an accompanying Teacher's Book for each.
- Complete course audio is available to download from esource.cambridge.org using the activation code inside the front cover of the Student's Book or Teacher's Book.
- The *Unlock* Teacher's Books contain step-by-step lesson plans, additional activities, common student errors and teaching tips.
- Unit Review tests, mid-level and end-of-level tests are available to download from esource.cambridge.org using the activation code on the last page of the Teacher's Book.
- *Presentation Plus* **software for interactive whiteboards** is available for both Student's Books.

LISTENING AND SPEAKING

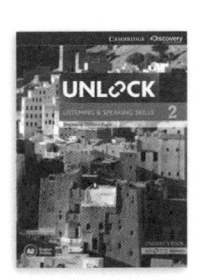

READING AND WRITING

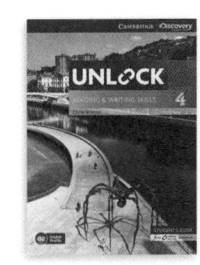

HELPING ARABIC SPEAKERS DEVELOP LITERACY IN ENGLISH

WHAT IS 'LITERACY'?

Literacy, simply put, is the ability to read and write. It can be used to describe competence in a first language (L1) or a second language (L2).

Reading and writing

There is a major difference between the literacy skills of reading and writing, and the other two language skills, listening and speaking.

Reading and writing:

- require guidance, learning, practice and a good deal of effort to master in both the L1 or L2.
- are code based and developing these skills is neither particularly natural nor easy.
- develop through the student becoming skilled at understanding a code (reading) and producing it (writing).

To add to the challenges, reading is usually done in an 'asynchronous' manner (i.e. the writer is not present with the reader, and therefore cannot receive real-time feedback on the extent to which the communication is effective) and 'internal', in that it is not visible to the world, which makes it more difficult to address from a teaching perspective. (This is particularly the case with silent reading). For both L1 and L2 students these skills require dedicated teaching and support, with many hours of effort and practice necessary in order to achieve proficiency.

Listening and speaking

Listening and speaking skills, on the other hand, develop naturally and universally in the L1 context without the need for any formal input or teaching. In the L2, these skills can be acquired with a less concerted effort than that required for reading and writing, through conversation and exposure to aural input. Such input is readily available in comfortable settings like watching TV or listening to the radio. Similarly, trying out newly-developed speaking skills often brings immediate and positive results in an authentic, communicative setting.

The integration of the skills

Reading and writing skills should not, however, be thought of as isolated from listening and speaking. Listening skills, for example, support reading, and in the early stages of literacy development, students can develop their skills effectively through utilizing two channels of input, by reading and listening at the same time. Auditory and phonological processing are also important elements of reading development. These refer to the systems used by the brain to recognize and interpret the sounds the ear hears. They are also applied in reading, in that the reader recognizes and 'sounds out' the sounds and words in their head, enabling access to meaning stored in the brain. Speaking and reading, i.e. reading aloud, can also aid reading development in the early stages.

It is sometimes assumed that literacy skills developed in the L1 are freely available for use in the L2. In contexts in which the writing systems are similar, this is largely true. In other contexts, it may be true in relation to broader literacy skills operating at a text level, such as understanding text layout and drawing on prior knowledge to help with understanding a text. However, depending on the student's L1, using the L1 literacy skills in the second language at a sound, spelling, word and syntactic level may be difficult, as we shall see in the next section.

WHAT CHALLENGES DO L1 ARABIC STUDENTS FACE WITH ENGLISH LITERACY DEVELOPMENT AND WHY?

Students with Arabic as their L1 face a variety of challenges when learning English. The two languages do share some similarities: they are both alphabetic, with letters building to words, and words combining to form syntactic blocks to make sentences, rather than character-based (like Chinese, for example). Both languages have some direct phonetic relationships between sounds and letters. However, as most students and teachers will be aware, the written languages are very unlike each other in other respects, and it is this distance, and the differences involved, which present the challenges for students. A summary of some of the main differences is below.

- English and Arabic have different alphabets.

- Some sounds exist in each language that do not exist in the other.
- There is a direct relationship between sound and spelling in Arabic (it is 'phonetic'), whereas English is less phonetic.
- Arabic is written from right to left, English from left to right.
- The two languages have different systems of punctuation, and English has capitalization whereas Arabic does not.
- Arabic words are structured around patterns of consonants (unlike English words). This leads to different eye movements and 'fixations' (moments when eyes are not moving across the text) from those required for reading in English.
- In Arabic, vowel letters are often not written.
- English and Arabic have different syntactic structures.
- The two languages have different text organization principles.

Each one of these differences makes the transference of literacy skills between the two languages more difficult, and, for L1 Arabic students of English, the result can be issues with all aspects of reading and writing at word, sentence and text levels. These include problems of recognition of letters in relation to sounds, issues with word recognition and comprehension, difficulties with letter formation, spelling and punctuation, and slow and inefficient reading and writing. For reading and writing to become enjoyable, fluent and productive, these differences need to be directly addressed through awareness-raising activities and focused, systematic practice.

WHAT ARE SOME SIGNS OF UNDERDEVELOPED LITERACY SKILLS?

Spelling issues

Teachers who have worked with lower level L1 Arabic students will immediately recognize the signs of underdeveloped literacy skills. Perhaps the most noticeable form in which they appear is spelling errors. Below are examples of errors made by real students grouped to show the possible causes of the error. Some are related directly to Arabic as the L1, and others are more generally connected with literacy development.

1 Consonant structure of words in Arabic

The reliance on consonants to give the meaning of the word can lead L1 Arabic students to remember consonants and their rough order far more clearly than the vowels that go between them. Examples:

pepol — *people*
boday — *body*
cutner — *country*
letal bet — *little bit*
xlrtr — *accelerator*

2 Over-application of rules

This is a common phenomenon with students of all different L1s: a rule is learned, in this case a spelling pattern, and then applied to many different, inappropriate situations. Examples:

Pattern	Examples	Student errors	
spelling /aɪ/ with *ai*	Dub**ai** Th**ai**land **ai**sle Shangh**ai**	on other s**ai**de r**ai**c excirc**ai**z	*on other side* *rice* *exercise*
spelling /əʊ/ with *ou*	although	cl**ou**se	*close*
words ending with *e*	lik**e** hop**e**	work**e** friendship**e** snik**e** out	*work* *friendship* *sneak out*

3 Constructing words phonetically

As noted above, Arabic is more phonetic than English, resulting in a common student strategy of spelling out the sounds, sometimes building onto known words (as in the final example here). Examples:

egzampol — *example*
compeuter — *computer*
vyou — *view*

4 Letter and letter-sound confusion

The letters *d* and *b* are sometimes confused when written (this can also be seen in L1 English students as they develop literacy). Example:

duiesines — *business*

Similarly, the letters *p* and *b* can be confused. However, this latter issue is largely to do with the absence of /p/ from Arabic, and, therefore, the problem also manifests itself in speaking. Examples:

pest — *best*
bob in my head — *pop in my head*

In the final position, /t/ and /d/ can also cause problems. Both these consonant sounds exist in Arabic, but /d/ remains unvoiced at the end of the word, so English words ending in /d/ are often pronounced with the /t/ sound. Examples:

goot   good
bat   bad

5 Approximations

Students often make attempts at spelling based on their incomplete and/or inaccurate recall of the sound and spelling of the words. It is not uncommon to see the same word spelled two or three different ways in a text produced by a student with underdeveloped literacy. Examples:

ides   ideas
raeons   reasons
bauesa   because
sfie   safe

Even the most seemingly difficult to decipher words often have an underlying rationale to the spelling. This can be seen here, particularly with the first word, which combines letter confusion, reliance on consonants and phonetic 'sounding out'. Examples:

dikchr   picture
sand vidyo   send video

Handwriting issues

Other easy-to-see signs of literacy development can be seen in handwriting. Common phenomena are as follows:

- writing unevenly and not on the line

You most to be healthy and do the excircaiz.

(You must be healthy and do exercise.)

- producing back to front letters

I like to take a dikchr and sand vidyo on my phone.

(I like to take a picture and send video on my phone.)

- writing with no space between words

Healsoeats fruitandvegetable.

(He also eats fruit and vegetables.)

- using a mixture of uppercase and lowercase letters, or differently-sized letters

I gaVe you egZAmpoL.

(I gave you an example.)

Reading issues

As mentioned earlier, reading issues are less directly visible to the teacher than writing ones. However, the effects of lack of automaticity (the ability to do something quickly and automatically, without conscious thought) with word recognition are clear, because students read slowly and are unable to engage with the text on any meaningful level. This can lead to a reluctance to read at all.

Asking students to read aloud is a good way to diagnose problems with reading. A student who ignores punctuation is probably reading mechanically, without understanding. Skipping words and a lack of appropriate chunking of language into meaningful units are also signs of lack of comprehension and ineffective eye movement, while misreading words or substituting others which have some similar letters indicate that the student has not mastered word recognition.

Effective readers use what is known as the 'dual-route' method. One of the two routes is to decode and 'sound out' individual letters to form words, while the second route is to recognize whole words almost instantly. Both routes operate together, supporting each other, and both need to be mastered for reading fluency. For new or low-frequency words, students will use the first route, while for many high-frequency words, they must learn to recognize and access the meanings without sounding them out to operate the second route. These high-frequency words are known as 'sight words', and many of them are non-phonetic or follow more complex spelling rules that prevent lower-level readers sounding them out accurately; for example, *know* and *was*. Recognizing the shape of the word and the letters are enough to trigger understanding of the whole word. The more words that students can turn into sight words the better.

Slow reading can prevent comprehension. Our working memory, which we use to hold the meanings of the string of words we are reading, is not able to hold many words at one time, and reading slowly means that earlier parts of a sentence are forgotten before the sentence is finished.

Knowledge of syntax and understanding of text organization are also areas which can affect reading fluency. Fluent readers constantly predict upcoming words based on their knowledge of syntax, and use text organization to help understanding. This knowledge will not be gained easily at lower levels; it is a developmental process that requires attention to the grammar and syntax of the language as well as to the generic features of texts.

WHAT CAN TEACHERS DO TO SUPPORT LITERACY DEVELOPMENT?

Teachers can play a large part in helping students become literate in English, given an understanding of the issues, and a suitable 'toolkit' of activities and strategies. Students need to have frequent opportunities for targeted practice in order to master specific skills, and so develop the secure foundations in literacy on which to build their language learning. The teacher's role is to identify the areas to develop, and provide focused, systematic practice that students feel is relevant, achievable and effective. Teachers need to be supportive and patient, recognizing that students work and develop at different rates, and that achieving literacy in an L2 is a substantial feat. Ultimately, teachers need to value this literacy work, and emphasize its importance to students; literacy skills really are the building blocks for successful language development.

Literacy development in an L2 requires different considerations and input from in the L1. Materials designed specifically for L1 literacy development are generally for young students and also often contain higher-level, less frequent vocabulary which the students will be familiar with from aural input (e.g. stories). Using appropriate materials and techniques designed for literacy development in English as an L2 is the ideal. These materials should be at the language level of the student (in other words, using familiar vocabulary and known grammar structures), and must be age-appropriate in terms of design and themes. At times it may be necessary to introduce a wider range of words to more fully demonstrate particular spelling patterns, but these should be chosen on the basis that they can be efficiently and effectively illustrated, so avoiding the need for further cognitive work on meaning.

We now present a basic toolkit of exercise types for teachers to use to develop literacy. Aside from underpinning the work done throughout *Unlock Basic Literacy*, these are strategies which teachers can adopt and apply to pre-existing materials, making 'just in time' interventions. After listing the toolkit exercises and examining their rationale, we will look at sequences of exercises from *Unlock Basic Literacy*, showing how they support students in developing literacy.

Toolkit – exercise types

- **Tracing** – Students trace letters and then words in order to practise letter formation. Initial directional lines on letters focus students on the correct production. The activity also helps students to notice the word and engage with the meaning, spelling and pronunciation of the word, and its position in the sentence. This latter function is similar to highlighting words with pens.

- **Word shapes** – Word shapes indicate the number and position of the letters in a word, and support the student in the writing of the word. They also encourage the development of whole-word recognition for sight words; that is, seeing and 'reading' the word in one block, essentially the ultimate aim for reading efficiency.

- **Writing staves** – Lines for writing guide early writers as to where to position the writing, and encourage straight, even, appropriately-sized writing.

- **Word stress circles** – The pronunciation and also the spelling of words is reinforced with the use of word stress circles, which identify the number of syllables in a word and also the main stress within the word. By knowing these two features of words, students are able to more accurately read, process, remember and then reproduce (i.e. write and say) them.

- **Identification of word boundaries** – Sentences with no spaces between words encourage students to apply their literacy skills in different ways. They can read for whole words and find the boundaries, or use their spelling/sound awareness to sound out words and find the boundaries. Knowledge of suffixes and prefixes also comes into play here, along with syntactic knowledge at a sentence level, with students able to draw on their grammatical expectations of a sentence.

- **Cover and complete** – This staged sequence for mastering spelling recognizes that students need more than one opportunity to produce a word to begin learning to spell it. They also need to move beyond copying to actually producing it, albeit with word shape support. In addition, the repeated spelling of the word focuses on free spelling from the end of the word back to the beginning ('back chaining'), which provides repeated, effective practice of the part of the word most often forgotten.

Exercise sequences

Unlock Basic Literacy uses regular exercise sequences to develop literacy. The same exercise types and order are repeated to help students become confident with the activity types and truly engage with the literacy focus.

Sound and Spelling

Two or more Sound and Spelling sections are built in to each unit, and they are key components of the systematic literacy development offered by *Unlock Basic Literacy*. The sections take a sound/spelling relationship as the focus, and then present and practise the different elements of this. The sound/spelling relationship focuses on vowels (e.g. *ea*), consonants (e.g. *p*) or consonant clusters (e.g. *br*). Each section, regardless of focus, follows a similar form.

The example here focuses on the long *e* (i.e. *e* after a vowel – in this case *o* or *u* – plus consonant). Exercise 7 highlights one of the spelling patterns beginning with a familiar word (phone), which has been learned as a vocabulary item prior to this lesson. Students listen and trace; meaning is clarified through illustrations. This is then repeated with the *u_e* pattern, again taking a known word as the starting point. Exercise 9 allows students to practise discriminating between short and long vowel sounds in relation to the spellings *o* versus *o_e* and *u* versus *u_e*. This moves from recognizing the differences in the context of words to identifying the actual word heard. Finally, in Exercise 11, students complete the correct spelling, using the audio as input. The list of words moves from the familiar (home, student) to the less familiar (perfume, hole, globe, dune).

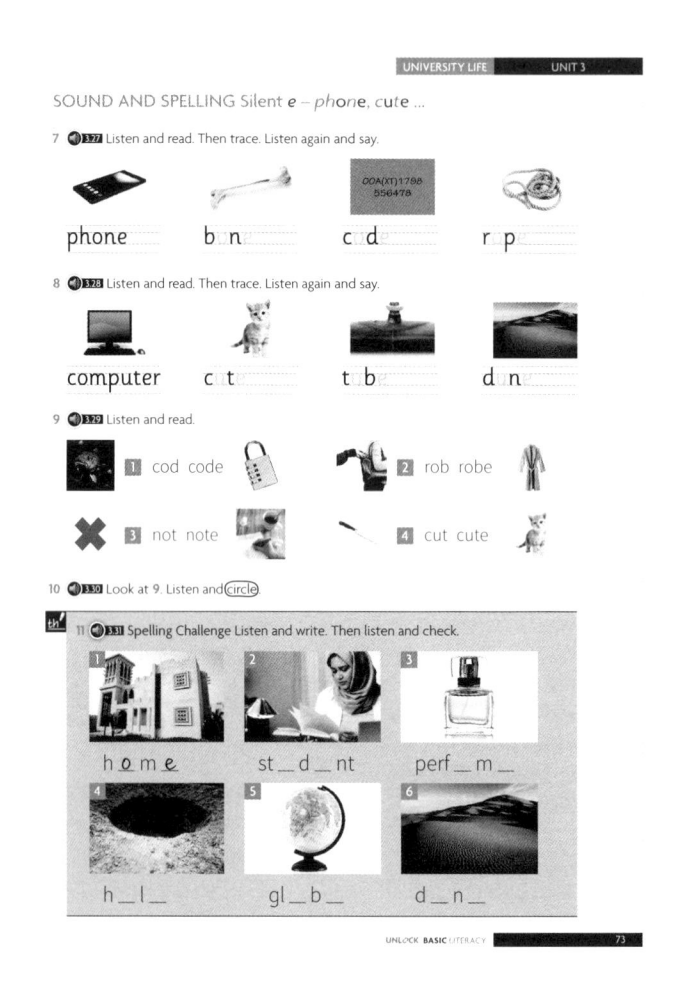

A similar approach is taken in the sequence below, except that here the focus is consonant clusters. First, words from the previous lesson are shown in familiar sentences, with listening and writing support. Students then listen to and engage with further examples of the spelling patterns, using familiar and less familiar words with visual support. Finally, students correct the known words by spelling the consonant clusters correctly within the context of words.

SOUND AND SPELLING *st*, *tr*, *str*

5 Listen and read. Then trace. Listen again and say.

station   train   street

6 Listen and read. Then trace.

The train station is on this street.

7 Listen and read. Then trace. Listen again and say.

1 student   stairs   star
2 tree   traffic   trolley
3 strong   string   straight

8 Spelling Challenge Look and correct. Then listen and check.

1 tirain ___train___   2 satation _____
3 setreet _____   4 sutednt _____

In addition to the full-page Sound and Spelling lessons, occasional additional sections and Review sections appear throughout the book. The additional Sound and Spelling sections focus briefly on spelling patterns which have emerged from that particular lesson and need pointing out for students. The example focuses on three different spellings of /f/.

SOUND AND SPELLING *f*, *ph*, *ff*

3 Listen and read. Then trace. Listen again and say.

1 five   2 photographer
3 officer   4 family
5 phone   6 difficult

The Sound and Spelling Reviews recycle spelling patterns from previous units, presenting them within known words and pointing them out within the context of new vocabulary from the current unit. Students recognize, match, listen and say the words.

SOUND AND SPELLING REVIEW

2 Match and write. Listen and check. Then say.

write   listen   blog   website
app   use   game   webinar

1 fifty ___listen___   2 bag _____
3 ten _____   4 name _____
5 five _____ _____
6 hot _____   7 June _____

Key Words for Literacy

As well as strategic work on spelling patterns and sound-spelling relationships, *Unlock Basic Literacy* also works systematically with 'sight words', identified in the book as 'key words for literacy'. These words are usually high-frequency but with fewer or even no predictable or identifiable spelling patterns. They are often also 'grammar' words, carrying little meaning in themselves, but important for the sentence context. L1 English students – children at school – learn these as sight words; that is, they learn to read and spell them automatically as one block, without decoding them through pattern identification. The approach taken in *Unlock Basic Literacy* is to provide staged engagement with small groups of these words. The sight words in these sections will already have appeared in the unit.

The students' first interaction with the words in the Key Words for Literacy sections gives them the opportunity to recognize the target word in a string of similar words, in particular, words with similar beginnings. This encourages the student to see the whole word: shapes and letters. The sequence then uses the 'Cover and complete' exercise (as outlined in the Toolkit section). Finally, the students produce the words within a sentence context, using audio to check their answers.

Our corpus-informed research tells us that if students learn the 60 words below, they will have mastered more than a third of all the words in academic English.

the	an	other
of	which	his
and	at	its
in	were	had
to	have	only
a	we	two
is	can	there
that	their	may
for	I	would
as	has	some
with	but	will
on	more	no
be	one	he
are	between	into
was	also	about
from	all	time
not	they	when
this	than	who
it	been	where
or	these	both

Conclusion

Some students face real and persistent challenges with basic English literacy and they and their teachers may struggle to know how to approach these challenges. We believe that there are a variety of practical strategies and activity types which teachers can use to help students along the road to mastery of the foundations of literacy. Teachers and students can be confident that addressing literacy using these ideas and methods will be a worthwhile, time-efficient way of developing the literacy foundations that will support students as they progress in their future English studies.

Emma and Gary Pathare
Unlock Basic Literacy Author Team

TEACHING TIPS

UNLOCK BASIC SKILLS AND UNLOCK BASIC LITERACY

For pre-A1 students from a non-Roman alphabet background, learning English presents a number of specific challenges. *Unlock Basic Skills* has been designed to be supportive to students facing this challenge. *Unlock Basic Literacy* follows the same syllabus and focusses specifically on the needs of Arabic L1 beginners, with the aim of developing literacy.

The two course components can be used flexibly to create the course that is right for your students.

Starter Units

The *Unlock Basic Literacy* Starter Unit is designed to meet the needs of students who are unfamiliar with the written form of English. The activities here provide a step-by-step introduction to:

- Reading and writing left to right
- Recognizing numerals and uppercase and lowercase letters
- Forming numerals and uppercase and lowercase letters with correct stroke order
- Awareness of the relative heights and positions of letters
- Consonant and vowel sounds

Use the *Unlock Basic Literacy* Starter Unit ahead of the *Unlock Basic Skills* Starter Unit with students who you know need input in these areas.

Alternatively, the Starter Unit in *Unlock Basic Literacy* can be used to diagnose any remedial work required with:

- Recognizing numerals and uppercase and lowercase letters
- Forming numerals and letters of the alphabet with correct stroke order
- Awareness of the relative heights and positions of letters

You could use the *Unlock Basic Skills* unit section by section and follow up on any challenging areas using the *Unlock Basic Literacy* unit in class, or set as homework for weaker students.

Units 1–10

Each lesson and unit of *Unlock Basic Skills* builds from language input and practice to more extended skills work. *Unlock Basic Literacy* follows the same patterns but focusses on the written and phonological aspects of the language.

Using the books together

In each unit, vocabulary and structures are presented and practised across four lessons of each unit. The typical relationship between the two books is shown in the chart below.

	Unlock Basic Skills Listening and Reading 1–3 Language Focus	*Unlock Basic Literacy* Listening and Reading 1–3 Language Focus
Vocabulary	• Vocabulary presentation • Awareness of sound and spelling, word stress and capitalization	• Recognizing written form of new vocabulary • Written practice with new vocabulary • Focus on sound and spelling, word stress and capitalization
Vocabulary and structures in context	• Meeting vocabulary and new structures in the context of short reading and listening texts • Full presentation of new structures • Controlled written and spoken practice of new structures • Awareness and practice of punctuation	• Reading comprehension of new vocabulary and structures • Awareness raising / review of the meaning and form of new structures • Controlled and highly supportive written practice of new structures • Awareness raising and practice of writing features such as contractions and full forms, word boundaries, word order and punctuation
Writing and speaking	• Freer, often personalized, written practice of new language, such as sentence completion and table completion • Freer more extended spoken practice, often personalized, of new language	• Writing full, often personalized, sentences using the target language from the lessons
Sound and Spelling	• Systematic focus on sound and spelling relationships • Further enhance listening and speaking comprehensions	• Systematic focus on sound and spelling relationships • Focus on automating recognition of sight words

In the final two lessons of each unit academic skills are developed in more extended tasks, bringing together the language from the unit.

Unlock Basic Skills	*Unlock Basic Literacy*
Academic Listening and Speaking • Vocabulary and structures review • Listening skills development with extended listening • Critical thinking preparation for speaking task • Pronunciation • Speaking task	*Listening focus and key words for literacy* • Reviewing written form of vocabulary • Extended listening with written support • Focus on automating recognition of sight words
Academic Reading and Writing • Vocabulary and structures review / Pre-teaching • Reading skills development with extended reading texts with an academic focus (with audio support) • Focus on spelling of vocabulary for writing task • Critical thinking preparation for writing task • Focus on academic writing skills • Writing task – more extended genre writing practice within a supportive frame	*Reading and Writing* • More extended reading comprehension • Reading skills development with extended reading texts with an academic focus • Written error correction tasks • Scaffolded writing tasks – more extended genre writing practice within a supportive frame

With stronger classes you could use *Unlock Basic Skills* lessons ahead of *Unlock Basic Literacy*; covering one Lesson of *Unlock Basic Skills* and then the corresponding lesson of *Unlock Basic Literacy*. Students could work more independently in the *Unlock Basic Literacy* lessons, using the book largely as a workbook. This provides students with individual additional practice and deeper understanding and familiarity with the written and phonological forms. In the Reading and Writing lessons in *Unlock Basic Literacy* you can omit the use of audio in the Reading sections if your group is ready for this challenge.

With weaker classes you could plan your lessons using both books, working systematically through presentations in *Unlock Basic Skills* and then the corresponding practice sections in *Unlock Basic Literacy*. Alternatively, literacy tasks could be set for homework or individual work in class for weaker students.

Using *Unlock Basic Literacy* ahead of *Unlock Basic Skills*, or as a stand-alone course

For students whose language skills are imbalanced (strong speaking and listening, weak reading and writing), *Unlock Basic Literacy* can be used in class or for self-study, to focus entirely on developing their weaker skills more fully.

For complete beginners with little to no knowledge of English, *Unlock Basic Literacy* can be used ahead of *Unlock Basic Skills* or as a stand-alone course in the classroom to develop literacy. In order for students to find the *Unlock Basic Literacy* content manageable, they need additional support with the vocabulary and structures, which are more thoroughly presented in *Unlock Basic Skills*. In the relevant lessons of these teaching notes there are stages for Vocabulary Pre-teaching / Review which exploit the *Unlock Basic* flashcards. Go to esource.cambridge.org to print the flashcards. There are also procedures for each NOTICE feature, which is where the structures are highlighted.

LEAD-INS AND OPTIONAL ACTIVITIES

Throughout the teaching notes in this Teacher's Book are Lead-ins and Optional activities. Some of these activities are very flexible and can be used with a wide range of language. The instructions for this type of activity are included below.

Flashcards

Some of the Lead-ins and Optional activities require flashcards, a very useful teaching tool with pre-A1 students. All of the flashcards needed for the activities have been provided for you to print out and use at:

esource.cambridge.org

VOCABULARY PRE-TEACHING / REVIEW

1 Most of the sets of flashcards have pictures on one side and words on the other. Show students the picture side of the flashcards one by one. Ask students: *What's this?* If students are mostly confident with the vocabulary set, you can move on to step 5.

2 If students do not know the words, go through the cards again one by one. This time also show them the word side as you say the word, and draw attention to the spelling. Ask students to repeat each word after you.

3 Shuffle the cards and display them one by one. Don't say the words; elicit them from the students, allowing them to see both sides of the cards.

4 Shuffle the cards again and show the picture side one by one. See if students can remember the words. If they can't, say the first sound in the word, e.g. /hɒ/ (hospital). Continue until students can recall most of the words without prompting.

5 Use one of the flashcard activities below to test students' recall of the set.

Flashcard contents

Set	Topic
0.1	Numbers 0–10
0.2	Alphabet
0.3	Instructions
0.4	Numbers 11–20
0.5	Sound and Spelling Starter
0.6	Greetings
1.1	Personal details 1
1.2	Countries
1.3	Personal objects 1
1.4	Personal details 2
2.1	Family
2.2	Personal objects 2
2.3	Numbers 20–100
2.4	Academic Reading and Writing pre-teaching (*Unlock Basic Skills* only)
3.1	University subjects
3.2	Days of the week
3.3	Adjectives 1
3.4	Time
4.1	Adjectives 2
4.2	Pronouns
4.3	Adjectives 3
5.1	Jobs
5.2	Phrases 1
5.3	Phrases 2
5.4	Months
6.1	Food and drink
6.2	Phrases 3
6.3	Phrases 4
6.4	Feelings
7.1	Places 1
7.2	Places 2
7.3	Places 3
7.4	Directions
8.1	Personal objects 3
8.2	Calendar
8.3	Frequency
8.4	Spending
8.5	Currencies
8.6	Big numbers
9.1	Phrases for technology 1
9.2	Phrases for technology 2
9.3	People Singular vs Plural
9.4	People
10.1	Free time activities 1
10.2	Free time activities 2
10.3	Clothes
10.4	Colours

Extra cards for *Unlock Basic Literacy* only and extra cards for *Unlock Basic Skills* only

Learning styles and motivation

Including a variety of activities in your lesson planning to suit different student styles is a great way to keep all the members of the class motivated. Regularly changing the pace and focussing attention away from the book will make learning more engaging and less predictable. Most students respond to several styles so the following activities will be suitable for all classes (providing they are suitable for your teaching context).

Flashcard activities

Team pelmanism
Shuffle each set of flashcards but keep them separate. Divide the class into two groups: Group A and Group B. Give each group a set of cards. Ask a student from Group A to hold up a card. Group B students should find the matching card and hold it up. You may wish to give a time limit of 10 or 15 seconds. If Group B are correct, they win the cards. If not, the teams put the cards back in the pile. Then Group B hold up a card and Group A try to find the matching card. The group with the most cards at the end of the game is the winner.

Find the card
You will need some sticky tack and flashcards with words and pictures separately. Stick the pictures randomly around the walls of the classroom. Hold up the word cards one by one. Do not read it aloud. Students sound out the words then move or point to the correct picture.

Memory game
You will need the cards with pictures only. Review all of the words. Then place the cards out of sight. Ask students to work in pairs and write down as many of the words as they can remember. Monitor and help with spelling.

Missing cards
Display the whole set of flashcards at the front of the room. Ask students to turn around or close their eyes, then remove a flashcard and place it out of sight. Students turn back or open their eyes. The first student to tell you which card is missing wins the card.

Slow reveal
You can use this technique with pictures or with words. You will need something to cover cards with, such as a large folder.

Books closed. Hold up the first card behind the folder so that students cannot see it. Slowly pull the card out to your right, so that students can see a little bit of the picture, if you are using pictures, or perhaps the first letter, if you are using words. Encourage students to guess the words on the card. Slowly reveal more and more of the card until a correct answer is given. Award the card to the student who guessed correctly and repeat for all the cards in the set.

Eliciting structures
You will need the cards with words and pictures separately.

Hold up the cards and elicit a known structure with that vocabulary item, e.g. book: *Can I have a book please?* brother: *My brother is a doctor.* This is a very flexible activity which can be used to focus on a specific structure, like a substitution drill. Alternatively, it can be used to review a lot of language at once. If you wish, you can make the activity a competitive game.

Chain sentences
You will need the cards with pictures only. Display a single flash card. Elicit the words and then display a second flashcard next to it. Elicit the first structure which brings the two words together (e.g. *a school and a university*). Display a third flashcard and elicit a chain (e.g. *a hospital, a school and a university*). Now repeat the sequence with one, two and then three flashcards, but elicit the chains of items from the students. Now show a fourth flashcard on its own, and elicit the whole chain. (This is a memory game as well as focussing on the vocabulary and structures in the lesson). Continue for the whole set of flashcards. If no student can remember the sequence, support them by quickly flashing up a flashcard.

Then move on to structure 2. Shuffle the flashcards to keep the activity cognitively challenging. Repeat the procedure above. Finally move on to structure 3.

Sound and Spelling
You will need the cards with pictures only. Hold up the cards one by one. Elicit the letter(s) you are focussing on, e.g. *b*, the sound /b/ and the word *bus*. If you like you could show the matching word card to confirm students' answers. This activity can be used as a competitive team game. Award a point for each correct answer.

Collaborative vocabulary and spelling test
You will need the cards with pictures only. Go through the flashcards and review each vocabulary item orally by asking students to name what they see. Students work in small groups. Ask each

group to choose one student to be their writer. Tell the writers to write the numbers, (e.g. 1–12 or however many items you are testing) on a page in their notebook. Tell students they are going to look at the cards and write the words. Remind students to include any small grammar words, e.g. *a/an* or prepositions.

Display the flashcards one by one. Remember to note down the order you show them in. Students work in their groups to name the things they see and write the words. Groups swap notebooks. Write the answers on the board. Tell groups to check the other group's answers – giving one point for the correct word and one point for the correct spelling. The team with the most points wins.

Other activities

Alphabet vocabulary
Books closed. You will need one or more sets of alphabet flashcards (enough to give each group of three students five cards). Take out the Xs and the Zs.

Demonstrate the activity. Write the letter *c* on the board and look around you. Say: *something in the university, c /k/ …* If students do not volunteer ideas, say: *classroom!* Elicit at least one idea from the students (e.g. *computer, chair*). Divide the class into groups of three and give each group an equal number of the flashcards. Tell the group they need to think of something in the university that begins with each letter they have and write it down. The group that finishes first is the winner. Monitor and help as necessary. When a group finishes, check their list.

Alphabet categories
Write the categories on the board. Concept check these by giving an example and then eliciting two more examples. Write these on the board.

Tell students you are going to call out a letter of the alphabet, and they should think of something in each category which begins with that letter. Demonstrate the activity with the first letter in the list. Only use letters with examples which have been included in the course so far (i.e. the ones in the list.) However, accept any valid words the students give you.

When you have worked through all the letters, elicit sentences with the words on the board. If possible with the set, elicit individual sentences which use words from more than one category.

Alphabet memory game
To review the words that students have learned so far, play an alphabet memory game. Write the alphabet on the board and model the game; for example, point to A and say: *apple*; then indicate a student and the letter B on the board, elicit a word starting with *B*, e.g. *bag*; Elicit a chain of words, e.g. *apple, bag …* . The next student has to repeat the words heard so far and add a new word starting with the next letter of the alphabet, e.g. *apple, bag, computer*. Continue around the class in this way. Keep the chain going as long as possible. If students cannot remember the chain, you could prompt them or start from the next letter in weaker groups.

Aural dictation
Ask students to number the lines in their notebooks (for the number of sentences in the activity). Encourage students to listen carefully. Read the first sentence from the activity box in the unit aloud. Say: *Listen and write*. Read each sentence aloud at a normal speed. Do not pause between words. Repeat each sentence twice, or three times if the sentence is long or the class is weaker.

When students have written all of the sentences, write the sentences on the board. Students check their own answers, or swap notebooks and check each other's answers. Remind them to check punctuation as well as spelling.

Aural dictation (contractions)
Review on the board the contracted form and full written form of a contraction you are going to use. Point to the contraction and say: *Listen*. Point to the full form and say: *Write*. Ask students to number the lines in their notebooks (for the number of sentences in the activity). Encourage students to listen carefully. Read the first sentence from the activity box in the unit aloud. Read each sentence aloud at a normal speed, with normal sentence stress. Do not pause between words. Repeat each sentence twice. Monitor and check that students are attempting to write full forms.

When students have written all of the sentences, write the sentences on the board. Students check their own answers, or swap notebooks and check each other's answers. Remind them to check punctuation as well as spelling.

Aural gap fill
Encourage students to listen carefully. Read aloud the first sentence from the activity box in the unit, replacing the underlined words with a pause. If you like, you could count on your fingers to show there is a missing word. Ask students to raise their hands if they can say the whole, complete sentence. Repeat the sentence if necessary.

Continue the activity with the remaining sentences one by one. You could ask students to write down the missing words rather than say the sentences aloud. With strong classes, you can ask individuals or teams to write the whole sentences.

Running dictation

Make several, enlarged copies of the texts and label them clearly if different students are looking at different texts. Display these in different places around the class, away from where the students are sitting. Students work in pairs or groups of three. One student goes to the printed text and memorizes a few words or a sentence. Then they come back to their group and dictate the text. The other student(s) write down the words they hear. To set up the activity, demonstrate doing this on the board with a student as the writer (if it is appropriate in your context.) Set a time limit, for example, 10 minutes. Tell students to swap roles (writer and runner) every 2–3 minutes.

When the time is up, groups swap papers. Give out the correct texts to each group and ask them to check the accuracy of the writing and award a mark out of ten.

Mingle

Mingling activities are used to practise a variety of exchanges. Here is an example with questions. Ensure students know what question they are to ask by checking with individuals. Encourage students to stand up and walk around the classroom. Demonstrate this type of mingling activity the first time you use it by joining in for the first couple of turns. Use hand gestures to encourage students to circulate. Knock on your desk. Students stop, say hello, and ask their question to one nearby student. The other student replies and asks their own question. When you knock on the desk again, they say goodbye and walk around again. Knock on the desk again, and they stop and speak to a new student.

Alternative to mingling: If mingling activities are not appropriate for your context, ask students to sit in groups in a circle and speak to the person to their left. Then change direction. Then swap seats.

Classroom messages

If students are spread out in the room, ask them to move. They should be close enough to the student next to them to lean over and speak quietly to them. If there is room in your classroom, the students could sit in a circle or a long line.

Speak quietly to one student so that the other students cannot hear. Say a simple, familiar sentence, e.g. *How are you?* Encourage the student to repeat the same sentence very quietly to the next student, and so on. Monitor closely but do not correct students unless they have not understood the activity. When all the students have passed on the message, ask the last student to tell you the sentence they heard. Write this on the board and ask the first student if it is correct. Correct any mistakes as a class. Repeat the activity with the sentences in the activity box in the unit. You may change the order so that that the last student is now the first one.

False information

Students make changes to the material they are working out to create two or three false pieces of information amongst the true information. Students then read this aloud to a partner, a group or the whole class. The other students tell them which information was not true.

Bingo

Draw a grid on the board with two rows and four columns. Tell students to copy the grid into their notebooks. Tell them to write eight of the target items anywhere in the grid. With weaker classes you may wish to write up all of the target items on the board. Read out the target items one by one (keep a record of the items as you do so.). Encourage students to cross out the items in their grid as they hear them. The first student to cross out all their numbers shouts *Bingo!* Check the student's answers; if they are correct, they are the winner.

Text reconstruction

Tell students the subject you are going to talk about. Write relevant question words, e.g. *What, Where* and *What … like?* on the board. Elicit full questions from the students, e.g. *What is it? Where is it? What is it like?* Don't answer the questions. Write them on the board.

Read your text below aloud to the students and ask them to make notes to answer their own questions. Tell them not to worry about spelling and grammar. Read the text aloud twice. Then ask students to share their notes with you. Reconstruct your text on the board as students share different parts of their notes with you.

LEARNING OBJECTIVES FOR PRE-A1 STUDENTS

Learning objectives in the pre-A1 classroom

Although there are no Learning objectives in the *Unlock Basic Literacy* Student's Book, the *Unlock Basic Literacy* Teacher's Book provides lesson-by-lesson Learning objectives which can be used both at the beginning and end of each lesson. Choosing to communicate Learning objectives is motivating to students because the Learning objectives give them a clear way to measure their progress. They also give individual activities within a lesson a clear sense of purpose.

Communicating Learning objectives

Learning objectives tend to be expressed in language which may not yet be familiar or comprehensible to your students. If you speak the students' L1, you could translate the objectives and write them on the board. If you cannot or do not wish to use L1 in the classroom, you could use the following procedure:

Write the examples of the target language on the board and demonstrate what students will learn as below. Read each objective aloud in English as you do so.

Vocabulary sets / Keywords for literacy: Show the flashcards briefly and point to the examples on the board.

Punctuation: Circle examples of the punctuation on the board.

Listening and reading: Use a gesture to communicate the skills whilst indicating the text or the script in the Student's Book.

Writing: Say: *Write* and write the target structures for writing on the board.

Sound and Spelling: Use gestures to indicate the sound and spelling whilst saying the sounds aloud and writing the corresponding letters on the board.

Measuring progress

Monitoring at every stage of the lesson is the key to recognizing how well students are progressing with their objectives. If you have communicated the Learning objectives to students, you can round off each lesson with an objectives review. Encourage students to reflect on the objectives and communicate to you how confident they feel about each one. You could use a sliding scale on the board, for example:

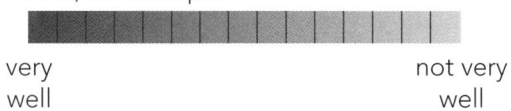

very well   not very well

Gauge the students' feelings regarding each objective and assure students they will get the opportunity to review and practise any areas they are not yet confident in in future lessons. There are also Review tests, which are designed to be used after the students have completed each unit of the Student's Book. Each Review test checks students' knowledge of the key language areas taught in the unit and practises the Literacy, Sound and Spelling, Pronunciation and Writing Skills from the unit. Go to esource.cambridge.org to download the printable Review tests and the Review test audio.

COMMUNICATING INSTRUCTIONS AND DEMONSTRATING ACTIVITIES IN THE PRE-A1 CLASSROOM

Grading your language

It is important not to overwhelm students with language in the classroom. Be particularly aware of common phrasal verbs in your speech. For example, instructions such as **Pick up** your book and **Get up** and **walk around** are unlikely to be understood without demonstration.

Use the simplest, most familiar language you can to communicate with students, but do not grade your language so that it is unnatural. For example, if you are asking questions about a picture, *Where is he going?* will be understood through the meaning of the content words (*where, he, go*); students do not need to be familiar with the present continuous to understand this. This Teacher's Book provides examples of language you can use for particular situations.

Non-verbal communication

Your role as the teacher in the pre-A1 classroom is perhaps more central than at other levels. In addition to reading rubrics aloud, it is important that you demonstrate activities. In general, the non-verbal techniques below can be helpful. Always accompany these with the spoken words.

- Use gestures and props such as books and headphones to communicate rubrics: *read, write, listen, do not write, do not speak*, etc.
- Use culturally appropriate gestures and/or facial expressions to accompany phrases: *That's right. That's not right. What's this? Which one? Is this yours? Whose is this? What's wrong with this sentence? Is this right or wrong? Work in pairs. Work in a group of three.* etc.

- Use gestures or clapping to communicate language points such as contractions, intonation and word and sentence stress.
- Use symbols on the board to communicate: Right (✓), Wrong (✗), Same (=), Different (≠), Ask me a question (< ?]), Say / Tell me / Describe ([>), etc.

Use the examples in the Student's Book to demonstrate the procedure for exercises. Model the activity by demonstrating the example and pointing out relevant sources of information on the page, such as vocabulary sets and grammar tables.

Setting up speaking activities with a model is particularly important. You may wish to take on the role of both students, changing where you are standing to indicate different speakers. Alternatively, you can demonstrate the full activity with a student.

Concept checking

Checking understanding of new lexis with pre-A1 students can seem challenging. However, as new language at this level is often concrete in meaning, it is often a straightforward task. Here are some techniques you can use:

Pictures in the Student's Book and pictures on flashcards *What's this? What are these? Is this (a tree)? Is he old? Is it busy?*

Questions *(go to work) Do I go to work on Thursday?* (Yes) *Saturday?* (No) *Do I go to work in the evening?* (No).

Substitution drills (See the section on Drilling in Teaching Pronunciation, below.)

Similar words You can use words which students have already learned. For example, when learning *photographer*, you can remind students that they know *photograph*.

● COMMON STUDENT ERRORS

Throughout this Teacher's Book there are boxes which tell you about typical errors your students may be prone to (depending on their L1). These are informed by the Cambridge Learner Corpus, a bank of official Cambridge exam papers. The highest frequency errors made by students have been included, allowing you to work on these in a remedial way, should you notice these errors occurring as you monitor.

TEACHING PRONUNCIATION

Unlock Basic Literacy features a focus on Sound and Spelling in every unit. In Sound and Spelling, students focus on common spellings of individual sounds and variations in the way individual letters and combinations of letters are pronounced. Focussing on these common sound and spelling relationships is helpful for accurate reading and writing as well as listening and speaking. There is also a Spelling challenge in very unit.

Drilling

Drilling refers to activities in which the same thing is repeated several times in order to practise it. Drilling new language is important – it exposes students to the sounds of new language, provides a focus on accuracy in a very controlled way and builds confidence with both the form and the sounds in subsequent practice and communicative use.

Simple drills

To conduct a drill, model the target language or play the audio and encourage the students to repeat it. Choose individual students to repeat the words and then encourage the whole group to repeat. You may wish to break down longer phrases into chunks, e.g. *fruit / vegetables* ➔ *fruit and vegetables* ➔ *eat fruit and vegetables*. Focus on word and sentence stress by clapping or punching the air on stressed syllables. With sounds that your students find particularly difficult, model the phoneme then the word, e.g. /fr/ /fruit/ /v/ /vegetables/.

Substitution drills

Substitution drills are a useful technique for practising longer sentences and structures in a very controlled manner. Drill a sentence, for example, *I like driving at weekends*. Then call out a variant of one part of the sentence, e.g. *He*. Then students replace *I* with *He* in the sentence and make any other necessary grammatical changes: *He likes driving at weekends*. In the beginning, choose the same variant part to change, e.g. the subject (*I, He, We You, Ahmed, My father*). As students grow more familiar with the activity you can vary other parts of the sentence (e.g. *walk in the park* ➔ *He likes walking in the park at weekends; not like* ➔ *He doesn't like walking in the park at weekends*.)

Back chaining

Back chaining is used to practise spelling in 'Cover and complete' exercises (see p. 9). It can also be used to practise longer sentences and questions. The procedure focuses on practising the sentence from the end back to the beginning. Write the sentence or question you would like students to practise on the board. Cover it except for the last word. Students practise saying the last word. Then uncover one more word so that the last two words are uncovered. Students practise saying the last two words together. Continue word by word until the whole sentence has been uncovered and the students have practised it. An alternative method is to write the sentence one word at a time, starting at the end, instead of writing the whole sentence and covering it.

WORDLISTS

Although there are no wordlists in the *Unlock Basic Literacy* Student's Book, the *Unlock Basic Literacy* Teacher's Book provides unit-by-unit wordlists on p. 142–143 which can be used both at the beginning and end of each lesson. The wordlists at the end of each unit are composed of the new vocabulary which students have practised in the unit. There are many ways that you can work with vocabulary. Encourage the students to learn the new words by setting regular tests. You could also ask the students to choose e.g. five words from the unit vocabulary to learn. You could also get your students to practise writing the words using the extra handwriting practice pages in the *Unlock Basic Literacy* Student's Book. The wordlists are in alphabetical order, but you can also ask students to focus on particular topic groups of words, e.g. colours or clothes. At the end of each unit, make sure students practise the new words and a selection of words from previous units. If you are using the *Unlock Basic Skills* Student's Book, you can refer students to the wordlists and glossary there.

EXTRA HANDWRITING PRACTICE

On pp. 197–200 of the *Unlock Basic Literacy* Student's Book there are some pages with writing staves for extra handwriting practice. These include the guide lines and direction arrows. See p. 9 for information about the purpose of writing staves. Many exercises in the Student's Book have writing staves provided, especially earlier in the course. You can use these extra handwriting practice pages to give weaker students and classes more support when a Student's Book exercise does not provide writing staves. As the course progresses, you should steadily reduce the use of writing staves so that students do not become overly reliant on them. An extra handwriting practice page is provided on p. 22 for you to photocopy.

DIRECTION ARROWS

Unlock Basic Literacy supports students with left to right eye-movement when engaging with the English language by including direction arrows for some exercises. Students will see the largest number of direction arrows in the Starter Unit.

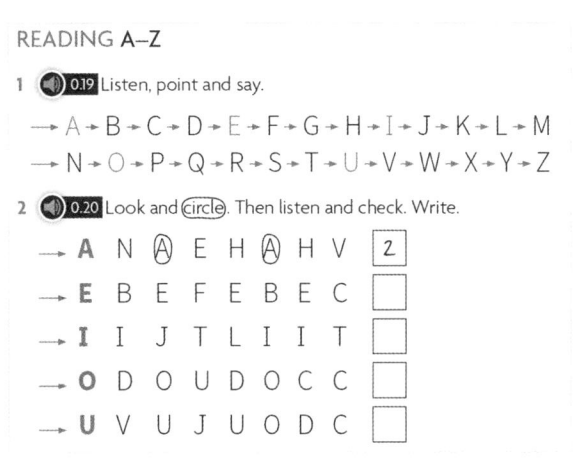

Units 1–5 provide direction arrows in most reading and writing exercises, which are mainly reading and writing exercises where the amount of text is larger. As students' literacy, reading and writing skills improve over the duration of the course, the need for direction arrows reduces and so Units 6–10 contain significantly fewer examples of these, mainly in more challenging writing exercises.

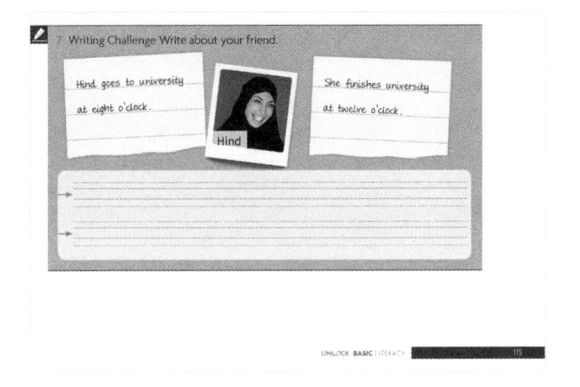

EXTRA HANDWRITING NOTES

MIXED ABILITY CLASSES

Unlock Basic Literacy supports students with different learning abilities and at different levels of English from complete beginners to students who have already had some minimal contact with the English language.

The Starter Unit, which is divided into shorter, more manageable sections with chunks of language rather than lessons, allows teachers to either do all exercises one after the other or to cover sections they know their students need to learn, improve on or revise depending on their students' needs. For more information on the Starter Unit, please see p. 13.

Unlock Basic Literacy also contains more challenging exercises for writing and spelling that can be used with stronger students. For more information on Writing and Spelling challenge exercises, see below.

All of the main reading texts are accompanied by an audio version, especially to assist weaker students. Using these in class is highly recommended for all classes, but you might sometimes decide to leave them out with stronger classes or if you do not have time. You can also use them for homework, by asking students to use them for reading or listening practice and for revision.

Main exercise instructions in this Teacher's Book often provide variations or additional steps in conducting an activity depending on the ability of the students and class. Such variations will start with 'In weaker classes,' or with 'In stronger classes,'.

CHALLENGE EXERCISES

Writing challenge exercises

Every unit has lots of achievable, scaffolded and well-structured writing exercises for students of all abilities in the class. Each unit also contains at least two writing exercises called Writing challenge, which are more challenging and may suit slightly stronger students. These are stand-alone exercises, towards the end of a lesson, that always appear in a box and so are easy to find. They get progressively more challenging from unit to unit, starting from completing sentences with words and moving on to writing between two and four full sentences. With weaker classes, you may decide not to use these, as there are other writing opportunities (achievable to all students) in each unit, or you may decide to do the Writing challenge exercises together as a class. With stronger students, you may wish to ask students to do them if they finish previous exercises earlier (while other students are still working). If your whole class is stronger, you may wish to use them together as a class at the point the Writing challenge appears in the Student's Book. You may also want to give these as homework to some or all of the students in your class.

Writing challenge exercise contents

Unit 1	
Exercise 10, Student's Book p. 32	Write a sentence with your name.
Exercise 10, Student's Book p. 35	Complete four short sentences with words.
Exercise 6, Student's Book p. 37	Write a sentence with your teacher's name.

Unit 2	
Exercise 9, Student's Book p. 49	Write two sentences about your family member.
Exercise 7, Student's Book p. 51	Write two sentences with *Our* and *Their*.
Exercise 6, Student's Book p. 56	Complete two sentences about your friend.

Unit 3	
Exercise 10, Student's Book p. 64	Write two sentences about your studies.
Exercise 7, Student's Book p. 69	Complete a question and write two sentences about a university subject.

Unit 4	
Exercise 7, Student's Book p. 80	Write two sentences about your country.
Exercise 6, Student's Book p. 85	Write two sentences about a city.

Unit 5	
Exercise 10, Student's Book p. 96	Write three short sentences about a person's job.
Exercise 8, Student's Book p. 99	Write two sentences about your city.

Unit 6	
Exercise 7, Student's Book p. 115	Write two sentences about a person's university.
Exercise 5, Student's Book p. 117	Write two sentences about people's eating and drinking habits.

Unit 7	
Exercise 9, Student's Book p. 131	Write two sentences about your city.
Exercise 6, Student's Book p. 134	Write three sentences about a city.
Unit 8	
Exercise 8, Student's Book p. 144	Write three sentences about someone's possessions.
Exercise 4, Student's Book p. 149	Answer three questions in a survey.
Unit 9	
Exercise 7, Student's Book p. 160	Write four sentences using adverbs of frequency.
Exercise 7, Student's Book p. 163	Write two longer sentences with *can* and *but*.
Unit 10	
Exercise 8, Student's Book p. 176	Write four sentences about your free time.
Exercise 7, Student's Book p. 179	Write four sentences about your friend's free time.

Spelling challenge exercises

Each unit in Unlock Basic Literacy has at least one Spelling challenge exercise, which is slightly more difficult than other Sound and Spelling exercises. These are stand-alone exercises that always appear in a box and so are easy to find in a lesson. They get progressively more challenging from unit to unit, starting from completing individual letters in words and moving on to correcting spelling mistakes and writing whole words. Most Spelling challenge exercises have audio support. Just as with Writing challenge exercises, you may decide to adapt the way you use them depending on the needs of your students and class, or how much class time you have. However, it is better to do the Spelling challenge exercises in class rather than at home for homework, so that pronunciation can be monitored and corrected.

Spelling challenge exercise contents

Unit 1	
Exercise 8, Student's Book p. 41	*hat, hot, bill, bell, bag, bug, desk, disk, boss, bus*
Unit 2	
Exercise 11, Student's Book p. 57	*date, lime, cape, pipe*
Unit 3	
Exercise 11, Student's Book p. 73	*home, student, perfume, hole, globe, dune*
Unit 4	
Exercise 7, Student's Book p. 88	*teacher, desert, jeep, beach, family, sea*
Unit 5	
Exercise 10, Student's Book p. 102	*cries, washes, flies, watches*
Unit 6	
Exercise 8, Student's Book p. 118	*dinner, fish, chips, cheese, green, tea*
Unit 7	
Exercise 10, Student's Book p. 128	*start, park, airport, work*
Exercise 8, Student's Book p. 137	*train, station, street, student*
Unit 8	
Exercise 7, Student's Book p. 150	*day, games, train, pay, newspaper*
Unit 9	
Exercise 10, Student's Book p. 166	*play, glasses, blog*
Exercise 10, Student's Book p. 169	*fridge, watch*
Unit 10	
Exercise 7, Student's Book p. 182	*watch, student, drink, lunch*

FONT, LETTER AND HANDWRITING VARIETIES

Unlock Basic Literacy provides opportunities for students to familiarise themselves with different font sizes as well as variations of letters (e.g. *a* and α) and handwriting (cursive (i.e. longhand, more joined) vs print (i.e. block letters)).

Font sizes

Different font sizes are used in all units ranging from smaller ones in exercise instructions to slightly larger ones depending on the purpose of their use. Reading texts contain a range of font sizes so that students are exposed to different styles of texts. Most writing exercises contain a slightly larger or significantly larger font size, depending on the unit, level of difficulty or amount to write. For example, all of the final writing tasks in the units use a larger font size to help students with their handwriting, but Writing challenge exercises have a slightly smaller font size to encourage students to write in a more natural, more literacy-advanced way.

Letter variations

Some letters have a slightly different format depending on their font and whether they are meant to be printed or whether they are supposed to imitate handwriting. Introducing variations of letters is beneficial for students as it will help them when progressing to higher levels where they see different font styles. Please see some examples of variations below:

y and y

ƒ and f

α and a

Cursive vs print handwriting

Unlock Basic Literacy mainly uses print handwriting for texts, instructions and most exercises. Students, however, see examples of cursive handwriting whenever there are handwriting examples given in exercises.

Providing both handwriting types is important in developing literacy skills. Cursive handwriting can be perceived as more natural with run-on words. Showing examples of cursive handwriting prepares students to read different texts with different types of handwriting. It is, however, more challenging to read, so print handwriting is more common in *Unlock Basic Literacy*.

AUDIO SCRIPTS IN UNLOCK BASIC LITERACY STUDENT'S BOOK

Most texts that have an audio version are present in the lessons on the pages of the Student's Book, and therefore have not been included in the Audio scripts pages at the back of the Student's Book. Sometimes, the audio text is slightly longer than the text on the page or contains information that students should not see before the audio is played. In such situations, audio scripts are provided in the Audio scripts pages at the back of the Student's Book.

STARTER UNIT THE BASICS

> **Learning objectives**
>
> - Read and write from left to right
> - Recognize and say basic introductions – *Hello. I'm …*
> - Recognize and write the numerals 0–10
> - Understand basic classroom instructions – *Look. Read. Listen. Write. Point. Say.*
> - Recognize and write the English alphabet (lowercase and uppercase)
> - Recognize and say consonant sounds
> - Gain awareness that individual vowels make more than one different sound
> - Recognize the written forms of numbers 0–10
>
> See p. 19 for suggestions on how to use these Learning objectives in your lessons.

LEFT-TO-RIGHT READING AND WRITING

1 The aim of this activity is to train students to move their eyes from left to right when reading. Draw a line across the board moving from left to right. Add some arrows above the line going from left to right. On the board, point at the line from right to left and say: *Arabic*. Then point at the board from left to right and say: *English*. Focus on the left end of the line by pointing. Say: *Look*. Move your hand across the line to the right end. Exaggerate looking from left to right along the line as you do this. Repeat several times. Leave this line on the board for Exercise 2.

Model looking at the line in the book whilst tracing it with a finger from left to right. Students work individually. Allow some time to repeat the action several times.

2 The aim of this activity is to train students to move their hands from left to right when writing. Draw another line over the top of the line on the board (from Exercise 1) starting at the left. If it is appropriate in your context, invite a few students to come to the board, one by one, to trace the line. Guide them to move their arms in the correct direction.

Model tracing the line in the book with a finger from left to right. Students work individually and trace the two lines. Monitor and check students are tracing the line in the correct direction.

3 The aim of this activity is to familiarize students with up and down directional strokes typical of the Roman alphabet when writing from left to right. Draw the first two lines in the book on the board using a dotted line.

Draw another line over the top of the dotted lines from left to right. If it is appropriate in your context, invite a few students to come to the board, one by one, to trace the lines. Guide them to move their arms in the correct direction.

Students work individually and trace the first two lines in the book. Monitor to check they start and end in the correct place. Students can repeat using the same lines.

Draw the third line in the book on the board using a dotted line. Demonstrate tracing this line. Emphasize starting at the top of each individual line, making a down stroke and then lifting the pen off the line to start at the top of the next line. If it is appropriate in your context, invite a student to come to the board and continue, making sure they follow the correct process.

Students work individually and trace the third line in the book. Monitor and check for correct downward strokes.

Draw the fourth line in the book on the board using a dotted line. Demonstrate tracing the first part of this line. If it is appropriate in your context, invite a student to come to the board and continue, guiding them to move their arms in the correct direction.

Students work individually and trace the fourth line in the book. Monitor and check they start and end in the correct place.

> **Literacy tip**
>
> All English letters start at the top with a down stroke; the pen or pencil moves from top to bottom. This downward movement requires less physical effort and, therefore, such letter formation enables faster and more fluent handwriting. Monitor students' hand movements carefully at the beginning stages of writing to check that students are following this movement. Establishing good habits now will make the learning process faster. Some students may resist if they already have their own method. If so, stress the importance of getting it right if they want their handwriting to be understood.

THE BASICS STARTER UNIT

SPEAKING AND LISTENING *Hi. Hello. I'm ...*

1 🔊 0.1 The aim of this activity is to recognize a basic self-introduction with *hello*. Focus on the photograph. If your students are familiar with some spoken English, you could elicit who the people are (students or friends). Play the audio. Elicit some of the names they heard.

2 🔊 0.2 The aim of this activity is to practise saying a basic self-introduction with *Hello. I'm ...* and gain confidence with the sounds. Focus on the photograph of the man. If your students are familiar with some spoken English, you could elicit who he is (a teacher). Play the audio. Repeat: *Hello. I'm (Mrs/Mr) ...* and model using your own name. Write: *Mr and Mrs* on the board. Point at the photograph of the male teacher in the book and say: *Mr*. Point at the photograph of the female teacher in the book and say: *Mrs*. Drill *Hello. I'm ...* adding various names of students in your class. See p. 20 for advice on drilling.

3 🔊 0.3 The aim of the activity is for students to practise introducing themselves to others with *Hello. I'm ...* Play the audio and indicate students should say their own names. Repeat the audio (or say it yourself) and elicit names from individual students. Then address a student at one end or side of the classroom. Say: *Hello. I'm (your name).* and encourage them to reply using culturally appropriate gestures. Indicate that the student should turn to the next student and say: *Hello. I'm ...* and encourage the next student to reply. Continue until all students have had the opportunity to speak.

READING Numbers 0–10

1 🔊 0.4 The aim of this activity is to understand the written numerals 0–10 and to present their names in English aurally. Draw rows of circles on the board.

O
OO
OOO

Point at the single circle and say: *1*. Write: *1* on the board. Repeat with *2* and *3*. Count the circle in sequence. Point to the numerals again and say them.

Focus on the diagram in the book. You could try to elicit all the names of the numbers from students to assess their existing knowledge. Model looking and pointing as you say numbers 0–3. Play the audio. Students listen and point. Monitor and encourage students to follow the numerals from left to right, pointing as they hear them.

2 The aim of this activity is to recognize the written numerals in different contexts. Focus on an example of a number in the classroom, e.g. on a door or the cover of a textbook. Look around and encourage students to point to any other numbers they can see around the classroom, e.g. on posters or on a phone.

Focus on the first picture (10) and the row of numbers above. Say: *Match* and follow the line with your finger from the picture to the number 10 above. Students work individually and complete the exercise. Then students work in pairs and check their answers. Check answers as a class by pointing at a number on the row at the top and encouraging students to point to the correct picture. You can say the numbers as you do this, to reinforce the names aurally.

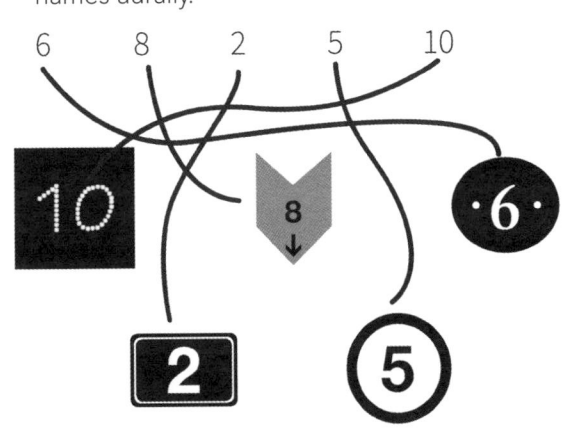

UNL⌀CK BASIC LITERACY TEACHER'S BOOK   **27**

3 👤👥 The aim of this activity is to recognize the written numerals in different fonts and recall their meaning. Focus on the *2* on the left and the rectangle containing 2 dots. Say: *Match* and trace the line from left to right with your finger. Students work individually and complete the exercise. Then students work in pairs and check their answers. Go through answers as a class by displaying a completed exercise if possible, or by drawing the answers on the board.

LISTENING AND SPEAKING Numbers 0–10

1 🔊 0.5 👤 The aim of this activity is to practise saying the names of the numerals in sequence. Write the numbers 0–10 on the board in a line from left to right. Point at each number in sequence and say the word.

Focus on the line of numbers in the book and point to the left end of the line. Play the audio for students to listen and point to the numbers. Repeat the audio. Students listen and say the numbers. Monitor and correct any pronunciation errors after the activity by modelling the numbers and drilling them. See p. 20 for advice on drilling.

2 🔊 0.6 👥 The aim of this activity is to recall the names of the numerals and practise saying them out of sequence. Return to the line of numbers on the board. Point at each number in sequence and say the word. Repeat the numbers, this time out of sequence. Then point and elicit the names of numerals at random from the class.

Focus on the numerals in the box in the book. Play the audio for students to listen and point. Students work in pairs and take turns to point at a numeral and say its name. Demonstrate this activity with a student. Monitor and correct errors with vocabulary and pronunciation.

WRITING Numbers 0–10

1 👤 The aim of this activity is for students to trace and copy numerals 0–10. Write: *0* on the board, starting at the top of the number. Add a dot to show where you started. Repeat for numbers 1–10, so you finish with a line of numbers with a dot on each. Under each number, quickly reproduce the number in a dotted line. If it is appropriate for your context, invite a student to the board to trace the numbers. Make sure they start at the top of each number and that their strokes are in the correct direction and complete.

Focus on the numerals in dark blue in the book and the numbers to trace. Say: *Look and trace* as you mime the actions. Students work individually. Monitor and check students' writing strokes. Write: *0* on the board in a continuous line. Demonstrate looking at the first *0*, then copy it several times. Say: *Look and copy* as you model the exercise. Students work individually. Monitor to check for correct strokes and that the numerals are the correct height and position on the handwriting lines.

2 🔊 0.7 👤 The aim of this activity is for students to write numerals 0–10 from visual input out of sequence. Focus on the example (10). Count out the dots in the rectangle. Students work individually and complete the exercise. Play the audio for students to check their answers and write the answers on the board.

Answers
3 5 7 0 2
4 6 1 8 9

3 🔊 0.8 👤👥 The aim of this activity is for students to practise writing the numerals 0–10 from aural input and out of sequence. Focus on the first photograph and point out the tick box and the number there. Say: *3*. Play the audio and indicate students should trace the numeral. Play the audio again. Students work individually and complete the exercise. Students work in pairs and compare their answers.

Answers
8 6 5 10 7

Optional activity

You will need a blank piece of paper. Students will need a photocopiable page with handwriting lines that can be downloaded from esource.cambridge.org.

Write the numerals 0–10 out of order on a piece of paper and show this to students briefly. Turn it over so only you can see it. Encourage students to pick up their pencils, then cup your ear and say: *Listen and write*. Mime writing. Read your line of numbers out, pausing to allow students to write each one. Show students your paper again for them to check answers (you could write the numbers up on the board in larger classes). Students work individually and write a line of numbers using numerals 0–10 in a random order. Working in small groups, students take it in turns to say their line of numbers while the rest of the group writes the numbers in the order they hear them. Students then compare number lines to check answers.

THE BASICS **STARTER UNIT**

LISTENING AND READING
Instructions

1. 🔊 0.9 👤 The aim of this activity is to familiarize students with simple instructions used in rubrics. Write: *read* and *listen* on the board in lowercase letters. Hold up a book. Mime reading it. Say: *Read* and point to the word on the board. Show headphones or cup your ear. Say: *Listen* and point to the word.

   Focus on the photographs in Exercise 1. Play the audio. Individually, students listen and point at the pictures. Play the audio again. Students listen and repeat the words as they point.

2. 🔊 0.10 👥 The aim of this activity is for students to practise recognizing simple instructions used in rubrics aurally. Focus on the numerals next to the words. Point and read out the numerals only. Then point to item 1. Say: *1 listen*. Demonstrate the activity by tracing the line from *listen* to the matching photograph on the right. Play the audio. Students work individually and match the pictures to the words. Play the audio again if necessary. Students work in pairs and check their answers. Go through answers as a class by pointing at each picture in sequence down the page and saying the correct answer including the numeral. Encourage students to point to the correct picture in the book.

   Answers
   Pictures in order left to right, row by row, on the page:
   5 look 1 listen 3 read 2 say 6 point 4 write

3. 🔊 0.11 👤 The aim of this activity is for students to practise recognizing common combinations of instructions used in *Unlock Basic* rubrics aurally. Mime listening and reading. Say: *Listen and read*. Mime and repeat to show you are doing two things at the same time.

   Focus on the photographs and say: *1 Look and listen*. Encourage students to point to the correct picture and point out the completed number *1* in the tick box. Mime tracing the number. Play the audio. Students work individually and match the instruction to the correct picture. Play the audio again if necessary. Go through answers as a class. With stronger classes, elicit the instruction that each picture shows by pointing at the picture and encouraging them to say the words.

Answers
Pictures in order left to right on the page:
4 Listen and write. 3 Point and say. 2 Read and listen.

Literacy tip

Students need to develop the ability to rapidly recognize the instructions aurally so that the time taken to demonstrate each activity is reduced. In time the process will become automated and reading the written form of the rubric will not provide any extra learning burden during lesson time. Repeated practice in short bursts, with an increasing level of challenge, will help to build automatic recognition skills. The Optional activity below can be repeated at various points in the lesson and subsequent lessons to ensure all students are able to recognize the instructions automatically.

Optional activity

You will need printable Flashcards 0.3, words and pictures, which can be printed at esource.cambridge.org. and some sticky tack.

Stick the cards around the classroom a large distance apart. Say an instruction from the cards. Students point to the correct card. Then collect the cards. Stand at the front of the class and hold up the cards one by one. Students say the instructions. Do this with increasing speed. If appropriate for your context, individual students can take on the teacher's role of showing the cards.

READING a–z

1. 🔊 0.12 👤 The aim of this activity is to familiarize students with the names and forms of the lowercase letters. Write: *a b c* in large lowercase letters on the board. Especially at the beginning of the course, students practise writing *a*, not *a*. Say the letters and point to them one by one. With a stronger class, elicit the rest of the alphabet and write it on the board in lowercase letters.

   Focus on the alphabet in the book. Say the letters, pointing at each one. Say: *Listen and point*. Play the audio and monitor to check students are able to follow the letters in sequence from left to right.

2. 🔊 0.13 👤 The aim of this activity is for students to practise saying the names of the lowercase letters. Write: *a b c* in large lowercase letters on the board. Say the letters and point to them one by one. Encourage students to repeat the name of each letter as you say it.

   Focus on the alphabet line in Exercise 1. Say: *Listen, point and say*. Play the audio and monitor and check students are pointing at

UNL🔒CK BASIC LITERACY TEACHER'S BOOK

the correct letter. Note any pronunciation errors and drill the names of these letters individually after the audio has finished. See p. 20 for advice on drilling.

> **Optional activity**
>
> Students stand up. Go around the room and encourage each student to say a letter (in alphabetical order). If a student makes a mistake or pauses for too long, they sit down. You could do this in two steps:
> 1 with the alphabet written across the board (in lowercase letters)
> 2 with part or all of the alphabet erased.

> **Literacy tip**
>
> Students need to practise recognizing letters in sequences of letters. This will help to reinforce left to right eye movement before they move on to whole word and sentence reading. The type of activity in Exercises 6 and 8 will also help to develop 'automaticity' (the ability to do something with no effort) in letter recognition. This skill will help students become faster, more efficient readers. This is especially useful for Arabic L1 students (students whose L1 is Arabic) with all vowels and easily confused consonants.

3 (0.14) The aim of this activity is for students to recognize the written form of individual vowels in sequences of letters. Write: *a* in lowercase on the board with an arrow pointing to it from the left. Write: *a e a o a* (in a different colour if possible) across the board to the right. Say: *a a*, pointing left to right, first to the *a* at the beginning of the line next to the arrow and then to the first *a* in the sequence of letters. Circle the first *a* in the sequence of letters. Read out the other letters, circling all of the *a*s as you say them. Count the circled *a*s then write: *3* at the end of the line of letters.

Focus on the first row of letters in the book. Point out where students start on each line (on the left side). Students work individually. Monitor and help as necessary.

Play the audio for students to listen and check their answers. If necessary, go through answers as a class. Ask individual students to read out each line of letters and say the number at the end.

> **Answers**
>
> e: 2 i: 2 o: 1 u: 2

4 (0.15) The aim of this activity is for students to check their knowledge of the names of the lowercase English vowels. Focus on the line of letters. Students work in pairs and take turns reading the letters aloud. Play the audio for students to listen and check. Ask individual students to read out the line of letters.

5 (0.16) The aim of this activity is for students to recognize the written form of individual, often confused consonants in sequences of letters. Repeat the procedure in Exercise 3 with the sequences of letters. Use the first line of the activity to demonstrate the procedure.

> **Answers**
>
> p: 2 q: 3 b: 3 d: 2 g: 2 h: 2

6 The aim of this activity is for students to recognize the written form of individual lowercase consonants. Focus on the cloud of letters on the left. Encourage students to call out the letters one by one in any order. Then focus on the cloud of letters on the right. Encourage students to call out the letters on the right. Say: *the same: j j, f f, t t …* and point from one side to the other as you do so. Point out the completed example in the book by tracing the line from *j* to *j* left to right with your finger. Students work individually to complete the exercise and then compare their answers in pairs.

7 The aim of this activity is for students to recognize the written form of individual lowercase consonants. Repeat the procedure in Exercise 6 above.

8 (0.17) The aim of this activity is for students to recognize the written form of individual lowercase letters in written words and spell them out orally. Write: *say* on the board. Spell the word aloud. Encourage individual students to spell *say* orally.

Focus on the words in the book. Students work in pairs and take it in turns to spell out words orally. Play the audio for students to listen and check. Go through answers as a class, asking individual students to spell out each word.

WRITING a–z

1 The aim of this activity is for students to trace the lowercase alphabet, forming the letters correctly. Write: *a* in lowercase on the board. Add an arrow to show where you started and the direction of the first stroke and the second. Number the arrows 1 and 2. Under the letter, quickly reproduce the letter. If it is appropriate for your context, invite a student to the board

THE BASICS STARTER UNIT

to trace the letter. Make sure their strokes are in the correct direction and complete. If this is not appropriate, trace the letter yourself.

Focus on the letters in dark blue in the book. Say: *Start at the top*. Point out the arrows on each letter going down. Demonstrate writing letters on the board, each time pointing at the starting point, and repeating: *Start at the top*. Focus on the letters for tracing. Say: *Look and trace*. as you demonstrate by writing over the top of some of the letters on the board. Students work individually. Monitor and check students' writing strokes.

2 ◀) 0.18 The aim of this activity is for students to copy the lowercase alphabet and recall the name of each letter in sequence. Play the audio and encourage students to point at each letter as they repeat it aloud. Write: *a* in lowercase on the board. Elicit from students where to start the letter and the correct stroke order. Say: *Write*. Point out the completed example and the space for students to write. Students work individually. Monitor to check for correct writing strokes and that the letters are the correct height and position on the handwriting lines.

READING A–Z

1 ◀) 0.19 The aim of this activity is to familiarize students with the names and forms of the uppercase letters. Write: *A B C* in large uppercase letters on the board. Say the letters and point to them one by one. Encourage students to repeat the names of each letter as you say it.

Focus on the uppercase alphabet in the book. Say: *Listen, point and say*. Play the audio and check that students are pointing at the correct letter. Note any pronunciation errors and drill the names of these letters individually after the audio has finished. See p. 20 for advice on drilling.

2 ◀) 0.20 The aim of this activity is for students to recognize the written form of individual uppercase vowels in sequences of easily-confused uppercase letters. Write: *A* in large uppercase on the board with an arrow pointing to it from the left. Write: *N A E H A H V* (in a different colour is possible) spread across the board to the right. Say: *A A*, pointing left to right, first to the *A* at the beginning of the line next to the arrow and then to the first *A* in the sequence of letters.

Circle the first *A*. Read out the other letters, circling all of the *A*s as you say them. Count the circled *A*s then write: *2* at the end of the line of letters.

Focus on the first row of letters in the book. Point out where students start on each line (on the left side). Students work individually. Monitor and help as necessary.

Play the audio for students to listen and check their answers. If necessary, go through the answers as a class. Ask individual students to read out each line of letters and say the number at the end.

Answers
E: 3 I: 3 O: 2 U: 2

3 ◀) 0.21 The aim of this activity is for students to recognize the written form of individual easily-confused consonants in sequences of letters. Repeat the procedure in Exercise 2, above. Use the first line of the activity to demonstrate the procedure.

Answers
C: 3 D: 3 Q: 2 G: 2 S: 3

4 The aim of this activity is for students to recognize the written form of individual uppercase consonants. Focus on the cloud of letters on the left. Encourage students to call out the letters one by one in any order. Then focus on the cloud of letters on the right. Encourage students to call out the letters on the right. Say: *These are the same: YY, XX, MM* and point from one side to the other as you do so. Point out the completed example in the book by tracing the line from *Y* to *Y* from left to right. Students work individually to complete the exercise and then compare their answers in pairs.

5 The aim of this activity is for students to recognize the written form of individual uppercase consonants. Repeat the procedure in Exercise 4 above.

6 The aim of this activity is to recognize the written uppercase letters in different contexts. Focus on an example of uppercase Roman letters in the classroom, e.g. on the front of the textbook. Look around and encourage students to point to any other uppercase letters they can see around the classroom, e.g. on posters, on devices and appliances.

Focus on the first picture (EXIT) and the row of letters to the left in the book. Say: *Look and circle*. Name the first letter aloud (E) then trace the line of letters along until you find E and trace a circle around it with your finger. Then return to the second letter (X) and repeat. Repeat for *I* and *T*. Students work individually and complete the exercise. Students work in pairs and check their answers. Go through answers as a class by pointing at each sign (1–4) and asking students to spell out the word orally. Write the rows of letters on the board with the correct letters circled for students to check their answers.

| Answers
2 GO 3 STOP 4 LOGIN

7 (0.22) The aim of this activity is for students to recognize uppercase letters in common acronyms. Write: *TV* on the board and draw a quick picture of a television. Spell out the word aloud. Encourage individual students to spell it out orally.

Focus on the pictures and the acronyms in the book. Students work in pairs and take it in turns to spell the acronyms orally. Play the audio for students to listen and check. Go through answers as a class, asking individual students to spell out each acronym.

WRITING A–Z

1 The aim of this activity is for students to trace the uppercase alphabet, forming the letters correctly. Write: *A* in uppercase on the board. Add an arrow to show where you started and the direction of the first stroke and the second. Number the arrows *1* and *2*. Under the letter, quickly reproduce the letter. If it is appropriate for your context, invite a student to the board to trace the letter. Make sure their strokes are in the correct direction and complete. If this is not appropriate, trace the letter yourself on the board.

Focus on the letters in dark blue in the book. Say: *Start at the top*. Demonstrate writing some letters on the board, e.g. *A H K*, each time pointing at the starting point and repeating: *Start at the top*. Focus on the letters for tracing. Say: *Look* and *trace*, as you demonstrate by writing over the top of some of the letters on the board. Students work individually. Monitor and check students' writing strokes.

2 (0.23) The aim of this activity is for students to copy the uppercase alphabet and recall the name of each letter in sequence. Play the audio and encourage students to point at each letter as they repeat it aloud. Write: *A* in uppercase on the board. Elicit where to start the letter and the correct stroke order. Say: *Write*. Point out the completed example and the space in the book for students to write. Students work individually. Monitor to check for correct writing strokes and that the letters are the correct height and position on the handwriting lines.

WRITING Aa–Zz

1 The aim of this activity is for students to trace and copy the uppercase and lowercase forms of individual letters correctly and to reinforce their relationship to one another. Follow the procedure in Exercise 1 above.

2 The aim of this activity is for students to recall the forms of lowercase or uppercase letters in relation to their lowercase or uppercase equivalents and write them correctly. Write the letter *a* on the board. Then pretend to be thinking. Then write uppercase *A* to the left of the letter. Repeat for *B* (write lowercase *b* to the left) and *c* (write uppercase *C* to the right).

Focus on the completed examples for *A* and *B* in the book. Then point at the lowercase *c* and indicate the space to the left. Say: *Write*. Students work individually and complete the exercise. Monitor and check for correct writing strokes and position of the letters on the handwriting lines.

3 The aim of this activity is to recall correct letter forms and practise writing letters at their correct relative heights. Focus on the completed examples for *A a*. Then point at uppercase and lowercase *B b*. Say: *Write*. Students work individually and complete the exercise. Monitor and check for correct writing strokes and position of the letters in the boxes.

4 (0.24) The aim of this activity is to reinforce the variations in relative heights and positions of letters in relation to the line and each other. Draw four straight lines across the board, similar to one row of handwriting lines used in the book. Write: *a* in the correct position on the line. Then write: *c* on the correct position on the line. Write: *x o G L h b p y j* somewhere

THE BASICS STARTER UNIT

else on the board. Look at the lines and pretend to think. Then write: *x* in the correct position on the line. Continue with all the letters. Then draw a box around each letter. Draw attention to their relative heights using your hands.

Focus on the letters in the box in the book. Students work individually and complete the exercise. Monitor and check for correct writing strokes and choice of the letters in the boxes. Go through the answers as a class by writing them up in groups on the board (*b d g k n p s t y*).

5 👤 The aim of this activity is to write lowercase and uppercase versions of letters. Focus on the letters in the book. Students work individually and copy each letter. Monitor and check for correct writing strokes.

6 🔊 0.25 👤 The aim of this activity is to write uppercase and lowercase versions of all letters of the alphabet independently with aural input. Demonstrate listening and then writing letters by saying *k*, cupping your ear and then writing *K k* on the board, and then saying *m* and writing *M m* on the board.

Play the audio for students to listen and write. Play the audio again while writing the answers up on the board. Students check their own work.

Answers
Aa Pp Cc Ss Dd Bb Ee Ll Nn Oo Vv Uu Zz
Tt Ff Jj Gg Hh Ii Qq Rr Xx Ww Yy

SOUND AND SPELLING
Consonants

1 🔊 0.26 👤 The aim of this activity is to learn the consonant sounds in relation to words.

Write: *10* on the board and elicit the word *ten* (do not write this). Write: *z, n* and *t* and elicit which letter starts *ten*. Point at the letters, say their names and then the sound that they make. Repeat with *9* and *0*.

Focus on the first line in the book and read it aloud: *b* (say the letter), /b/ (say the sound), *bus*. Play the audio for students to look at the letter, listen to the audio and repeat. Demonstrate tracing the letter *b* in the second *bus*. Students trace the letter. When all students have traced the letter, ask one student to repeat the whole line, i.e. *b* /b/ *bus bus*.

Common student errors
Arabic L1 speakers often have difficulties distinguishing between /p/ and /b/, and /f/ and /v/ consonant sounds. This results in mistakes when recognizing or producing these sounds. In these two particular cases, the difference between the pairs is that the first sound is 'unvoiced' and the second is 'voiced'. The place that the pairs of sounds are produced in the mouth is the same. Therefore, asking students to look at your mouth as you produce the pairs of sounds will not help them. Instead, highlight that with the second of each pair of sounds (/b/ and /v/), vibration can be felt in the throat. Demonstrate putting your hand on your throat and making each sound. The difference can be clearly felt.

2 🔊 0.27 👤 The aim of this activity is to identify letters producing consonant sounds at the start of words. Draw a basic outline of a bus on the board and write: *us*. Pretend to be confused. Say: *us* /ʌs/. Point at the space before the letter *u* and elicit the letter *b*. Write: *b* and say: *bus*.

Focus on the letters in the box, the pictures and the words with missing letters in the book. Play the audio. Students work individually and complete the exercise. Play the audio again for students to listen and repeat. Go through answers on the board as a class.

Answers
p̲alm q̲ueen g̲as j̲eans k̲ilogram r̲adio W̲i-Fi

3 🔊 0.28 👤 The aim and the procedure of this activity are similar to those in Exercise 2 above. Focus on the letters in the box, the pictures and the words with missing letters. Students work individually and complete the exercise. Play the audio for students to listen and check. Go through answers on the board as a class.

Answers
h̲ello n̲ine s̲alad t̲en v̲ideo z̲ero

SOUND AND SPELLING
Vowels

> **◉ Common student errors**
>
> There are many more vowel sounds in English than in Arabic and this often results in students making pronunciation and spelling mistakes. There are several spelling patterns involving vowels which can help students to build their knowledge and confidence, and reduce the risk of spelling mistakes; these will be the focus of later units in this book. However, it is worth pointing out, without going into depth, that there can be differences in sounds made by vowels in English.

1 ◀) 0.29 The aim of this activity is to understand that vowels can represent different sounds in words. Write: *gas* and *palm* on the board. Say both words. Circle the *a* in both words and repeat the two words. Then say the two sounds of *a* on their own: /æ/ /ɑː/. Elicit if they are the same or different (different). You can communicate the idea of *the same* and *different* by drawing two circles next to each other and then a circle and a square. Point to these as you say the vowel sounds and look questioning. Students identify the circle and the square.

Focus on the vowels in orange, one at a time. Say them aloud. Then focus on the completed example. Point at the word *palm*. Trace a circle around the *a* in *palm* with your finger. Point at the two *a*s on the same row. Play the audio for students to complete the exercise. Monitor and check answers as a class.

READING AND WRITING
Numbers zero–ten

1 ◀) 0.30 The aim of this activity is to introduce the word forms of the numbers 1–10. Write the numerals *0, 4, 9, 10* on the board. Elicit the numbers in English and write the words *zero, four, nine, ten* next to the numbers. Point at the numeral *0* and say: *zero*, then point at the word and say: *zero*. Repeat for the other numbers. Now demonstrate tracing over the first letters only of each of the words.

Focus on the words and corresponding dots in the book, and read through the numbers tracing your finger along the words in the book as you say them.

Focus on the completed examples. Students work individually and complete the exercise. Play the audio for students to listen and repeat.

2 ◀) 0.31 The aim of this activity is to recognize the word forms of the numbers 1–10.

Focus on the written numbers and the completed example. Trace your finger along the line and say: *one, one*. Students work individually and match each word to the correct numeral. Play the audio for students to listen and check their answers.

1 MEETING PEOPLE

LISTENING AND READING 1

Learning objectives

- Understand basic introductions – *Hi. My name's …*
- Understand the question – *How do you spell that?*
- Spell out names
- Use capital letters on first words correctly
- Write your name in English
- Recognize and write full stops and question marks – *I'm Sami. How do you spell that?*
- Introduce yourself and spell out your name

See p. 19 for suggestions on how to use these Learning objectives in your lessons.

Lead-in

You will need enough blank pieces of paper for one per student. Put these on students' desks before the class. You will also need a piece of paper with your name written on it.

Choose one student and write his or her name on the board. Write the same name on a piece of paper and fold it. Repeat the procedure for one more student. Students choose one person in the class and write his or her name on a piece of paper. Collect all pieces of paper. To demonstrate the exercise, use a piece of paper with your name. Unfold it and show it to the class. Say your name aloud. Then react by raising your hand (if appropriate in your context) and say: *I'm* (say your name). Then take a random piece of paper and read another name aloud. The person with this name should raise his or her hand and say: *I'm* (name). Continue until all card names are used.

1 ◀) 1.1 Write: *1 I'm Fatima. 2 I'm Saif.* on the board. Underneath write: *Saif* and *Fatima* with a little box next to each. Say: *Read and match.* Point at sentence 1 and read it aloud. Point at the name underneath (Saif) and say: *Saif* in a questioning tone. Elicit: *no* from students. Then point at the second name underneath (Fatima) and elicit: *yes* from students. Write: *1* in the box next to *Fatima*. Repeat the procedure with the second sentence.

Focus on the photographs and the speech bubbles in the book. Ask a student to read the first speech bubble aloud. Repeat it and point to the photograph. Play the audio for students to listen and read the speech bubbles. Then point at the first speech bubble again and the name in it (Jamal). Point at *1* in the photograph and at *1* in the box next to the name badge with *Jamal* on it. Say: *Match.* Students work individually and read and match the name badges to the photographs. Allow students to make any corrections. Go through answers as a class.

> **Answers**
> Nasser 3 Amal 4 Hassan 2 Hessa 5

2 ◀) 1.2 Write: *A a* on the board. Next to it, write: *Aisha Al Bargi.* Point at the capital letter *A* and say it aloud. Move your pen slowly along the name while you read it aloud. Say: *Stop!* when you get to the first capital *A* in the name. Circle it and continue with the family name. Repeat the procedure for the remaining *A* and *a*s.

Focus on the letters and the arrows in the book. Students work individually, listen, read and circle the letters. Play the audio again if required and check answers as a class.

NOTICE

Focus on the NOTICE box. The aim of this NOTICE box is to teach the way in which the eye follows a text longer than one line. Point at numbers *1*, *2* and *3*. Then say: *Look* and point at the arrow from *1* to *2*, *2* to *3* until you finish at *4*. Say: *Read* and point at the lines from *1* to *4* once more.

3 Focus on the name with capital letters in bold. Ask a student to read it aloud. Say: *name* and point at it. Read it aloud again. Point out the capital letters to trace at the beginning of each name. Students work individually and trace the letters. Monitor and check students are tracing the capital letters correctly.

4 ◀) 1.3 Write your full name on the board. Erase the capital letters leaving a gap where the letters were. Indicate listening by cupping your ear and spell your name aloud. Write the missing letters on the lines.

Focus on the names in the book. Encourage students to guess what the names are, but do not tell them if they are right or wrong. Play the audio for students to write the missing letters. Students work in pairs and check their answers. Monitor and correct errors with the names of the letters.

> **Answers**
> Badir Al Faris Hessa Al Jawa Rowdah Al Kaabi

5 🔊 1.4 👤 Focus on the photographs and the speech bubbles. Play the audio for students to listen and read. Point out both instances of *How do you spell that?* and read these aloud. Write the question on the board. Say your name. Read the question again and spell your name. Write it on the board with a dash (-) between the letters. Write on top of the letters once more to demonstrate tracing. Students then work individually and trace the letters in their books. Monitor and check students are tracing correctly. When they finish, play the audio again.

6 🔊 1.5 👤 Write: *Hessa* on the board. Elicit if it is correct, i.e. with a capital letter, by saying *yes* in a questioning tone. Circle the double s. Say the spelling: *capital H, e, double s, a* and write a tick (✓) on the board. Repeat, this time saying *s s* instead of *double s*, and indicate that this is wrong by writing a cross (✗) on the board.

Play the audio. Students listen and circle double letters. Play the audio again for students to check. Go through answers as a class.

> **NOTICE**
>
> Focus on the NOTICE box. Read it aloud and point out the double phrasing. Look at the example name *Mohammed* in Exercise 6. Show how double letters are circled.

7 🔊 1.6 👤 Focus on the first photograph and read the speech bubble. Spell out and write the name on the board. Underline the initial capital. Point at the first photograph and read the speech bubble. Ask a student to read the next speech bubble. Repeat the procedure with one more student. Say: *Listen and write the name.* Play the audio. Students write the name. Play the audio again and monitor to check the names spelling and use of capital letters.

> **Answers**
>
> 2 Ameena 3 Qassim 4 Rosa

> **Optional activity**
>
> Demonstrate the exchange with a stronger student. Say: *I'm (your name).* Elicit: *How do you spell that?* by writing the first letter of your name on the board followed by gaps and pointing at the missing letters. Spell your name aloud, indicating students should write their names. Write your name on the board for students to check. Students work in pairs. Students say their names and ask: *How do you spell that?*, noting down the spelling of their partner's name. Students swap partners. If it is appropriate in your context, invite various students to come to the board to write the names of the people they heard. Go through the spellings of students' names as a class.

> **NOTICE**
>
> Focus on the NOTICE box. Read it aloud and point out the use of full stops in affirmative sentences and the question mark in the question. Ask a student to read the text aloud.

8 👤 Write: *My name's* (your name). on the board. Draw students' attention to the capital letter at the beginning of the sentence and the full stop at the end. Write: *How do you spell that* (without the question mark) and write a dash to indicate something is missing. Elicit that the question needs a question mark (?).

Focus on sentence 1 in the book. Point at the full stop at the end. Students work individually and write a full stop or a question mark at the end of each sentence. Go through answers as a class.

> **Answers**
>
> 2 . (full stop) 3 ? (question mark)

> **NOTICE**
>
> Ask a student: *What's your name?* Elicit: *My name's …* Write the answer on the board: *My name's* (name). Erase the apostrophe s and write: *is*. Say: *Say My name's, write My name is.*
>
> Focus on the NOTICE box. Allow a minute for students to read the information.

9 🔊 1.7 👤 Write: *MynameisSaudAlFaris.* on the board. Move the pen along the sentence and draw a vertical line after *My*. Move the pen again and encourage students to shout *Stop!* at the word boundaries.

Focus on the completed example in the book. Students work individually and draw lines between the words in the sentences. Monitor and help as necessary. Go through answers on the board.

> **Answers**
>
> 2 I am Ameena Al Ghanim.
> 3 My name is Rosa Golijan.
> 4 How do you spell that?

> ⦿ **Common student errors**
>
> **Punctuation:** Arabic L1 and Turkish L1 students often forget to capitalize the pronoun *I*. It is important to focus on *I* and its spelling. Point the pronoun *I* out in sentences to practise the correct spelling of it as often as possible.

MEETING PEOPLE UNIT 1

WRITING CHALLENGE

10 Focus on the photograph of a student. Point at it and say: *Khalid Al Faris*. Ask a student to read out the model text. Focus on the rubric. Say: *Write about you*. Students work individually and write their names in a full sentence. Monitor and help as necessary. Check that students are writing in the correct position on the lines. Students swap notebooks with a partner and check each other's writing for correct language, spelling, punctuation and use of capital letters.

LISTENING AND READING 2

Learning objectives

- Understand information on contact cards – *first name, family name, phone number, email address*
- Read and understand how to ask for other people's contact details – *What's your number?*
- Understand the difference between *his* and *her*
- Understand and say phone numbers – *0544 343 009*
- Read and understand other people's details – *His name is Abdullah. Her phone number is 0873 590 321.*
- Use capital letters and full stops on sentences

See p. 19 for suggestions on how to use these Learning objectives in your lessons.

Lead-in

Create a name wall. Students write their names (*My name is …*) on large strips of paper. Monitor and check for correct use of capital letters and full stops.

Display the alphabet on individual cards around the room. Students add their sentences under the correct letter, e.g. *A – My name is Ahmed*. Students read their sentences aloud.

Vocabulary Pre-teaching / Review

You will need printable flashcards with numbers 0–10 (Flashcards 0.1), which can be printed at esource.cambridge.org.
Follow the procedure on p. 15.

1 ◀) 1.8 Write: *0 1 2* on the board. Put boxes with the corresponding number of dots in them in a random order above the numerals (as in Exercise 1). Point at *0* and match it to the empty box. Repeat the procedure with *1* and *2*.

Focus on the numbers in the box. Say: *Listen and write* and point at the empty boxes underneath the dots. Play the audio for students to listen and write the numerals in order underneath the dots. Go through answers as a class.

2 ◀) 1.9 Write: *344* on the board. Point at each numeral and say: *three double four*. Ask students to repeat as a class. Repeat with more examples, e.g. *1566* (one, five, double six), *899* (eight, double nine), *055266* (zero, double five, two, double six).

Focus on the photographs and the numbers in the book. Trace the line connecting the photograph of Sultan with his number (05 927 3401). Say: *Listen and match*. Play the audio for students to listen and match the numbers and the photographs.

Play the audio again if required. Pause after each dialogue and ask individual students (or the whole class) to repeat. Go through answers as a class.

Answers

Bushra 09 527 8440
Abdul Rahman 095 278 4410
Sheikha 059 273 4401

3 ◀) 1.10 Write: *097* on the board. Point and say: *098*. Say: *yes or no?* in a questioning tone (no). Cross out *7* and elicit: *8* from students. Write: *8* above the crossed out *7*.

Focus on the completed example in the book (Mehmet). Point at the wrong number. Say: *039 282 9460* in a questioning tone. Point at the wrong numbers (*3* and *1*) and cross them out. Say: *Listen and correct*. Play the audio for students to listen and correct the numbers. Play the audio again if required. Write the correct numbers on the board. Students swap notebooks and check each other's answers.

Answers

2 Abdul Aziz 0181 285 2865
3 Fatima 07706 468 926
4 Latifa 01253 805 257

Optional activity

Say: *045 3288 196*. Students listen and write the number. Write the number on the board for students to check. Ask students to write three (invented) telephone numbers. Students work in pairs and take turns to say their numbers while the other one listens and writes. Students check their answers in pairs.

UNLOCK BASIC LITERACY TEACHER'S BOOK   37

4 Write: *What is your name* (without the question mark) on the board. Point to the end of the question and say: *yes or no?* in a questioning tone. Elicit that the question mark is missing. Write it at the end of the question. Write: *My name is Ahmed* (without the full stop) on the board and point at the end of the sentence to elicit what is missing. Write the full stop at the end.

Focus on the sentences in the book. Students work individually and add full stops or question marks. Monitor and help students as necessary. Go through answers as a class.

Answers
2 . (full stop) 3 ? (question mark) 4 . (full stop)

5 (1.11) You can use Flashcards 1.4 to pre-teach this vocabulary set. Write your full name (first and family) on the board. Ask: *first name?* and guide students to your first name. Repeat with your family name. Write the @ symbol and say: *at*. Write: *.co.sa* and say: *dot co dot S-A*. Encourage students to repeat.

Focus on the information on the first ID card in the book. Read and show the completed example. Students work individually and match sentences 2 and 3 to the correct information.

Focus on the second ID card in the book. Students work individually and match the information with sentences 4, 5 and 6. Play the audio for students to listen and check. Go through answers as a class.

Answers
2 rahman@alkaabi.co.em. 3 *019 234 7921.* 4 *Sheikha.* 5 sheikha@alshahrani.co.sa. 6 *04875 267 930.*

NOTICE

Focus on the NOTICE box. Demonstrate the difference between *his* and *her* by indicating different students and saying: *His/Her name is …* In a single gender class, point at the pictures in Exercise 5 and elicit: *his* and *her*. Ask students to repeat *his* and *her* after you.

6 (1.12) Focus on the photographs. Point at the first one and say: *Her first name is Fatima*. Point at sentence 1 and then at photograph 1. Play the audio for students to listen and read. Encourage students to read along (silently) while listening. Say: *Read and match*. Students work individually, read and match the sentences to the photographs. Go through answers as a class. Focus on *Her* in the first sentence. Demonstrate tracing the word in the book. Repeat with the pronouns in the other sentences. Students work individually and trace the letters. Monitor and help as necessary.

Answers
a 1, 3 b 2, 4

7 Write: *his* on the board. Write these words: *hi his hiss has his*. Point at the first word you wrote (hi) and elicit the pronunciation. Move your pen slowly along the line of words, encouraging students to shout *Stop!* when you get to *his*. Circle: *his* and then continue along the line until students shout *Stop!* at the second *his*.

Focus on the words in bold in the book. Students work individually and read and circle the words.

8 Remind students how to form *h*, *i* and *s* with correct strokes on the board. Focus on the first word *his* in the book. Then demonstrate covering it with a piece of paper. Point to the second column and the letters *hi*. Elicit the next letter (s). Demonstrate writing it carefully in the book. Students continue to move across the columns, completing the words. Monitor and check that students are working from left to right. Encourage correct stroke direction and correct height and position of the individual letters.

9 Remind students how to form *h*, *e* and *r* with correct strokes on the board. Repeat the procedure in Exercise 8 with *her*, *number* and *first*.

10 (1.13) Focus on the words in the box and the gapped sentences. Students work individually, read the sentences and complete the gaps. Play the audio for students to listen and check their answers. Write the sentences on the board. Ask a student to read the sentences aloud.

Answers
1 first 2 His 3 Her 4 number

MEETING PEOPLE UNIT 1

LISTENING AND READING 3

Learning objectives

- Name countries – Mexico, India, Saudi Arabia, Turkey, Japan, the UK, Bahrain, Portugal
- Understand the difference between *She is* and *He is*
- Read and understand someone's nationality – *He's from Turkey. She's from Mexico.*
- Write about your teacher's nationality using the full form of *be* – *He is from Saudi Arabia.*
- Gain awareness of the sounds of the letters *b* and *p* – *B*ahrain, *P*ortugal

See p. 19 for suggestions on how to use these Learning objectives in your lessons.

Lead-in

Write: *His name is … / Her name is …* on the board (depending on the class you teach). Choose a student from the class, but don't say this person's name yet. Say: *His name is … / Her name is …* and start spelling the name aloud one letter at a time. Encourage students to guess the name after the first letter. If they cannot guess at this stage, say: *His name is … / Her name is …* and give two letters. Continue giving letters until students guess the name. Repeat the procedure with a few more names. This exercise can also be conducted as a competition, by dividing the class into small groups. Give one point to the group that guesses the correct name first.

Vocabulary Pre-teaching / Review

You will need printable flashcards with countries (Flashcards 1.2), which can be printed at esource.cambridge.org. You need the sides of the cards with both flags and words.

Follow the procedure on p. 15.

Write: *Saudi Arabia* and *the UK* on the board. Point at both words in each country and count the words to help students understand that these countries consist of two words.

1 🔊 1.14 Before class, draw word shapes on the board for *Turkey*, *Bahrain* and *Saudi Arabia*. You will need a world map for this activity. Point at Turkey on the map. Elicit the name of the country. Write it on the board. Repeat with Saudi Arabia and Bahrain. Ask students which word shape resembles the name of each country. Write them in, emphasizing the stroke direction.

Focus on the completed example in the book. Say: *Write*. Students work individually and write the countries. Monitor and check how students are writing. Play the audio for students to listen to the countries.

Answers

2 the UK 3 India 4 Japan 5 Bahrain 6 Turkey
7 Portugal 8 Mexico

NOTICE

Write: *turkey* on the board. Cross out the lowercase *t* and write a capital *T* above it. Focus on the countries in the book and point out that they all begin with a capital letter. Ask students to underline all the capital letters in the countries in Exercise 1.

2 🔊 1.15 If your name has more than one syllable, say it, emphasizing the stressed syllable. If your name has one syllable, choose the name of a student that has more than one syllable. Use bubbles to demonstrate the stress patterns of the names, e.g. *Peter: Oo, Sachiko: Ooo*, and ask students to identify which fits your or your student's name. Repeat with *Japan* and *Turkey*.

Focus on the stress patterns at the top of the columns in the book. Play the audio for students to listen and repeat.

Literacy tip

Stressed syllables are very significant in English literacy, as they determine the vowel sound in many words. Raising awareness of them is an important first step. Most students should be able to hear them if the model given is clear and exaggerated.

3 🔊 1.16 Focus on the photographs and the sentences. Point out the first sentence and the *1* written in the box next to the photograph. Point out the first *She's* and the woman in the photograph to help students with the exercise by recognizing gender. Say: *Listen and match*. Students match the sentences to the photographs. Play the audio for students to complete the exercise. Go through answers as a class.

Answers

2 Rosa 3 Greg 4 Levent

NOTICE

Focus on the NOTICE box. Read out the examples, stressing *he* and *she*. Say: *Say He's / She's. Write He is / She is*. Write examples with the contracted form and *from* + a country on the board, pointing out the capital letters at the beginning of the sentences.

UNLOCK BASIC LITERACY TEACHER'S BOOK

4 🔊 1.17 👤 Focus on the icons (for gender and country) next to each sentence. Point at *He* and *She* in each sentence. Then point at the first picture and say: *He? She?* in a questioning tone. Students circle the correct pronoun. Say: *Read and circle*. Students work individually, look at the pictures with flags and circle the correct words. Play the audio for students to listen and check their answers. Say: *Trace* and demonstrate with your pen tracing the example. Students work individually and trace the pronouns they have circled. Monitor and encourage correct direction of lines.

> **Answers**
> 2 He is 3 He is 4 She is

5 🔊 1.18 👤 Focus on the photographs and the sentences. Elicit: *he* and *she* for the correct photographs (a *he*, b *she*). Read sentence 1. Show how *she* matches the photograph of the woman. Say: *Listen and match*. Play the audio for students to listen, read and match. Go through answers as a class. Play the audio again for students to repeat the sentences.

> **Answers**
> a 2, 3, 5 b 1, 4, 6

WRITING CHALLENGE

6 👤 Point at yourself. Say: *from?* and write your country. Say: *student or teacher?* and elicit the answer (*teacher*). Say: *She or He?* and elicit the answer. Write all three words you elicited on the board (country of origin, *teacher*, *She/He*).

Focus on the photograph in the book. Ask a student to read the model sentence aloud. Focus on *He*, the capital letter and the full stop at the end of the sentence.

Students work individually and write a sentence about their teacher. Monitor and help as necessary.

SOUND AND SPELLING *p, b*

7 🔊 1.19 👤 Say the two sounds /p/ and /b/ and ask students to repeat. Write: *p* on the board and say the sound /p/ again. Repeat the procedure for *b* /b/. Ask students to look at Exercise 1 and find the countries that start with *p* and *b* (Portugal, Bahrain).

Focus on the pictures and the phrases in Exercise 7. Play the audio for students to listen and read. Then point out the letters for tracing. Students work individually and trace the letters.

8 🔊 1.20 👤 Write: *pen* and *book* on the board, using a different colour pen for the *p* and *b* if possible. Say the words with the /p/ and /b/ sounds clearly pronounced. Erase the rest of the words leaving just the first letters. Pronounce each sound one at a time and ask students to indicate which it is on the board. Repeat a few times.

Focus on the two columns of words in the book. Play the audio for students to look and listen. Play the audio again and students listen and repeat.

> **Optional activity**
>
> Use the words in Exercise 8. Students work in pairs and test each other on the two sounds /p/ and /b/. Students take it in turns to say one word. Their partner identifies which sound they hear (/p/ or /b/). Continue until students have used all of the words.

9 🔊 1.21 👤 👥 👥👥 Focus on the question and the flags and say: *country?* Demonstrate the first example by showing the path *push, bee, back, pear* that takes students to *Bahrain*. Say these words aloud while pointing at the words. Play the audio for students to listen and draw a line from word to word. Play the audio again for students to listen and check. Go through the answer as a class. Play the audio again for students to repeat, focusing on correct /p/ and /b/ sounds. Play the game several times with students tracing the path with their fingers or a pencil. In stronger classes, students can play the game in pairs or small groups, with one student saying the words and the others tracing their journey. Points can be awarded for the person who calls out the answer first.

> **Answer**
> Japan

MEETING PEOPLE   UNIT 1

LANGUAGE FOCUS

Learning objectives

- Name study objects – *library card, student ID card, pen, pencil, book, notebook, mobile phone, dictionary*
- Read and understand a polite way of asking for objects – *Can I have a pencil, please?*
- Gain awareness of sounds and spelling of short vowels

See p. 19 for suggestions on how to use these Learning objectives in your lessons.

Lead-in

To practise the sounds /p/ and /b/ with the new vocabulary, write: *pen* on the left-hand side of the board and *ben* on the right-hand side. Say: *How do you spell that?* Elicit the spelling of both words. Say: *pen*. Ask students to listen and choose the right spelling by pointing at the correct word (*pen*). Cross out the word *ben*.

Vocabulary Pre-teaching / Review

You will need printable flashcards with everyday objects (Flashcards 1.3), which can be printed at esource.cambridge.org.

Follow the procedure on p. 15.

To help students remember some of the new vocabulary, point out the spelling patterns in *pen* and *pencil*, *book* and *notebook*. Write: *pen* on the board in one colour and point at the flashcard that shows a pen. Using a different colour if possible, add *-cil* to *pen* to create *pencil* and point at the flashcard that shows a pencil. Repeat the procedure with the words *book* and *notebook*.

1 🔊 1.22 👤 Focus on the word shapes in the book. Play the audio for students to listen and read. Students complete the exercise by first tracing, then copying, the words. If students are proficient with handwriting, they could go immediately to the copying stage. Monitor and check for correct directional strokes and writing on the line.

2 🔊 1.23 👤 Place an ID card, a pen, a notebook and a pencil on the table. Say: *Can I have a pen, please?* Indicate the pen. Say: *Can I have a notebook, please?* Indicate the pencil and say: *yes or no?* in a questioning tone (no). Repeat a few times with different objects to check students' understanding of the study objects.

Focus on the first photograph in the book. Say: *library card?* (no). Say: *mobile phone?* (yes). Say: *Look, read and circle.* Students work individually, read the sentences and circle the correct objects. Play the audio for students to listen and check. Go through answers as a class.

Answers

2 a student ID card   3 a pen   4 a pencil

⬤ Common student errors

The word *please* is frequently mispelled by Arabic L1 students. This is the typical error: *pleas*.

To focus students on this word, write this line of words on the board:

please   pleas_   plea_ _   ple_ _ _

Focus on the first word. Ask students to spell it aloud. Erase the word. Ask students to complete the first gap. Then erase the word. Continue like this until students are able to write the whole word with no prompts. If students make mistakes, go back a word and repeat the procedure.

Optional activity

The aim of this exercise is to drill the question *Can I have a …, please?* Students work in pairs and gather a collection of objects in the vocabulary set (book, pen, mobile phone, notebook, etc.). It does not matter if they do not have all the objects. Students take turns asking for different objects using *Can I have a …, please?* Their partner hands them the correct object.

3 🔊 1.24 👤 Show students a book and elicit: *book*. Write: *book* on the board, emphasizing correct letter formation for *b*. Repeat the procedure with *pen*.

Focus on the words in the book. Play the audio for students to follow the words. Students trace the *b*s and *p*s in the words. Play the audio again for students to repeat the words, focusing on correct pronunciation of /p/ and /b/ sounds.

4 👤 Focus on the crossword and point at the photograph of the pen. Point at where the word is written in the crossword. Focus on the photograph of the student ID card and elicit the missing letters. Students work individually and complete the crossword. Go through answers as a class. Point at the orange box running vertically and elicit the word (pencil).

Answers

st**u**dent ID c**a**rd
notebook
dictionary
library card
mobile phone
Word in the box: pencil

UNL*O*CK BASIC LITERACY TEACHER'S BOOK   41

5 🔊 1.25 👤 Ask a student: *Can I have a pen, please?* Encourage the student to give you a pen and then encourage them to ask for the same pen back using the same question. When they do, give them the pen and say: *Here you are.* Write it on the board. Ask a different student: *Can I have a book, please?* Once you get a book, encourage the same student to ask for it back. This time say: *No, sorry* and keep the book. Write: *No, sorry.* on the board.

Focus on the photographs and the sentences in the book. Say: *Listen and read.* Play the audio for students to listen and follow the text. Play the audio again for students to listen and repeat. Invite students to ask you for different objects and respond accordingly, either by giving them the object or not.

6 👤 Write: *mopile* with a cross (✗) next to it on the board. Elicit the mistake and its correction. Cross out the word and write the correct form (mobile).

Focus on the first sentence and the mistake in the book. Show how it is crossed out and the correct form written next to the sentence. Students work individually and correct the mistakes in the sentences. Go through answers as a class.

> **Answers**
> 2 notebook 3 dictionary 4 book 5 please

SOUND AND SPELLING
Short vowels

> **Literacy tip**
>
> Arabic has far fewer vowel sounds than English and only three short vowel sounds. Spelling with vowels is difficult for Arabic L1 students and vowels are frequently written interchangeably. In English there are often more ways than one of spelling the same sound. However, there are recognizable patterns which, once students are aware of them, give the confidence and knowledge needed for students to improve their spelling.
>
> Major factors altering the production of a vowel, and therefore its sound, are the jaw and the tongue. Vowel production is more internal and the differences can be much less visible to students than the difference between /p/ and /v/, for example. However, once they are made aware of these factors, students are more empowered to produce and recognize differences in vowel production.

7 🔊 1.26 👤 Write: *Aa have, Ee ten, Ii his, Oo doctor, Uu bus* on the board. Point at *Aa* on the board and then point at *have*. Move your pen along the word and encourage students to shout *Stop!* when you reach the vowel *a*. Repeat the procedure for the rest of the words with their respective vowels.

Focus on the pictures and the sentences in the book. Play the audio for students to listen and read. Then point out the letters for tracing. Students work individually and trace the letters.

SPELLING CHALLENGE

8 🔊 1.27 👥 Focus on the two columns of words and photographs in the book. Say: *hat* and point at the word *hat* in the book. Say: *hot* and point at the word *h_t*. Say: *hot* a couple of times. Model the words, exaggerate the mouth movements on the vowel sounds, e.g. the dropped jaw with *hot*. Elicit the missing letter (o) and ask students to write it in their books. Say: *Listen and write.* Play the audio for students to listen and complete the words. Students compare answers in pairs and then listen again if required.

> **Answers**
> h<u>a</u>t h<u>o</u>t
> b<u>i</u>ll b<u>e</u>ll
> b<u>a</u>g b<u>u</u>g
> d<u>e</u>sk d<u>i</u>sk
> b<u>o</u>ss b<u>u</u>s

LISTENING FOCUS

> **Learning objectives**
>
> - Understand a dialogue in which a student applies for an ID card
> - Understand personal questions – *What's your phone number?*
> - Read sentences with *he, his* and *he's*
>
> See p. 19 for suggestions on how to use these Learning objectives in your lessons.

> **Lead-in**
>
> **Back chaining** Follow the procedure on p. 20.
> 1 *Can I have a pencil?*
> 2 *What's your name?*
> 3 *Where are you from?*
> 4 *What's your phone number?*

MEETING PEOPLE — UNIT 1

1 🔊 1.28 Focus on the pictures. Elicit where the people in picture 1 are (university, library). Play the audio for students to look and listen.

2 🔊 1.29 Focus on the sentences. Read the completed example aloud. Play the audio for students to listen and circle the correct words. Students compare their answers in pairs. Play the audio again for students to check their answers.

> **Answers**
> 2 Paddy 3 UK 4 443 218 5 pen

3 Focus on the pictures in Exercise 1. Elicit questions the two people might say. Write some questions on the board (e.g. *What's your first name?*). Focus on the completed example in Exercise 3. Show how it relates to picture d. Students work individually and complete the exercise, matching pictures to questions. Go through answers as a class. In stronger classes, you could play the audio again while students follow the dialogue questions in Exercise 3.

> **Answers**
> 2 e 3 c 4 a 5 b

4 🔊 1.30 Write this sentence on the board with no spaces: *Canlhavealibrarycard,please?* Move your pen along the sentence, encouraging students to say: *Stop!* where the first word ends. Mark a vertical line at that point. Continue until all the correct word boundaries have been marked.

Students work individually to complete the exercise in the book. Monitor and help as necessary. Play the audio for students to check. Go through answers as a class.

> **Answers**
> 2 Where are you from? 3 What's your name?
> 4 Can I have a pen?

> **Optional activity**
> Write three questions on the board: *What's your name? Where are you from? What's your phone number?* Divide the class into Student As and Student Bs. Ask Student As to ask the questions and Student Bs to answer. Then students swap roles. Monitor and help as necessary.

⊙ KEY WORDS FOR LITERACY

> **Learning objectives**
> - Read, spell and pronounce key words for literacy – *he, she, you, have, the*
> - Complete sentences with the key words for literacy
>
> See p. 19 for suggestions on how to use these Learning objectives in your lessons.

1 🔊 1.31 Write: *he* on the board. Write these sentences: *He's Sultan. He's from the UAE.* Point at the first word you wrote (he) and elicit the pronunciation. Move your pen slowly across the sentences, encouraging students to shout *Stop!* when you get to the word *he*. Circle it in both sentences. Read the sentences aloud.

Focus on the words in bold in the book. Say: *Listen, read and circle.* Play the audio. Students work individually and listen, read and circle the words.

2 Write: *he* on the board. Write these words: *he her here his he*. Point at the first word you wrote (he) and elicit the pronunciation. Move your pen slowly across the sentences, encouraging students to shout *Stop!* when you get to the word *he*. Circle it twice.

Focus on the words in bold in the book. Say: *Read and circle.* Students work individually, read and circle the words. Go through answers as a class.

3 Remind students how to form the letters *h, s, e, y, o, u, a, v* with correct strokes on the board.

Focus on the lines of words in the book. If necessary, prompt students to use something to cover the words on the left as they complete each one. Students work individually and complete the words. Monitor and check that students are working from left to right. Encourage correct stroke direction and correct height and position of the individual letters.

4 🔊 1.32 Write: *you* on the board in a box. Erase one letter at a time and then try to elicit the missing letter(s).

Focus on the sentences in the book. Students complete the exercise individually. Play the audio for students to listen and check.

> **Answers**
> 2 the 3 He 4 She

UNLOCK BASIC LITERACY TEACHER'S BOOK 43

READING AND WRITING

Learning objectives

- Understand basic academic words – *student, teacher, email, library*
- Read and understand a simple email with personal details
- Read for detail
- Complete a student's ID card
- Use capital letters on first names correctly – *Murat*
- Complete four sentences about yourself – *My name is … I am from … I am a … My phone number is …*

Lead-in

Divide the board in two halves vertically. On the left, write the word *teacher* in a circle in the centre. Draw lines coming out from the circle in a spidergram. Elicit names of other teachers in your school or university. Write the names at the ends of the lines. On the right side of the board, write the word *student* in a circle in the centre. Draw lines coming out from the circle in a spidergram shape. Ask students to say their names. Write the names at the ends of the lines.

1 Focus on the photographs. Elicit words about what is in the photographs to check students' existing knowledge. Focus on the completed example by pointing at picture d, *1 email*, and the completed tick box. Tell students to read the words and match them to the photographs. Go through answers as a class.

> **Answers**
> 2 a 3 b 4 e 5 c

2 🔊 1.33 Ask students to read through the words in the box. Focus on the first word (library) and go through the text, using your finger to demonstrate reading the complete line from left to right before going to the line below. Point out the circled examples of the word. Repeat the procedure with the word *student* as a class. Say: *Look* (pointing at the words in the box), *read and circle* (pointing at the text). Students work individually and complete the exercise. Monitor to check students are reading left to right.

Answers

```
●●●
To:       University (Library)
From:     laila@college.com
Subject:  (Library) card
```

→ Hello,
→ I am a new (student). I need a (library) card.
→ My first (name) is Laila. My family (name) is
→ Abdulla. I am from the UAE.
→ My (teacher) is Mrs Hind.
→ My phone number is 059 201 3382.
→ My (email) address is laila@college.com.
→ Thank you.
→ Laila Abdulla

3 Focus on the first sentence. Point at the text in Exercise 2. Read the sentence: *Laila is a new student*. Focus on the circled word *student* underneath the sentence. Indicate that the answer *student* in the first item is also circled in the text to help them find the answers more quickly. Students work individually, read each sentence, look at the text in Exercise 2 and find the place in the text where the answer is given. Students circle the correct options. Go through answers as a class. Ask students to write the correct options in the gaps. Monitor and help as necessary.

> **Answers**
> 1 UAE 2 card 3 email address

4 Write: *omar, oman, khalid* on the board. Point at each word and ask students what it is (first name). Then write a cross (✗) above each word indicating that there is a mistake. Elicit that the words need capital letters. Cross out the first lowercase letters and replace with capitals. Erase the words.

44 UNLOCK BASIC LITERACY TEACHER'S BOOK

MEETING PEOPLE　　UNIT 1

Focus on the words in the box and the name *Omar* written on the student card in the book. Students work individually and complete the card. Monitor and help as necessary. Students compare their cards in pairs.

> **Answers**
> Family name: Khalid
> Country: Oman

5 🔊 1.34 Write: *MynameisOmarKhalid.* on the board. Move the pen along the sentence and draw a vertical line after *My*. Move the pen along again, encouraging students to shout *Stop!* at each word boundary. Draw lines between the words.

Focus on the completed example in the book. Students work individually and divide the words in the sentences. Monitor and help as necessary. Go through answers as a class.

> **Answers**
> 1 My name is Omar Khalid.
> 2 I am from Oman.
> 3 I am a student.
> 4 My phone number is 0437834323.
> 5 My email address is omar1999@edu.com.

> **◉ Common student errors**
> Punctuation: Arabic L1 and Turkish L1 students frequently make mistakes when writing *I'm* with an apostrophe (e.g. *I'am*). *I'm* is a very high-frequency phrase, so it is crucial to pay attention to its spelling from the very beginning.
> When you see that you are teaching a lesson with a lot of sentences with *I'm*, write it on the board. Every time a student is meant to write a sentence with *I'm*, point at it on the board to help them with the spelling.

6 Write: *my name is Omar Khalid.* on the board. Elicit the mistake (no capital at the beginning). Remind students about capitals on country names and for the pronoun *I*.

Focus on the first example in the book. Students work in pairs and complete the exercise. Students compare their answers in small groups. Go through answers as a class.

> **Answers**
> 2 I am from <u>O</u>man.
> 3 <u>I</u> am a student.
> 4 My phone <u>n</u>umber is 0437834323.

7 Write your name, country of origin and *teacher* on the board. Use these words to say three sentences: *My name is* (your name). *I am from* (your country of origin). *I am a teacher.*

Focus on the notebook in the book. Say: *Write about you.* Students work individually and complete four sentences. Monitor and help as necessary. Students swap notebooks and check each other's writing for correct language, spelling and punctuation.

> **Model answer**
> My name is Mansour Al Naimi. I am from Qatar. I am a student. My phone number is 70158090.

> **Optional activity**
> Photocopy one page with writing lines from p. 22 for each student. Distribute to the class. Divide the class into Student As and Student Bs. Ask Student As to read their sentences in Exercise 7 to Student Bs. Student Bs write down the name, country and the phone number. Encourage Student Bs to ask Student As for the spelling to make sure their writing is correct. Students swap roles. Monitor and help as necessary.

> **Objectives review**
> See Teaching tips on p. 19 for ideas about using the Objectives review with your students.
>
> **WORDLIST**
> See Teaching tips on p. 21 for ideas about using the Wordlist on p. 142 with your students.
>
> **REVIEW TEST**
> See esource.cambridge.org for the Review test and ideas about how and when to administer the Review test.

2 PEOPLE AND THINGS

LISTENING AND READING 1

Learning objectives

- Name members of the family – grandmother, grandfather, mother, father, brother, sister
- Read and understand sentences in which people introduce family members – This is my brother.
- Differentiate between titles – Mr, Mrs, Dr
- Use capital letters in titles correctly – Mr, Mrs, Dr
- Gain awareness of sound and spelling of the letters th
- Write two sentences introducing a family member – This is my sister. Her name is Manal.

See p. 19 for suggestions on how to use these Learning objectives with your students.

Lead-in

Write these gapped sentences on the board:

_____ am from the UK. (I)
His family _____ is Al Mady. (name)
My phone _____ is 059 201 3382. (number)
I _____ a student. (am)
Laila needs a library _____. (card)
_____ first name is Yehya. (My)

Students work in pairs and think of the words that complete the gaps. Students do not write anything at this stage, just think of the options. Elicit the correct answers as a class. Write them in the gaps. Underline the first letters of these words: from, Al, My, I, Laila, and Yehya. Ask students what word these letters create (family). Tell students that they are going to learn vocabulary on the topic of family in this lesson.

Vocabulary Pre-teaching / Review

You will need printable flashcards with the family words (Flashcards 2.1), which can be printed at esource.cambridge.org.

Follow the procedure on p. 15.

If appropriate, bring photographs of your family to class. Show students the photographs and say: father (name), mother (name), sister (name), brother (name). Show the photographs again, but this time say only the name. Check if students remember who the people are and if they are able to tell you the family words in English.

1 ◄))2.1 Focus on the photographs. Point at Ahmed and say: What's his name? Elicit: Ahmed. Point at the picture of his mother and elicit: mother. Try this with other words to check students' existing knowledge. Play the audio for students to listen and look at the photographs and words. Write: father on the board and then demonstrate tracing the word, pointing out the correct place to start. Students trace the words. Monitor and help as necessary. Play the audio again for students to listen and repeat.

2 ◄))2.2 Draw the word shape for sister on the board. Complete the first four letters and elicit the final two to complete the shape. Point out that all the letters sit on the line and t ascends above the middle line.

Focus on the first photograph and sentence in the book. Demonstrate completing the words. Students work individually and read and complete the sentences. Play the audio for students to listen to the full sentences.

Answers

2 father 3 brother 4 mother 5 grandfather
6 grandmother

SOUND AND SPELLING th

3 ◄))2.3 Write: mother on the board. Trace: th in a different pen if possible. Say the sound /ð/ and then say the whole word. Students make the sound and say the word with you. Play the audio. Students work individually, listen and trace the letters. Play the audio again for students to listen and repeat.

4 ◄))2.4 Write: mo_ _ er on the board. Elicit which two letters are missing (th). If appropriate in your context, invite a student to the board to complete the word. Otherwise, complete it yourself. Students write the letters individually. Play the audio for students to listen and write. Say the words and drill them as a class and individually, focusing on pronouncing the /ð/ sound. Play the audio again for students to listen and repeat.

PEOPLE AND THINGS — **UNIT 2**

5 🔊 2.5 Write your first and last name on the board. Add the labels *first name* and *last name* below the names. Focus on the photographs and the names. Elicit the first name and last name for each person. Complete the first item together, matching *Dr Allen* to *Maya Allen*. Students work individually and match the photographs to the names with titles. Play the audio for students to listen and check. Go through answers as a class and then drill pronunciation. (These are sight words that have almost no letter/sound information.) Elicit that *Mr* is for men, *Mrs* is for women and *Dr* is for both. You could also point out, if appropriate, how *Miss* (unmarried women) and *Ms* (women, married or not) are used. However, these titles are not used in this unit.

> **Answers**
> 1 c 2 a 3 d 4 b

> **NOTICE**
> Focus on the NOTICE box and point out that the correct use of titles (including *Mr* and *Mrs*) is with the last name, not the first name.

6 Write: *Mrs* on the board. Write these titles in a line: *Mr, Mrs, Dr, Mrs, Mr*. Point at the first title you wrote (Mrs) and elicit the pronunciation. Move your pen slowly across the titles, encouraging students to shout *Stop!* when you get to *Mrs*. Circle it twice.

Focus on the words in bold. Students work individually and read and circle the words. Go through answers as a class.

7 🔊 2.6 Focus on the first photograph and the name beneath it. Read through the sentences and point at the word *his*. Point at the photograph and again at the word *his*. Say: *his*. Point at the options. Say: *Mr? Mrs?* Elicit the correct answer (Mr) and point at the completed example. Students work individually, look at the photographs, read the text and choose the correct options. Monitor and help as necessary. Play the audio for students to listen and check their answers.

> **Answers**
> Dr Davey Mrs Spring Mr Rashid

> **Optional activity**
> Prepare some photographs of famous people who students will know (e.g. Cristiano Ronaldo, female singers or actresses well-known in your country), but avoid unmarried women at this stage as students are not practising *Miss* and *Ms*. Write: *Mr, Mrs, Dr* on the board. Show students a photograph and elicit the first and last name. Elicit the correct title (e.g. *Mr Ronaldo*).

8 Write: *this is my brother.* on the board and elicit there is a mistake (no capital T) by writing a cross (✗) next to the sentence. Cross out the *t* and write: *T* above it.

Focus on the first sentence in the book. Students work individually, read each sentence and find and correct the mistake. Students compare their answers in pairs. Go through answers on the board as a class.

> **Answers**
> This is my teacher.
> Her name is Maya Allen.

WRITING CHALLENGE

9 Focus on the photograph of a student. Point at the photograph and say: *Rashid Ali*. Ask a student to read out the model text. Focus on the rubric and read it aloud. Students work individually and write two sentences using *This is* and *His/Her name is …* Monitor and help as necessary. Check that students are writing in the correct position on the lines. Students swap notebooks and check each other's writing for correct language, spelling and punctuation.

LISTENING AND READING 2

> **Learning objectives**
> - Recognize the plural and singular form of the verb *be* – *I'm, We're*
> - Understand how to make a noun plural – *student, students*
> - Understand the difference between full and short verb forms for the verb *be* – *We're, We are*
> - Read and understand about groups of people – *We're students. They're teachers.*
> - Write two sentences about two teachers – *Our teachers are from the UK and Oman. Their names are Mrs Smith and Mr Rashid.*
>
> See p. 19 for suggestions on how to use these Learning objectives with your students.

Lead-in

Divide the board into two halves. Draw word clouds on both halves. Write: *He's my ...* in one cloud and *She's my ...* in the second. Demonstrate by saying: *He's my grandfather*. Elicit more sentences and write them in the word clouds. Students work in pairs and think of as many words as possible to finish the sentences in each word cloud. (Possible answers: *He's my grandfather / father / brother / teacher / doctor / university teacher. She's my grandmother / mother / sister / teacher / doctor / university teacher.*)

1 (2.7) Point at yourself and say: *I'm from* (your country). Indicate two students from the same country as you (if possible) and say: *They're from* (their country). Indicate yourself and the two students and say: *We're from* (country).

Say: *Listen and read*. Play the audio for students to listen and read. Point at the completed example and demonstrate tracing *I'm*. Say: *Trace*. Students work individually, read the sentences again and trace the words. Monitor and check that students are using correct stroke direction. Then students read the words and repeat.

NOTICE

Write: *I am a teacher.* on the board. Indicate two students in the class. Write: *They are students.* Underline the plural *s* in *students*. Connect *they* to the *s* with a line. Read both sentences again and ask students to repeat after you.

Focus on the NOTICE box. Ask a student to read the sentences and check pronunciation.

2 (2.8) Write: *I am / We are a teacher.* on the board. Ask students to give you the correct answer (I am). Circle it. Write: *I am / They are students.* on the board and again ask students to give you the correct answer (They are). Circle it.

Focus on the first photograph and the sentences in the book. Read through the sentences, focusing on the completed examples and emphasizing the pronouns. Play the audio for students to listen and underline the correct option. Go through answers as a class. Students work individually and trace the answers. Monitor to ensure correct directional strokes.

NOTICE

Write: *I am* and *I'm* on the board and read them aloud. Say: *Say I'm and write I am*.

Focus on the verbs in the NOTICE box. Allow students a minute to read the information. Ask a student to read the contractions aloud.

3 (2.9) Write: *I am* on the board. Cross out *a* and write in the apostrophe. Demonstrate the first example in the book on the board. Demonstrate correct use of strokes and how and where to write the apostrophe.

Students work individually, look at the photographs, read and complete the words in the sentences. Monitor and check for correct strokes and apostrophes in the correct position. Play the audio for students to listen.

Answers
She's He's We're They're

4 (2.10) Write: *Wearestudents.* on the board. Move the pen along the sentence and draw the first line after *We*. Move the pen again and encourage students to shout *Stop!* at each word boundary. Add vertical lines between the words.

Focus on the completed example. Point out how lines mark spaces between words. Explain that the contracted form (*I'm*, *We're*, etc.) is considered as one word. Students work individually through the other sentences. Monitor and help as necessary. Go through answers as a class. Play the audio for students to listen and repeat.

Answers
2 They're from Japan. 3 I'm from the UAE.
4 She's a teacher. 5 We're from Saudi Arabia.
6 They are students.

Optional activity

The aim of this activity is to practise speaking naturally by focusing on speed and basic linking of words. Students may question why there is no break between words when spoken, so it is important to raise awareness of this feature of English as early as possible.

Write these sentences on the board:

I'm a teacher.

They're from Saudi Arabia.

They're students from Saudi Arabia.

Repeat each sentence at normal speed and then gradually slow it down until it starts to break up. Say it again at normal speed. Repeat the procedure for all three sentences. Ask students to practise saying the sentences aloud following the same procedure.

5 Write: *My* on the board. Say: *My name's* (your name). and point at yourself. Write: *My name is* (your name). on the board. Point at the first *My* you wrote and then at the one in the sentence. Circle the one in the sentence.

PEOPLE AND THINGS — UNIT 2

Focus on the words in the box in the book and then the text. Say: *Read and circle*. Students work individually, read the text and circle the words. Go through answers as a class.

> **NOTICE**
>
> Write: *I am a teacher. My name is* (your name). on the board. Underline *I* and *My*. Draw a line connecting them.
>
> Focus on the NOTICE box. Read the sentences aloud. Ask students to repeat after you. Write them on the board. Draw lines connecting *We* with *Our* and *They* with *Their*.

6 👤 Indicate two students in the class. Write: *They aer from* (the country they are from). on the board. Underline *aer* and write a cross (✗) above it. Indicate the mistake and elicit the correct answer (are). Write it on the board.

Focus on the completed example. Students work individually and correct the mistakes. Write the sentences with mistakes on the board and elicit corrections. Mark them clearly on the board, in a different colour if possible. Check that students have corrected the sentences in their books.

> **Answers**
>
> 2 I <u>am</u> from Oman. 3 <u>Our</u> teachers are from the UK.
> 4 <u>Their</u> names are Ali and Obaid. 5 He is a <u>teacher</u>.
> 6 She is a <u>student</u>.

> 👁 **Common student errors**
>
> **Spelling:** The word *their* is in the top 20 misspelled words by Arabic L1 students. This is the typical error: *thier*.
>
> Write on the board:
>
> their thei_ the_ _ th_ _ _
>
> Focus on the first word. Ask students to spell it out. Then erase the word. Ask them to spell the word out again and complete the first gap when they are successful. Then erase the word. Continue like this until students are able to write the whole word.

WRITING CHALLENGE

7 👤👥 Focus on the photographs of two teachers. Point at the photographs and say: *Their names are Mrs Smith and Mr Odeh.* Ask a student to read out the model text. Focus on the rubric and read it aloud. Students work individually and write two sentences using *Our* and *Their*. Monitor and help as necessary.

Check that students are writing in the correct position on the lines. Students swap notebooks and check each other's writing for correct language, spelling and punctuation.

LISTENING AND READING 3

> **Learning objectives**
>
> - Name a number of common possessions – *camera, bag, mobile phone, computer, television, car*
> - Revise numbers from 0–10
> - Write numbers from 0–10
> - Form regular plural nouns – *mobile phones, bags*
> - Write two sentences about your family's possessions – *We have three computers. We have two televisions.*
> - Gain awareness of word stress
>
> See p. 19 for suggestions on how to use these Learning objectives with your students.

> **Lead-in**
>
> The aim of this activity is for students to revise writing the numerals 0–10 from aural input out of sequence. Say: *Listen and write*. Say the sequences below for students to listen and write in their notebooks.
>
> 2 4 6
> 3 5 7
> 0 1 0
> 9 6 3
>
> Students work in pairs and compare their answers. Write the sequences on the board for students to check. Add a gap at the end of each sequence and indicate that there is a number missing. Demonstrate with the first sequence by writing *8*. Ask students to write the missing number for each sequence. Go through answers as a class. The missing numbers are *8, 9, 1, 0*.

> **Vocabulary Pre-teaching / Review**
>
> You will need printable flashcards with common possessions and numbers (Flashcards 2.2 and 0.1), which can be printed at esource.cambridge.org.
>
> Follow the procedure on p. 15.
>
> Using the flashcards with numbers, start with the side that has the numeral on it, not the word. Show students a random number and a random common possession. Ask students to say the number and the possession aloud (e.g. *9, bag*). Say: *one bag*, (number on the flashcard) *bags*, stressing the *s*. Ask students to repeat after you. Repeat the procedure for a few more words and then change the side of the flashcard from the number to the word. Pre-teach how to write the numbers using the same procedure.

UNLOCK BASIC LITERACY TEACHER'S BOOK   49

1 🔊 2.11 👤 Focus on the numerals in the box and the written forms. Students work individually and complete the number row with the numerals. Play the audio. Drill the numbers if appropriate by asking students to cover the numerals and read the written forms.

> **◉ Common student errors**
>
> **Spelling:** The word *two* is in the top 20 mispelled words by Arabic L1 students. This is the typical error: *tow*.
>
> Write on the board:
> two tw _   t _ _
>
> Focus on the first word. Ask students to spell it out. Then erase the word. Ask them to spell the word out again and complete the first gap when they are successful. Then erase the word. Continue like this until students are able to write the whole word.

2 🔊 2.12 👤 Put two mobile phones (or two books – yours and a student's) on a student's desk. Say: *one, two. Two mobile phones (books)*. Add another phone (or book) and repeat the counting. Elicit: *three*. Say: *three mobile phones (books)*.

Focus on the photographs. Students work individually, count and write the numbers. Play the audio for students to listen and check. Go through answers by asking students to spell out the numbers. Write the words on the board.

3 🔊 2.13 👤 Write: *onetwothree* on the board. Move the pen along the sentence and draw a vertical line after *one*. Move the pen again and encourage students to shout *Stop!* at each word boundary. Add lines between the words.

Focus on the line of words in the book. Show how lines mark spaces between words. Students work individually along the line. Monitor and help as necessary. Play the audio for students to listen and check. Go through answers on the board.

4 👤 Remind students how to form *o, e, u, i* and *n, t, w, f, r, g, h* with correct strokes on the board.

If necessary, prompt students to use something to cover the words on the left as they complete each one. Monitor and check that they are working from left to right. Encourage correct stroke direction and correct height and position of the individual letters.

> **NOTICE**
>
> Write: *one computer* on the board. Underline: *one*. Next to it, write: *three computers* and underline: *three* and *s* in *computers*. Draw a line connecting *three* and *s*.
>
> Focus on the NOTICE box. Read the phrases aloud. Ask students to repeat after you. Write them on the board. Draw lines connecting the numbers and the *s* in the nouns.

5 🔊 2.14 👤👥 Focus on the first example in the exercise. Say: *Listen*. Read the question aloud and point at the question mark. Say: *Trace*. Demonstrate tracing the word *cars* in the book. Play the audio for students to listen and read. Students work individually and trace the words. Monitor and help as necessary. Students check their answers in pairs. Play the audio again for students to listen and repeat.

6 👤 Put one thing on your desk, e.g. one bag. Say: *I have one bags*. Write it on the board. Circle the word *bags* and write a cross (✗) above it. Elicit the correct word for this sentence (*bag*) and write it above the cross. Say: *I have one bag*.

Students work individually and complete the exercise by circling the incorrect words and writing the correct form. Write the sentences with mistakes on the board. Ask a student to correct each one, if appropriate, or ask for corrections from the class.

> **Answers**
>
> I have two ba<u>gs</u>.
> We have four television<u>s</u>.
> We have one <u>computer</u>.

7 👤 Write: *have / eight cameras. / I* on the board. Elicit the correct order for the words (*I have eight cameras.*). Write the answer on the board.

Focus on the jumbled words in the book. Students work individually, look at the words and re-order them. Monitor and check students are using capitals and full stops correctly. Go through answers on the board, using different colours if possible to highlight the subject pronoun / verb pattern.

> **Answers**
>
> 2 We have two televisions.
> 3 I have four bags.
> 4 I have seven mobile phones.

PEOPLE AND THINGS   UNIT 2

Optional activity

Write: *How many … do you have?* at the top of the board. Below, write a word cloud with these words inside: *cameras, library cards, bags, mobile phones, computers, television*. Students work in pairs and use the words in the word clouds to create questions about possessions. Students ask each other about the number of things they have (e.g. *How many bags do you have? I have three bags.*). Monitor and note any grammar or pronunciation mistakes you hear. At the end of the exercise, write the mistakes on the board, cross them out and elicit corrections.

SOUND AND SPELLING
Word stress

Literacy tip

In unstressed syllables the vowel sound is reduced. In many cases the resulting sound is known as the schwa /ə/ (e.g. the final syllable in *teacher* and *computer*). This sound can be spelled in many ways and is a common cause of spelling errors, as it is usually not clear which vowel should be used to spell it. There are no solid rules to present to students for this area. However, developing awareness of word stress and its features helps students in these ways:

- Developing syllable awareness helps students to read words and to produce them accurately.
- Developing vowel reduction awareness helps students to decode what they hear and relate it to the written word.
- Developing awareness that the reduced vowel has no fixed spelling shows students the importance of learning the complete spelling of words from the visual form, rather than relying on a rough phonetic transcription of what they hear (which often leads to missing out vowels when spelling, e.g. *teachr*).

8 ◆) 2.15 Draw circles on the board corresponding to the syllables of your name if it is more than one syllable (e.g. oOo *Mohammed*). If your name is one syllable, use the name of a student. Say the name, strongly exaggerating the stress while pointing at each circle. Get students to repeat as a class and then individually. Students then say their own names in the same way. Write the relevant number and size of circles and compile a list of names on the board.

Focus on the photographs and words in the book and their stress patterns. Play the audio for students to listen and follow the stress patterns. Play the audio again for students to repeat.

9 ◆) 2.16 Write on the board the three syllable patterns in the book, numbered *1, 2, 3,* and write three words (*teacher, grandmother, television*) under them, respectively. Say the words aloud and write the corresponding number next to each one (*teacher [1], grandmother [2], television [3]*).

Play the audio for students to look at the words and listen. Then ask students to read the words and match them to the corresponding pattern. They can also do this exercise in pairs. Play the audio again for students to listen and check their answers. Go through answers as a class. Play the audio again if required.

Answers

television [3] Mexico [2] sister [1] family [2]
grandfather [2] brother [1] father [1] mother [1]
student [1]

10 ◆) 2.17 Write the first two stress patterns on the board. Say: *family* and write it on the board. Focus on the corresponding stress pattern (Ooo). Circle: *family*. Say: *sister* and write it on the board. Point at the stress pattern (Ooo) and say: *yes or no?* in a questioning tone. Then say: *grandmother* and write it on the board. Point out that it follows the same pattern as family. Circle: *grandmother* to show it matches the pattern. Drill the pronunciation of *sister* and *grandmother* as a class and individually to practise the pattern.

Students work individually, look at the pattern, read the words and circle the two with the same stress pattern. Play the audio for students to listen and check their answers. Play the audio again and write the words under the correct stress pattern on the board. Drill the words.

Answers

2 brother, Turkey 3 grandfather, family 4 student, doctor

LANGUAGE FOCUS

Learning objectives
- Read and write numbers 1–100
- Read and understand about age of people and objects – *He is twenty years old.*
- Recognize the difference between *one year old* and *three years old*
- Discriminate between *-teen* and *-ty* in numbers – *thirteen/thirty, fourteen/forty*
- Write two sentences about a person in your family and this person's age – *This is Majid. He is twenty years old.*
- Gain awareness of words with *silent e*

See p. 19 for suggestions on how to use these Learning objectives with your students.

Lead-in
The aim of this lead-in exercise is for students to revise the numbers 0–10 out of sequence. Students stand up. Students will be saying the numbers in order as fast as they can, starting from 10 and going down to 0. Say: *10* and then nominate (or throw a ball for a student to catch) a student to say the next number.

Elicit the number 9. Repeat the procedure for the rest of the numbers. Once you reach 0, start from 10 again. If a nominated student makes a mistake, this person should sit down. Continue the exercise until all students are sitting down or until you repeat all the numbers twice.

Vocabulary Pre-teaching / Review
You will need printable flashcards with bigger numbers (Flashcards 0.4 and 2.3), which can be printed at esource.cambridge.org. You need the sides of the cards with both numerals and words.

Follow the procedure on p. 15.

Write these numbers on the board: fifteen, eleven, fourteen, nineteen and twelve. Ask students to work in pairs, read the numbers and put them in order. Go through answers as a class (eleven, twelve, fourteen, fifteen, nineteen).

1 (2.18) Say the first two numbers aloud while students follow in the book. Then point at the next number and say: *Listen. Thirteen* and let them write: *3*. Say: *Look and listen.* Play the audio for students to listen and look at the dots and the written forms. Students work individually and complete the numbers. Write on the board the numbers and the full words next to the numbers, for students to check and correct their spelling. Point out the similarities, e.g. *six/sixteen* by circling and connecting them, and the differences, e.g. *five/fifteen*, *three/thirteen* by underlining them.

NOTICE
Write: *thirteen* on the board. Underline *-teen*. Next to it, write: *fourteen* and underline: *-teen*.

Focus on the NOTICE box. Read the numbers aloud. Ask students to repeat after you. Ask students to look at Exercise 1 and underline all instances of *-teen* in numbers 12–19.

2 (2.19) Write: *seventeeneleven* on the board. Above this, write: *17 11*. Say: *17 11*. Draw a line after *seventeen*.

Focus on the numbers and the written forms. Students work individually, look at the numbers and find and connect the written form by drawing a line. Play the audio for students to listen and check. Write the numbers on the board for students to check.

Answers
eleven   thirteen   nineteen   twelve   eighteen   fourteen   sixteen   fifteen

3 (2.20) Focus on the completed example and point out how it is crossed out in the box. Students work individually and add the numbers to the boxes. Play the audio for students to listen and follow. Students then work individually and trace the word shapes. Monitor and check for correct letter formation.

4 (2.21) Write: *13* and *30* on the board. Say: *30* and elicit which number you said by pointing at each number and asking: *yes or no?* Try this a few times, changing numbers, and then write: *thirteen* and *thirty*. Repeat the procedure with the written forms. Underline the ending of both words (*-teen* and *-ty*).

Focus on the completed example. Students work individually and complete the exercise by looking at the numbers and circling the correct option. Play the audio for students to listen and check. Students work individually and trace the numbers. Monitor and check for correct letter formation. Drill the pronunciation of the pairs of numbers.

5 (2.22) Focus on the first photograph: Osama. Read out the two sentences and point to the age. Point out the completed example. Students work individually, look at the photograph and the number, and write the number in full. Students check their answers in pairs. Play the audio for students to listen and check.

PEOPLE AND THINGS — UNIT 2

WRITING CHALLENGE

6 Focus on the photograph of Majid. Point at the photograph and say: *This is Majid. He is twenty years old.* Ask a student to read out the model text. Focus on the rubric and read it aloud. Students work individually and write two sentences. Monitor and help as necessary. Check that students are writing in the correct position on the lines. Students swap notebooks and check each other's writing for correct language, spelling and punctuation.

> **Optional activity**
>
> Write the ages of members of your family in a column (rounded to the nearest 10 if over 20) and then the appropriate words jumbled in another column, e.g. *father, mother, brother, sister.* Ask students to guess who is which age. (This could be reversed, so you write the words in the table and students guess the ages, either from numbers on the board or freely guessing.)

SOUND AND SPELLING
Silent *e* – n*a*me, n*i*ne …

> **Literacy tip**
>
> The silent *e* is a very useful rule to point out. Many words include vowel + consonant + the letter *e* together in a syllable; for example *name, nine, mobile.* The final *e* is not pronounced, but it makes the vowel sound in the syllable the same as the name of the first vowel letter.
>
> name /neɪm/
>
> a /eɪ/
>
> This is common in high-frequency words with the letters *a* (*name*), *i* (*nice*) and *o* (*home*). It is less common for the letter *u* (*tube*) and it is quite rare for the letter *e* (*these*).

7 (2.23) Write: pl_n_ on the board. Say: *plane.* Elicit the first missing letter (a). Say: *plan.* Then elicit the second missing letter (e). Say: *plane.* Cover the final *e* with your hand, and repeat *plan.* Ask students to repeat. Then uncover and say: *plane.* Students repeat. Demonstrate how to write *a* and *e* with correct line directions.

Play the audio for students to listen and read the words. Students work individually and trace the letters. Monitor and check for correct letter formation. Write all the words on the board. Point at the photographs to check meaning. Ask students to read and say the words aloud. Play the audio again for students to listen and repeat.

8 (2.24) Write: n_n_ on the board. Say: *nine.* Elicit the first missing letter (i). Elicit the second missing letter (e). Write them in the gaps on the board.

Play the audio for students to listen and read the words. Students work individually and trace the letters. Monitor and check for correct letter formation. Write the words on the board. Point at the photographs to check meaning. Play the audio again for students to listen and repeat.

9 (2.25) Write: *plan plane hat hate* on the board. Say: *plane.* Point at *plan* and say: *yes or no?* (no) Point at the word *plane* and say: *yes or no?* (yes) Circle: *plane.* Repeat the procedure with *hat* and *hate.* Focus on the pictures and the words. Play the audio for students to listen and read.

10 (2.26) Focus on the pictures and words in Exercise 9. Say: *Listen and circle.* Play the audio for students to listen and circle the word they hear. Go through answers as a class.

> **Answers**
>
> 1 plan 2 hate 3 cane 4 pin

SPELLING CHALLENGE

11 (2.27) Focus on the photographs and the words underneath. Demonstrate the first example by writing d_t_ on the board. Say: *date* and point at the gaps. Elicit the missing letters (a, e) and complete the word.

Play Part 1 of the audio for students to listen and write the complete words. Point out the spelling pattern. Allow students time to check their answers in pairs before playing Part 2 of the audio, which includes the spelling. Go through answers as a class.

> **Answers**
>
> 1 d*a*t*e* 2 l*i*m*e* 3 c*a*p*e* 4 p*i*p*e*

LISTENING FOCUS

> **Learning objectives**
>
> - Understand descriptions of possessions – *This is my car. My car is from Japan.*
> - Listen for key information
>
> See p. 19 for suggestions on how to use these Learning objectives with your students.

Lead-in

Prepare flashcards with common possessions (Flashcards 2.2), which can be printed at esource.cambridge.org. You need the sides of the cards with photographs.

Take one flashcard and say: *How old is your* (object from the flashcard)? Give your answer: *My* (object name) *is two years old.* Write the dialogue on the board. Ask students at random about their objects. Show a few more objects and ask how old they are.

1 (◀) 2.28) 👤 Focus on the photographs and the information about them. Then read the first sentence aloud and point at the two photographs for students to match. Elicit the correct answer (b) by saying: *yes or no?* when pointing at each photograph. Students work individually, read the sentences and match the photographs. Play the audio for students to listen and check. Go through answers as a class.

> **Answers**
> 2 a 3 a 4 b 5 a 6 b

2 (◀) 2.29) 👤 Write: *Thisismygrandmother* on the board. Move the pen along the sentence and draw a vertical line after *This*. Move the pen again and encourage students to shout *Stop!* at the word boundaries. Add lines between the words.

Focus on the completed example in the book. Show how lines mark spaces between words. Students work individually through the other sentences. Monitor and help as necessary. Play the audio for students to listen and repeat. Go through answers as a class.

Focus on the photographs and the two completed boxes. Read the first sentence and point at photograph b. Say: *Read and match.* Students work individually, read the sentences again and match the photographs. Go through answers as a class.

> **Answers**
> 3 He is from Oman. (b)
> 4 This is my teacher. (a)
> 5 He is 79 years old. (b)
> 6 He is from the UK. (a)

Optional activity

Write these sentences on the board:
They from are the UK.
My television is 5 old years.
Many how mobile phones do you have?
He is years 17 old.
Our are names Olivia and Ali.
Car my is from Japan.

Read the first sentences aloud. Write a cross (✗) next to the sentence. Elicit the mistake and how to correct it (They <u>are from</u> the UK.). Students work in pairs and continue with the remaining sentences. Go through answers as a class. (My television is 5 <u>years old</u>. <u>How many</u> mobile phones do you have? He is <u>17 years</u> old. Our <u>names are</u> Olivia and Ali. <u>My car</u> is from Japan.)

👁 KEY WORDS FOR LITERACY

Learning objectives
- Read, spell and pronounce key words for literacy – *are, is, one, two, from*
- Complete sentences with the key words for literacy

See p. 19 for suggestions on how to use these Learning objectives in your lessons.

1 (◀) 2.30) 👤 Write: *our* on the board. Elicit the pronunciation /aʊər/. Write this sentence: *Our names are Maria and Anna.* Move your pen slowly across the sentence, encouraging students to shout *Stop!* when you get to the word *our*. Circle: *our* and read aloud.

Focus on the words in bold. Say: *Read and circle.* Students work individually, read and circle the words. Play the audio for students to listen and check.

2 👤 Write: *are* on the board. Write these words: *or are our or are our.* Move your pen slowly across the sentences, encouraging students to shout *Stop!* when you get to the word *are*. Circle it twice.

Focus on the words in bold. Say: *Read and circle.* Students work individually, read and circle the words. Go through answers as a class.

3 👤 Focus on the first line. Students work from left to right, covering and completing the words as they go. Monitor and help as necessary. Encourage correct stroke direction and correct height and position of the individual letters.

4 (◀) 2.31) 👤👥 Write: *are* on the board. Erase one letter at a time and elicit the missing letter until students can spell out the word.

Focus on the sentences. Students work individually, read the sentences and complete the words. Play the audio for students to listen and check. Students compare their answers in pairs. Go through answers as a class.

> **Answers**
> 2 from 3 one 4 is 5 two

READING AND WRITING

> **Learning objectives**
> - Revise the verb *be* for *he, she, we* and *they*
> - Use pronouns to help with understanding when reading
> - Read and understand a text about a class – *This is our class.*
> - Complete a text about a class – *We have ten computers.*
>
> See p. 19 for suggestions on how to use these Learning objectives with your students.

> **Lead-in**
> On the board write the names of your mother, father, brother, sister and two friends. Next to the first name, write: *mother*. Ask students to guess who your next three family members are. Point at the name of your first friend, write: *friend* next to it and ask: *family?* (no). Make sure students understand the meaning of this word by indicating two students in the class who are friendly and saying: *friends*. If necessary, ask students to check the meaning in the dictionary. Point at the last name and elicit the word *friend* again by pointing back at the previous name. Point (with a circular movement) at the names of your family members. Say: *family*. Point at your friends' names and say: *friends*.

1 Focus on photograph c. Say: *teacher?* Point at *1* and again at photograph c. Say: *Look and match*. Students work individually, look at the words and match the photographs. Go through answers as a class.

> **Answers**
> 2 a 3 e 4 b 5 d

2 🔊 2.32 Focus on the text. Point at the circled phrase in the first line and point to the same words in Exercise 1. (At this point, ignore the highlighted pronouns; they are used in the next exercise.)

PEOPLE AND THINGS — UNIT 2

Students work individually, read and find the other words from Exercise 1, circling them. Monitor and make sure students read from left to right. Play the audio for students to listen and read the text.

> **Answers**
> We have 30 *dictionaries*. We have six *computers*. *Our teacher* is from the UK. Her name is Mrs Randall. She is 40 years old. Carlos is from Mexico. He is nineteen. Riku and Taro are *friends*. They are from Japan. Riku is twenty-two years old. Taro is twenty-three years old.

> 👁 **Common student errors**
>
> **Sentence boundaries:** Arabic L1 students often have problems with sentence boundaries. Not beginning a new sentence when required is one of the most frequent errors of Arabic speakers. Arabic L1 students create sentences that are often too long, saying and writing a few sentences as if they were one, e.g. *We have thirty computers we have ten mobile phones we have two bags.* When reading texts with students, focus their attention on the full stops. Ask students to count the words in the sentence. This may help them understand that short sentences are easier to understand.

3 Focus on the highlighted pronouns in this exercise and the highlighted pronouns in the text in Exercise 2. Make sure students can see that they are the same. Point at the example, showing that *We* means *Our class* in the text. (If you can display the text on the board, indicate the relationship by circling and drawing a line from *Our class* to the highlighted *We*). Say: *Look* (point at the text in Exercise 2) *and match* (point at the sentences and people in Exercise 3). Students work individually, read the sentences and refer back to the text to match. Student check answers in pairs. Go through answers as a class.

> **Answers**
> 2 Mrs Randall 3 Carlos 4 Riku and Taro

4 Write: b r t h e r on the board. Write a cross (✗) next to it. Elicit the missing letter and its position (br<u>o</u>ther). Repeat the procedure with t h r t e e n (thi<u>r</u>teen).

Focus on the example and the individual letters. Students work individually, read the words and insert the missing letter. Go through answers on the board as a class.

> **Answers**
> 2 te<u>a</u>cher 3 stud<u>e</u>nt 4 cl<u>a</u>ss 5 comput<u>e</u>r

5 Write: *This is class.* on the board. Then write: *our* to the left of the sentence. Move your pen across the sentence in the book, encouraging students to shout *Stop!* where they think *our* goes (This is our class.) Write the correct sentence on the board.

Students work individually, read the sentences and add the missing word. Monitor and check that students are copying the words correctly. Go through answers as a class.

> **Answers**
>
> 2 We have 10 computers. 3 His name is Jack.
> 4 She is from the UK. 5 He is my friend.

6 Write the name of a friend on the board and say: *This is* (name of your friend). *She/He is my friend. She/He is from* (country of origin). Write the sentences on the board.

Focus on the gapped text and demonstrate writing in the gaps. Focus on the rubric and read it aloud. Students work individually and complete the text. Monitor and help as necessary. Check that students are writing in the correct position on the lines. Students swap notebooks and check each other's writing for correct language, spelling and punctuation.

> **Model answer**
>
> This is our class. We have five computers. This is my teacher. Her name is Jenny. This is Rowdah. She is my friend. She is from Saudi Arabia.

Optional activity

Aural gap fill: Follow the procedure on p. 17.

This is (our) class.   This is (my) mobile phone.
We (have) ten computers.   This (is) my friend.
(This) is our teacher.   She is 20 years (old).
I am (from) the UAE.

> **Objectives review**
>
> See Teaching tips on p. 19 for ideas about using the Objectives review with your students.
>
> **WORDLIST**
>
> See Teaching tips on p. 21 for ideas about using the Wordlist on p. 142 with your students.
>
> **REVIEW TEST**
>
> See esource.cambridge.org for the Review test and ideas about how and when to administer the Review test.

3 UNIVERSITY LIFE

LISTENING AND READING 1

Learning objectives

- Understand university subjects – *Maths, Chemistry, English, Biology, History, IT, Business, Japanese*
- Read and understand about the subjects people study – *I study Maths, English and Biology.*
- Use capital letters for the first letter in university subjects – *Maths*
- Gain awareness of the stress patterns in university subjects
- Understand how to use a comma in lists
- Write two sentences about what you study – *I am a student. I study IT, Business and English.*

See p. 19 for suggestions on how to use these Learning objectives with your students.

Lead-in

Write on the board these words with gaps:

s t _ d _ n t
t _ _ ch _ r
_ n _ v _ rs _ t _
s t _ d _ n t _ D c _ r d
l _ b r _ r _

Ask students to work in pairs and complete the gaps. Go through answers as a class, writing the missing letters in the gaps (student, teacher, university, student ID card, library). Circle the following letters in the words: ⓢtudent, ⓣeacher, ⓤniversity, stuⓓent ID card, librarⓨ. Ask students what word these letters create (study). Tell students that they are going to learn vocabulary on the topic of university.

Vocabulary Pre-teaching / Review

You will need printable flashcards with the university words (Flashcards 3.1), which can be printed at esource.cambridge.org.

Follow the procedure on p. 15.

Take in some subject books or use flashcards with photographs. Hold up the Maths book (or the flashcard) and elicit: *Maths*. Write it on the board. Continue with the remaining subjects. Read the subjects aloud for students to repeat. Erase each word one by one, hold up the flashcard (covering the word) and elicit the subject. Continue until all the words have been erased. Hold up each card again and try to elicit the subject and how it is spelled. Write each subject on the board.

1 🔊 3.1 👤 Focus on the pictures. Point at and read *1 (Maths)* aloud for students to repeat. Point at photograph d and say: *Look and match*. Students work individually, read the words and match them to the pictures. Play the audio for students to listen and check.

> **Answers**
> 2 e 3 b 4 f 5 h 6 c 7 g 8 a

NOTICE

Focus on the NOTICE box and point out that university subjects always begin with a capital letter. Ask students to underline the capital letters in the subjects in Exercise 1.

2 🔊 3.2 👤 Focus on the completed example. Play the audio. Students listen and read the words. Write: *Maths* on the board and then demonstrate tracing the word, pointing at the correct place to start. Students work individually and trace the words. Monitor and help as necessary, checking for correct stroke direction. Play the audio again for students to listen and repeat.

3 🔊 3.3 👤 Draw the word shape for *Maths* on the board, the same as the one in the book. Complete the first three letters (M a t) and elicit the final two (h s) to complete the shape. Point out that all the letters sit on the line and three go above the middle line (M t h). Remind students that all university subjects start with a capital letter.

Focus on the words to complete in the book. Play the audio for students to listen, read and complete the words.

Literacy tip

Stress patterns are important in literacy. There is always a vowel sound in every syllable, and the stress often determines the sound of the vowel (an unstressed vowel is often the schwa sound /ə/). Raising awareness will help students to understand how English sound/spelling relationships work.

4 🔊 3.4 👤👥 Write: *English* on the board. Say: *English* with clearly differentiated syllables. Ask: *How many?* pointing at each syllable, elicit: *two* and draw the stress pattern *Oo* above the word.

UNL⚆CK BASIC LITERACY TEACHER'S BOOK   57

Focus attention on the subjects in Exercise 1. Students work individually. They read each one aloud and write them in the correct column. Students work in pairs and compare their answers. Play the audio for students to listen and check.

> **Answers**
> Oo: Business
> Ooo: History
> oOoo: Biology
> oO: IT
> ooO: Japanese

5 (◆) 3.5 Focus on the second dialogue and the pictures. Read the second dialogue aloud. Point at the word *Japanese* and elicit which picture it refers to (a). Students work individually, read the dialogues, look at the pictures and match. Students compare their answers in pairs. Play the audio for students to listen and check. Go through answers as a class.

> **Answers**
> 1 b, c, f 2 d, e

NOTICE
Focus on the NOTICE box. Read the sentence aloud. Point out the comma and the word *and* in the sentence. Focus on the first dialogue in Exercise 5 and ask students to circle the comma and the word *and*.

6 (◆) 3.6 Write: *I study E_ _ _ _ _ _ , B_ _ _ _ _ _ _ and C_ _ _ _ _ _ _ _.* on the board. Elicit the missing subjects (English, Business, Chemistry). Trace the first letter: *E* and ask students to spell the word *English* aloud. Repeat the procedure with the words *Business* and *Chemistry*. Complete the words.

Focus on the subjects in the box. Say: *Trace and write*. Students work individually, read the sentence, trace the first letters and write the subjects. Students compare their answers in pairs. Play the audio for students to listen and check. Go through answers as a class.

> **Answers**
> I study English, Japanese and Maths.
> I study Business, Biology and Chemistry.

7 Write: *I study English Chemistry and History* on the board. Write a comma, a full stop and question mark above the sentence. Elicit where to put them (I study English, Chemistry and History.) They don't need the question mark, but they will do for question 4.

Students work individually, read the sentences and add commas, full stops and question marks in the correct positions. Go through answers as a class.

> **Answers**
> 1 I study Maths, English and Biology.
> 2 I study History, Chemistry and IT.
> 3 I study Business, Maths and Japanese.
> 4 What subjects do you study?

8 (◆) 3.7 Write: *IstudyJapanese,BusinessandIT.* on the board. Move the pen from left to right along the sentence and draw the first line after *I*. Move the pen again and encourage students to shout *Stop!* at the word boundaries. Add lines between the words.

Focus on sentence 1. Show how lines mark spaces between words. Students work individually through the other sentences. Monitor and help as necessary. Play the audio for students to listen and check. Go through answers as a class.

> **Answers**
> 1 I study Japanese, Business and IT.
> 2 I study IT, English and History.
> 3 I study Chemistry, Biology and Maths.
> 4 What subjects do you study?

9 (◆) 3.8 Write the letters of the alphabet on the board letter by letter, saying the letters for students to repeat. Write: *Maths* on the board, reading out the letters one by one. Elicit that it needs a capital *M*.

Say: *Listen and write*. Play the audio for students to listen and write the words. Students check their answers in pairs. Play the audio again if required. Go through answers as a class.

> **Answers**
> 2 Chemistry 3 English 4 Business 5 History 6 IT
> 7 Biology 8 Japanese

UNLOCK BASIC LITERACY TEACHER'S BOOK

UNIVERSITY LIFE · UNIT 3

WRITING CHALLENGE

10 Focus on the photograph. Point and say: *She is a student*. Ask a student to read out the model text. Focus on the rubric and read it aloud. Students work individually and write two sentences using university subjects. Monitor and help as necessary. Check that students are writing in the correct position on the lines. Students swap notebooks and check each other's writing for correct language, spelling and punctuation.

Optional activity

Collect students' work. Read their sentences aloud with the names missing. The class guesses who wrote each sentence. Make sure they know not to call out their own name.

LISTENING AND READING 2

Learning objectives

- Understand days of the week – *Sunday, Monday, Tuesday, Wednesday, Thursday, Friday, Saturday,*
- Understand the difference between *morning* and *afternoon*
- Use capital letters on days of the week – *Sunday*
- Read and understand where and when people's classes are – *Where is our English class? In room 7. When is our Business class? On Tuesday morning.*
- Understand how to use prepositions *on* and *in* when saying where and when people's classes are
- Write two sentences about subjects – *I study History on Wednesday morning. I study History in room 11.*

See p. 19 for suggestions on how to use these Learning objectives with your students.

Lead-in

Write: *university* in the middle of the board with eight lines coming from it. Write: *English* at the end of the first line. Students work in pairs and complete the spidergram with all the university subjects they know so far (Maths, Chemistry, English, Biology, History, IT, Business, Japanese). Do not allow students to look in the book. Elicit and write subjects on the board, asking students to spell them out.

Vocabulary Pre-teaching / Review

You will need printable flashcards with the days of the week (Flashcards 3.2), which can be printed at esource.cambridge.org.

Follow the procedure on p. 15.

Say: *It's* (the day of the week). Students repeat. Point forward and say the next day. Continue through the days of the week. Write them on the board in a column, starting with the first weekday in your country. Use capitals for the first letters. Draw a circle around the two weekend days in your country.

1 🔊 3.9 Write: *Su M Tu W Th F Sa* on the board. Say: *Sunday*. Elicit from students which calendar letters it refers to (Su). Repeat the procedure for *Wednesday* and *Saturday*.

Focus on the days of the week and the calendar letters. Say: *Match*. Students work individually and match the words to the calendar letters. Play the audio for students to listen and check. Go through answers as a class. Ask students to read the days of the week aloud.

Answers

Friday 6 Monday 2 Wednesday 4 Tuesday 3
Thursday 5 Saturday 7

👁 Common student errors

Punctuation: Arabic L1 students often do not remember to capitalize the first letter in days of the week, especially if these appear in the middle of the sentence, e.g. *On monday morning …* When writing sentences with days of the week, remind students to always check if they have used a capital letter.

NOTICE

Focus on the NOTICE box. Read the words aloud. Point out the capital letter in each day of the week. Ask students to look at Exercise 1 and underline the capital letter in each day of the week.

Optional activity

Write all the days of the week in a column on the board starting with *Sunday*. Students read the words aloud as a class. Erase one of the days except for the first letter. Students read the words aloud again as a class and try to remember the erased word. Repeat until all the words have been erased and only the first letters remain. Then erase the first letters in the same way. To finish, students say the days of the week in order while you write them on the board again.

UNL🔒CK BASIC LITERACY TEACHER'S BOOK

2 🔊 3.10 Write: *S, M, T, W, T, F, S* in a column on the board. Elicit the days of the week and their spellings. Write them on the board. Clearly show the direction of strokes as you write, particularly showing the difference between capital and lowercase letters (e.g. *M* is pointed, while *m* is rounded).

Focus on the words in the book. Students work individually and trace the letters. Monitor and check for correct stroke direction. Play the audio for students to listen and repeat.

3 🔊 3.11 Write: *Sunday* on the board. Write these words on the board: *Saturday Sunday Saturday Saturday Sunday*. Move your pen slowly across the sentences, encouraging students to shout *Stop!* when you get to *Sunday*. Circle: *Sunday* twice.

Focus on the words in bold. Say: *Read and circle*. Students work individually, read and circle the words. Play the audio for students to listen and check.

4 Draw a word shape for *Monday* on the board and write: *M* next to it. Say: *What day?* Elicit the correct answer (Monday).

Students work individually and complete the days of the week. Monitor and ensure correct directional strokes.

> **Answers**
> 2 Friday 3 Tuesday 4 Sunday 5 Thursday
> 6 Wednesday 7 Saturday

5 🔊 3.12 Write: *morning* and *afternoon* on the board. Write: *16:00* and *08:00* and show a clock on the wall or a watch. Elicit which time goes with morning (08:00) and afternoon (16:00). Say: *morning* and *afternoon* aloud for students to listen and repeat.

Focus on the pictures and the numbered words to trace. Students match the pictures and write the letters in the boxes. Go through answers as a class. Students work individually and trace the words. Play the audio for students to listen and repeat. Focus on the word stress in *afternoon* (ooO) and *morning* (Oo).

> **Answers**
> 2 a 3 c 4 d

6 🔊 3.13 Write: *Where is our English class? When is our English class?* on the board. Underline *Where* and *When* in the questions. Write the time and place of your English classes using *In room …* and *On* (day of the week) *morning/afternoon*. Underline *In* and *On* in the answers. Draw a line joining *Where* with *In* and *When* with *On*.

Focus on the timetable, the questions and the answers. Students work individually, read the questions and match them to the answers. Students compare their answers in pairs. Play the audio for students to listen and check. Go through answers as a class.

> **Answers**
> 2 On Tuesday afternoon.
> 3 In room 3.
> 4 On Monday morning.

> **NOTICE**
>
> Focus on the NOTICE box. Read the words aloud. Point out the prepositions *on* and *in*. Focus on Exercise 6 and ask students to circle the prepositions *on* and *in*.

7 Write: *Where? When?* on the board. Elicit which preposition goes with each question word (*in* with *where*, *on* with *when*).

Focus on the questions and the gapped answers. (Ignore the *Yes/No* options for now.) Show the completed example for the first question. Students work individually, read the questions and write *In* or *On* in the gap. Go through answers as a class.

> **Answers**
> 2 On 3 On 4 In

8 Focus on the timetable and the questions and answers in Exercise 7. Say: *Look. Yes? No?* Point at the completed example. Students work individually, look at the timetable, read the questions and answers and circle: *Yes* or *No*. Students work in pairs and compare their answers. Go through answers as a class.

> **Answers**
> 2 Yes 3 No 4 Yes

UNIVERSITY LIFE — UNIT 3

9 ◄)) 3.14 Write: *afternoon* and *I study English on Tuesday afternoon.* on the board. Move the pen along the sentence and circle the word *afternoon*. Read the sentence aloud.

Focus on the words before each sentence in the book. Say: *Read and circle.* Students work individually, look at the word and find it in the sentence. Monitor and help as necessary. Play the audio for students to listen. Go through answers on the board.

10 Write: *afternoon* on the board. Write: *after nine afternoon after none afternoon* on the board. Move your pen slowly across the words, encouraging students to shout *Stop!* when you get to the word *afternoon*. Circle it twice.

Focus on the words in bold. Say: *Read and circle.* Students work individually, read and circle the words.

11 Focus on the word shapes in the book. If necessary, remind students how to form *a, i, o* and *n, d* with correct strokes on the board.

Students work individually, cover and complete the words. If necessary, prompt them to use something to cover the words on the left as they complete each one. Monitor and check that they are working from left to right. Encourage correct stroke direction and correct height and position of the individual letters.

12 Write: *I study japanese in room 13.* on the board. Write a cross (✗) next to the sentence. Elicit where the mistake is (no capital in *Japanese*). Cross the word *japanese* out and correct it.

Students work individually, read the sentences and find and correct the mistake. Go through answers as a class.

> **Answers**
> 2 I study Business on Wednesday afternoon.
> 3 I study English on Tuesday morning.

LISTENING AND READING 3

Learning objectives

- Understand basic adjectives – *interesting, boring, easy, difficult*
- Read and understand people's opinions about subjects – *What's Maths like? It's easy.*
- Understand how to use the verb *be* in negative sentences – *It's not difficult.*
- Write two sentences about subjects – *What's Maths like? It is interesting. It is not boring.*
- Gain awareness of sound and spelling of letters *sh* /ʃ/, *ch* /tʃ/, *th* /θ/

See p. 19 for suggestions on how to use these Learning objectives with your students.

Lead-in

Write these sentences on the board:
I study Maths English and Business.
I study Japanese on Wednesday morning
Where is your History class

Next to the sentences write a cross (✗) to show students that each sentence has a mistake. Students work in pairs and find the mistakes. Elicit the correct answers and write them on the board (I study Maths, English and Business. I study Japanese on Wednesday morning. Where is your History class?).

Vocabulary Pre-teaching / Review

You will need printable flashcards with the basic adjectives (Flashcards 3.3), which can be printed at esource.cambridge.org.
Follow the procedure on p. 15.
Write: *2 + 3 =* on the board, look happy and say: *easy* and write *5*. Write: *interesting, boring, easy, difficult* on the board. Then call out names of subjects and get students to say one of the adjectives on the board, or more than one (e.g. *boring and difficult*), for each subject.

1 ◄)) 3.15 Focus on the pictures and the adjectives to trace. Play the audio for students to listen and read. Students work individually and trace the words. Monitor and check the correct handwriting. Play the audio again for students to listen and repeat.

> ### ⊙ Common student errors
>
> **Spelling:** The word *interesting* is in the top 20 misspelled words by Arabic L1 students. This is the typical error: *intresting*.
>
> Write on the board:
>
> interesting int_ r _ st_ing int_r_s_ _ _ _
> int _ _ _ _ _ _ _ _
>
> Focus on the first word. Ask students to spell it out. Then erase the word. Ask students to spell the word out again and complete the first gap when they are successful. Then erase the word. Continue like this until students are able to write the whole word.

2 🔊 3.16 👤 Draw the pattern Oo for *boring* on the board. Say: *interesting? boring?* Elicit the correct answer (boring) and write it on the board.

Play the audio. Students work individually, listen, read and match the words to the stress patterns.

> ### Answers
> interesting 2   easy 1   difficult 2

3 🔊 3.17 👤 Say: *What's Maths like?* Write: *What's _ _ _ _ _ like?* on the board. Point at the missing word and elicit the correct answer (Maths). Write the missing word (Maths) in the question.

Focus on the first dialogue and read it aloud. Play the audio for students to listen and read. Read the first dialogue again and point at the first picture. Say: *Listen and match*. Play the audio again for students to listen and match the dialogues to the pictures. Go through answers as a class.

> ### Answers
> 1 b   2 c, d

> ### NOTICE
>
> Write: *it is* on the board, erase the *i* in *is* and replace with an apostrophe. Repeat the procedure with *it is not* by erasing the *o* in *not* and replacing with an apostrophe.
>
> Focus on the NOTICE box. Read the sentences aloud. Point out the verb *be* with a full and short verb form. Ask a student to read the sentences aloud.

4 👤 Write: *It isn't difficult.* on the board. Erase *n't* and write: *not*. Focus on the completed example in the book. Students work individually, read the first sentence and complete the one underneath using a full verb form. Monitor students' handwriting. Go through answers as a class.

> ### Answers
> 2 It is easy.   3 It is not boring.   4 What is it like?

5 🔊 3.18 👤👥 Write: *It is easy.* on the board. Next to it write: *It ___ ___ difficult*. Point at *easy* and elicit what verb should be in the gapped sentence (is not).

Focus on the completed example. Say: *Read and circle*. Students work individually, read the sentences and circle the correct option. Students check their answers in pairs. Play the audio for students to listen and check. Students work individually and trace the correct options. Monitor students' handwriting.

> ### Answers
> 2 It is not   3 It is   4 It is

6 👤 Write: *diffcult* on the board. Write a cross (✗) next to the word. Elicit the correct spelling from students. Write the correct form on the board (difficult).

Focus on the completed example. Say: *Read and circle*. Students work individually, read the sentences and circle the mistake. Go through answers as a class. Say: *Correct*. Students correct the words. Write the correct answers on the board.

> ### Answers
> 2 easy   3 interesting   4 boring

WRITING CHALLENGE

7 👤👥 Focus on the model text. Ask a student to read it out. Focus on the rubric and read it aloud. Students work individually, complete the question and write two sentences using prepositions and adjectives. Monitor and help as necessary. Check that students are writing in the correct position on the lines. Students swap notebooks and check each other's writing for correct language, spelling and punctuation.

> ### Optional activity
>
> **Team pelmanism:** Follow the procedure on p. 16.
> It is easy.   It is difficult.
> It is interesting.   It is boring.
> It is not easy.   It is not difficult.
> It is not interesting.   It is not boring.

UNIVERSITY LIFE — UNIT 3

SOUND AND SPELLING *sh, ch, th*

Literacy tip

In English, two letters can make a single sound that cannot be represented by a single letter (e.g. *ch* /tʃ/ and *ng* /ŋ/). Two-letter sounds are called diagraphs. The silent *e* in English is a discontinuous diagraph – in other words, two letters that are not adjacent making a different sound. Diagraphs are not as commonplace in the Arabic writing system as they are in English, so they may be surprising for students.

8 🔊 3.19 Write: *teacher English three* on the board. Say the words. Circle: *ch* and say: *teacher* again. Say *ch* /tʃ/ for students to repeat. Demonstrate how to move your mouth and tongue, if appropriate. Do the same with the other two words and *sh* /ʃ/ and *th* /θ/.

Play the audio for students to listen and read. On the board, remind students what strokes to use for *c, t* and *h*. Students work individually and trace the letters. Monitor and ensure correct stroke direction. Make sure that they understand that it is the combination of two letters that makes the sounds. Play the audio again for students to listen and repeat.

9 🔊 3.20 Focus on the photographs and the words next to them. Read all the words aloud. Say: *Listen and read*. Play the audio for students to listen and read the words. Students work individually and trace the letters. Play the audio again for students to listen and repeat. Drill pronunciation.

10 🔊 3.21 Focus on the photographs and the words. Read the words aloud. Say: *Listen and read*. Play the audio for students to listen and read the words.

11 🔊 3.22 Write: *ship* and *chip* on the board. Say: *chip*. Elicit which word you said (chip). Circle it. Repeat the procedure with *chin* and *thin*.

Focus on the words in Exercise 10. Say: *Listen and circle*. Play the audio for students to listen and circle the word they hear. Play the audio again if required. Students check answers in pairs. Go through answers as a class.

Answers
1 ship 2 chin 3 thin 4 teeth

LANGUAGE FOCUS

Learning objectives

- Understand how to talk about time in English – *It is eight o'clock. It's eight-thirty.*
- Revise numbers 0–10
- Use the preposition *at* with times – *It's at ten o'clock.*
- Understand a question about time – *What time is our English class?*
- Revise sound and spelling of silent *e*

See p. 19 for suggestions on how to use these Learning objectives with your students.

Lead-in

You will need printable flashcards (Flashcards 0.1 and 0.4), which can be printed at esource.cambridge.org. You will need the sides of the cards with both numerals and written numbers 1–12.

Starting with the numbers in order, hold each card up for students to say aloud. Repeat with the cards out of order. Build up speed, quickly flashing the cards at students and focusing on individual students as well as the whole class.

Vocabulary Pre-teaching / Review

You will need printable flashcards with times (Flashcards 3.4), which can be printed at esource.cambridge.org.

Follow the procedure on p. 15.

Write these times on the board:

five o'clock

one o'clock

three-thirty

six-thirty

Ask students to listen carefully to what you say and point at the time on the board. Say the times out of order. Repeat the procedure with a different order.

1 Focus on the clocks and the words in the box. Point at the first clock, say: *two o'clock* and point at the completed example. Say: *Look and write*. Ask students to work individually, look at the clocks and write the missing numbers. Focus on the words *o'clock* and *-thirty*. Point at the full times in the first two clocks and times with *:30* in the second two to explain the meaning. Go through answers as a class. Write the correct times on the board.

Answers
2 <u>four</u> o'clock 3 <u>one</u>-thirty 4 <u>eight</u>-thirty

UNLOCK BASIC LITERACY TEACHER'S BOOK   63

2 🔊 3.23 👤 Focus on the clocks. Say: *Read and listen*. Play the audio for students to look at the clocks and listen to the times. Focus on the times written next to the clocks and show the line that matches the completed example. Point at the clock in *1* and ask what time it is (seven o'clock). Say: *Match*. Students work individually, look at the clocks and match the times. Go through answers as a class. Say: *Trace*. Students work individually and trace the letters. Monitor for correct stroke direction. Play the audio again for students to listen and repeat.

> **Answers**
> 2 It is nine-thirty.
> 3 It is three-thirty.
> 4 It is five o'clock.

3 🔊 3.24 👤 Write: *What time is it?* on the board and say it aloud. Look at your watch or clock. Say the time. (If it isn't on the hour or half past, you could use a clock that you can change the time on – the purpose is to teach the question at this point).

Focus on the clocks. Say: *Look and write*. Students work individually, look at the clocks and complete the times. Say: *Listen and check*. Play the audio for students to listen and check their answers. Go through answers as a class.

> **Answers**
> 2 It is twelve o'clock.
> 3 It is ten o'clock.
> 4 It is eleven-thirty.

4 🔊 3.25 👤 Focus on the timetable. Say: *When is the IT class?* Students look at the timetable and find the answer (On Tuesday morning). Point at the timetable, the questions and the answers. Say: *Read and match*. Students work individually, read the question, look at the timetable and match the questions and answers. Play the audio for students to listen and check. Go through answers as a class.

> **Answers**
> 1 On Tuesday morning.
> 2 It's at ten o'clock.
> 3 On Tuesday afternoon.
> 4 It's at three-thirty.

NOTICE
Focus on the NOTICE box. Allow a minute for students to read the information. Ask students to underline examples of *at* and *on* in the questions in Exercise 4. Drill *at* by asking questions, e.g. *What time is our* (a class they have) *class?*

👁 Common student errors
Missing words: Arabic L1 students often find the concept of prepositions challenging. They tend to make mistakes with the preposition *at* when talking about times. Two common mistakes include omission of this preposition or replacing it with the preposition *in*. Pay attention to what students use when talking about time and correct them when they make a mistake.

5 👤 Say: *What time is the* (subject) *class?* Write: *It's at nine clock.* Write a cross (**X**) next to the answer and elicit the mistake. (It's at nine o'clock.) Read the sentence aloud.

Focus on the sentences in the book. Say: *Read and circle*. Students work individually, read the sentences and circle the mistakes. Go through answers as a class. Say: *Correct*. Students work individually and correct the mistakes. Ask individual students to read out the correct answers and write the correct full sentences on the board.

> **Answers**
> 2 It is twelve-thirty. 3 It is five o'clock.

Optional activity
Information gap: Write two versions of the timetable on separate halves of paper as below. You will need one timetable half per student.

Tuesday
	Business
10:00	English
	Maths
3:30	Biology

Tuesday
8:30	Business
	English
12:00	Maths
	Biology

Together the two halves make a complete timetable. Students work in pairs with a different half of the timetable each. They complete the timetables by asking the question: *What time is … class?* Students check their answers by sharing their half of the timetable with their partner.

UNIVERSITY LIFE   UNIT 3

6 ◆3.26 Write a simple timetable on the board as in the book, e.g. *Thursday/1:30/Business*. Write: *What time is our Business class?* Elicit and write: *It is at one-thirty.* Focus on the preposition *at* and the hyphen in *one-thirty*.

Students work individually, look at the timetable, read and answer the questions. Monitor and help if necessary. Ask students to compare their answers in pairs. Play the audio for students to listen and check. Go through answers as a class.

> **Answers**
> 1 two o'clock
> 2 at nine o'clock
> 3 is at twelve-thirty
> 4 It is at three o'clock.

SOUND AND SPELLING
Silent *e* – *phone, cute …*

7 ◆3.27 Write: *phone* on the board. Say: *phone* and trace the letters *o* and *e* in a different colour if possible. Point at *e* in the word *phone* and say it aloud again, making sure students understand that it is silent.

Focus on the pictures and the words to trace in the book. Say: *Listen*. Play the audio. Students work individually and listen to the words. Say: *Trace*. Students work individually and trace the letters. Monitor handwriting. Play the audio again for students to listen and repeat.

8 ◆3.28 Write: *tube* on the board. Say: *tube* and trace the letters *u* and *e* in a different colour if possible. Point at *e* in the word *tube* and say the word aloud again making sure students understand that the *e* is silent. Repeat the procedure in Exercise 7, above.

9 ◆3.29 Focus on the pictures and the words. Read the words aloud. Say: *Listen and read*. Play the audio for students to listen and read the words.

10 ◆3.30 Write: *cod* and *code* on the board. Say: *code*. Ask students to show you on the board which word you said (*code*). Circle it. Repeat the procedure with *rob* and *robe*.

Focus on the words in Exercise 10. Say: *Listen and circle*. Play the audio for students to listen and circle the word they hear. Play the audio again if required. Students check answers in pairs. Go through answers as a class.

> **Answers**
> 1 code 2 rob 3 note 4 cute

SPELLING CHALLENGE

11 ◆3.31 Focus on the photographs and the gapped words. Play the audio. Students work individually, listen and write the missing letters to complete the words. Students check answers in pairs. Play the audio again if required. Go through answers as a class.

> **Answers**
> 2 st<u>ud</u>ent 3 perf<u>um</u>e 4 h<u>o</u>le 5 gl<u>o</u>be 6 d<u>u</u>ne

LISTENING FOCUS

> **Learning objectives**
> - Understand when people talk about subjects they study – *What subjects do you study? What is History like? Where is your English class?*
> - Listen for detail
> - Revise university subjects
> - Revise basic adjectives
>
> See p. 19 for suggestions on how to use these Learning objectives with your students.

> **Lead-in**
> Draw a word shape on the board for the word *interesting*. Write the alphabet above it. Ask students to call out letters. Cross out the letters as they say them. If they get one right, add it to the word shape. If someone says the word, write it in, and give them a point if vocabulary games are appropriate in your context. Repeat with word shapes for other adjectives and subjects (*boring, easy, difficult, Biology, History, Business, English*).

1 ◆3.32 Focus on the words in the box and the word shapes. Say: *Read and listen* and focus on the completed example. Play the audio. Students work individually and write the words. Monitor students' handwriting. Play the audio again for students to listen and check.

> **Answers**
> 2 interesting 3 boring 4 Business 5 English
> 6 difficult 7 easy

UNLOCK BASIC LITERACY TEACHER'S BOOK   65

2 🔊 3.33 👤 Focus on the dialogue. Say: *Listen and read*. Play the audio for students to listen and read the dialogue. Focus on the short answers and the options next to them. Make sure students understand that only one is correct. Say: *Read and underline*. Students work individually, read the text again and underline the correct answers. Play the audio again for students to listen and check. Go through answers as a class.

> **Answers**
> 1 History 2 Business 3 English

3 👤 Write: *Whatsubjectsdoyoustudy?* on the board. Move the pen along the sentence and draw the first line after *What*. Move the pen again, encouraging students to shout *Stop!* at the word boundaries. Add lines between the words.

Focus on the half-completed example in the book. Show how lines mark spaces between words. Students work individually through the sentences. Monitor and help as necessary. Write the sentences with spaces on the board for students to check their answers.

> **Answers**
> 1 What subjects do you study?
> 2 It is not boring.
> 3 It is difficult.
> 4 Where is your English class?

> **NOTICE**
> Focus on the NOTICE box. Read the words aloud. Point out that both forms have the same meaning.

4 🔊 3.33 👤 Focus on the sentences and answers in Exercise 3. Say: *Listen and match*. Play the audio for students to listen and match the answers.

> **Answers**
> 1 History, Business and English
> 2 History
> 3 Business
> 4 room 10

> **Optional activity**
> **Classroom messages:** Follow the procedure on p. 18.
> 1 Our class is at 2 o'clock.
> 2 It is not difficult.
> 3 It is interesting.
> 4 Our Business class is in room 5.

👁 KEY WORDS FOR LITERACY

> **Learning objectives**
> - Read, spell and pronounce key words for literacy – *it, at, in, on*
> - Complete sentences with the key words for literacy
>
> See p. 19 for suggestions on how to use these Learning objectives in your lessons.

1 🔊 3.34 👤 Write: *it* and *It is in room 6.* on the board. Point at the first word you wrote (*it*) and elicit the pronunciation. Move your pen slowly across the sentence, encouraging students to shout *Stop!* when you get to the word *it*. Circle it in the sentence. Read the sentence aloud.

Focus on the words in bold. Say: *Read and circle*. Students work individually and read and circle the words. Play the audio for students to listen to the sentences.

2 👤 Write: *it is it at it is* on the board. Point at the first word you wrote (*it*) and elicit the pronunciation. Move your pen slowly across the words, encouraging students to shout *Stop!* when you get to the word. Circle: *it* twice.

Focus on the words in bold. Say: *Read and circle*. Students work individually, read and circle the words.

3 👤 If required, remind students how to form *a, i, o* and *n, t* with correct strokes on the board. Ask students to work individually, cover and complete the words. If necessary, prompt them to use something to cover the words on the left as they complete each one. Monitor and check that they are working from left to right. Encourage correct stroke direction and correct height and position of the individual letters.

4 🔊 3.35 👤 Write: *it at in on* on the board. Focus on the sentences and the words on the board. Students work individually and complete the sentences. Play the audio for students to listen and check. Go through answers as a class.

> **Answers**
> 2 at 3 It 4 in

UNIVERSITY LIFE UNIT 3

READING AND WRITING

Learning objectives
- Revise the days of the week
- Scan a text for key words
- Read and understand an email with a timetable – *This is your timetable.*
- Complete a text about a class – *Our English class is on Thursday morning. It is at ten-thirty.*

See p. 19 for suggestions on how to use these Learning objectives with your students.

Lead-in
Elicit the days of the week and write them on the board at random. Ask a student: *What is today?* Write: *1* next to the correct day. Elicit the next day and write: *2* next to it. Continue until you have numbered all seven days of the week on the board.

1 Write the five vowels (*a, e, i, o, u*), on the board, using correct strokes. Say the vowels aloud. Write the consonants (*b, c, d, f, g, h, j, k, l, m, n, p, q, r, s, t, v, w, x, y, z*) underneath the vowels, saying each letter as you write it. Write the capital forms of *M, T, W, E, C* and *B*.

Students work individually and write the days of the week and the subjects. Monitor students' handwriting. Write all the words on the board for students to check.

Answers
Monday Tuesday Wednesday Thursday
English Maths Chemistry Business

2 (🔊 3.36) Focus on the email. Show how *Sunday*, the first word in Exercise 1, has been circled. Indicate that students must find all the other words from Exercise 1 by pointing at the words in Exercise 1 and the email in Exercise 2. Students work individually and read and circle the words in the email. Play the audio for students to listen and read the text. Go through answers as a class.

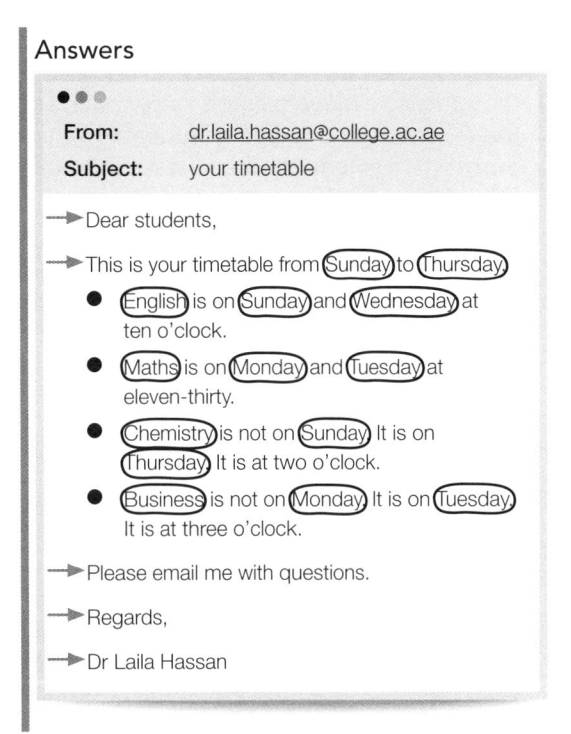

Answers

From: dr.laila.hassan@college.ac.ae
Subject: your timetable

→ Dear students,
→ This is your timetable from (Sunday) to (Thursday).
- (English) is on (Sunday) and (Wednesday) at ten o'clock.
- (Maths) is on (Monday) and (Tuesday) at eleven-thirty.
- (Chemistry) is not on (Sunday). It is on (Thursday). It is at two o'clock.
- (Business) is not on (Monday). It is on (Tuesday). It is at three o'clock.

→ Please email me with questions.
→ Regards,
→ Dr Laila Hassan

3 Focus on the timetable and the gaps. Make sure students understand that there is information missing from the timetable. Focus on the email in Exercise 2. Say: *Read again.* Students work individually and read the email again. In stronger classes, ask students to read the email aloud. Focus on the timetable. Say: *Complete.* Students work individually, look at the email and complete the timetable. Monitor and help as necessary. Students compare their answers in pairs. Write the answers on the board and indicate where they came from in the text.

Answers

	SUNDAY	MONDAY	TUESDAY	WEDNESDAY	THURSDAY
MORNING	English 10:00	Maths 11:30	Maths 11:30	English 10:00	
AFTERNOON			Business 3:00		Chemistry 2:00

UNLOCK BASIC LITERACY TEACHER'S BOOK 67

4 Write: *Our Japanese class is at Three-thirty.* on the board. Write a cross (✗) next to the sentence. Move your pen slowly across the sentence, encouraging students to shout *Stop!* when you get to the mistake (Three). Elicit that it should not be capitalized and correct it clearly.

Students work individually, read the sentences, circle and correct the mistakes. Students check answers in pairs. Go through answers as a class.

> **Answers**
> 2 English 3 at 4 Wednesday 5 two 6 afternoon

5 Focus on the timetable and the sentences in the model text. Make sure they see that the two are the same information. Point at the options to circle. Say: *Look, read and circle.* Students work individually, look at the timetable, read the text and circle the correct words. Write the sentences on the board and point out the capitals, full stops, apostrophes and hyphens. Go through answers as a class.

> **Answers**
> Our class is on Thursday morning. It is at ten-thirty.
> Our Maths class is on Thursday afternoon.
> It is at two o'clock.

6 Focus on the empty timetable. Elicit a possible first answer. Show that it should be real, not made up. Students work individually and make notes in the timetable. Then they complete the sentences using their notes and the model answer in Exercise 5 to help. Monitor and check spelling and correct strokes.

Ask students to read their sentences aloud. Tell them to listen for similarities to / differences from their own answers.

> **Model answer**
> Our English class is on Monday morning.
> It is at ten o'clock.
> Our Business class is on Tuesday afternoon.
> It is at three-thirty.

Optional activity

Make a few copies of the gapped notebook in Exercise 6. Dictate completed variations of these sentences, e.g. *Our Maths class is on Wednesday morning …* . Students listen and complete the sentences.

Objectives review

See Teaching tips on p. 19 for ideas about using the Objectives review with your students.

WORDLIST
See Teaching tips on p. 21 for ideas about using the Wordlist on p. 142 with your students.

REVIEW TEST
See esource.cambridge.org for the Review test and ideas about how and when to administer the Review test.

4 DIFFERENT COUNTRIES

LISTENING AND READING 1

Learning objectives

- Understand basic adjectives describing weather and countries – *big, small, hot, warm, cold, dry, wet*
- Read and understand sentences describing countries and weather – *The UK is cold.*
- Write two sentences using adjectives to describe your country – *I am from Singapore. It is warm and wet.*
- Understand sentences joined by a conjunction – *and Singapore is small and wet.*

See p. 19 for suggestions on how to use these Learning objectives with your students.

Lead-in

You will need a map to show to students. Point at the UK. Elicit which country it is. Write: *the UK* in the middle of the board. Elicit any words students associate with it, e.g. *London, football, queen*. Focus on the UK's size and write: *small* and *big* on the board. Explain the meaning using gestures or drawing a small and a big square next to the words. Elicit: *The UK is small*. Do this with another country, particularly in the local region.

Vocabulary Pre-teaching / Review

You will need printable flashcards with adjectives describing countries and weather (Flashcards 4.1), which can be printed at esource.cambridge.org.

Follow the procedure on p. 15.

Show a world map to students. Write all the adjectives on the board (*big, small, hot, warm, cold, dry, wet*). If appropriate in your context, invite students to come closer to the map. Say the first adjective aloud (*big*) and ask students to show you countries on the map that are big. Repeat the procedure with other adjectives. If coming closer to the map is not appropriate in your context, point at countries on the map yourself and ask students to match them to the adjectives on the board.

1 🔊 4.1 Focus on the pictures and the adjectives. Point at the picture of snow and say: *cold. Look and listen.* Play the audio for students to look at the pictures and words and listen to how they are pronounced. Students work individually and trace the words. Monitor and check students' handwriting. Play the audio again for students to listen and repeat.

2 🔊 4.2 Focus on the pictures and the sentences. Point at the picture of the UK. Elicit the word *cold.* Point at and read the first sentence aloud. Say: *Read and match.* Students work individually, read the sentences and match the photographs, writing the numbers in the boxes.

Play the audio for students to listen. Write the correct answers on the board with full sentences.

Answers
b 1 c 6 d 2 e 4 f 5

3 🔊 4.3 Write: *coldsmallcold* on the board. Move the pen along the sentence and draw a line after *cold*. Move the pen again, encouraging students to shout *Stop!* at the word boundaries. Add lines between the words.

Focus on the line of words in the book. Show how lines mark spaces between words. Students work individually through the lines. Monitor and help as necessary. Play the audio for students to listen and check. Go through answers on the board.

4 Focus on the adjectives. Ask students to work individually, cover and complete the words. If necessary, prompt them to use something to cover the words on the left as they complete each one. Monitor and check that they are working from left to right. Encourage correct stroke direction and correct height and position of the individual letters.

5 Say: *What is (your country) like?* Mime an adjective, e.g. *hot*, and elicit: *hot*. Write the question on the board and say it aloud again, then write: *It is hot.* Check that students understand the question by using more examples, if necessary. Elicit all the adjectives that they have studied and write them on the board (*big, small, cold, warm, hot, dry, wet*). Then write: *What is (another country they know) like? It is … and …* Elicit suggestions and write them on the board.

Focus on the adjectives in the box. Students work individually, look at the pictures and complete the sentences. Ask some students to read out their answers. Write a few on the board and see if everyone agrees.

UNL🔒CK BASIC LITERACY TEACHER'S BOOK

Suggested answers

2 cold 3 small 4 big

> **NOTICE**
>
> Focus on the NOTICE box. Read the sentences aloud. Point out the word *and* being used to join two sentences. Ask a student to read the sentence with *and* aloud.

6 🔊 4.4 👤👥 Focus on the completed example. Students work individually, read the sentences about countries and join them using the word *and*. Students compare their answers in pairs. Play the audio for students to listen and check. Write the sentences on the board.

> **Answers**
>
> 2 big and warm
> 3 is big and cold
> 4 Saudi Arabia is dry and hot.

WRITING CHALLENGE

7 👤👥 Focus on the photograph of someone in Singapore. Point at the photograph and say: *This is Singapore. It is warm and wet.* Ask a student to read out the model text. Focus on the rubric and read it aloud. Students work individually and write two sentences using adjectives describing their country and the weather. Monitor and help as necessary. Check that students are writing in the correct position on the lines. Students swap notebooks and check each other's writing for correct language, spelling and punctuation.

> **Optional activity**
>
> Write: *Qatar, Russia, India, Greece* on the board. Ask students to listen carefully to a sentence and choose a country on the board which matches the description. Read the sentences below one by one aloud. Elicit the correct answers.
>
> *It is hot and big.* (Greece)
> *It is hot and small.* (Qatar)
> *It is cold and big.* (Russia)
> *It is wet and big.* (India)

LISTENING AND READING 2

> **Learning objectives**
>
> - Use *in* to describe where a place is and *from* to describe where someone is from
> - Read and write positive and negative forms of the verb *be* – *It is in the UK. It is not in Mexico.*
> - Scan a text for country names
> - Understand the connection between spoken (contracted) and written (uncontracted) forms of the verb *be*
> - Practise writing sentences with full stops and capital letters
>
> See p. 19 for suggestions on how to use these Learning objectives with your students.

> **Lead-in**
>
> Show students three or four photographs of places that they will know around the local region or famous places in countries around the world (e.g. Big Ben in London, the UK). Elicit the countries and write them on the board. Point at each country and say: *It is in …* , *They are in …*, as appropriate. You could turn this into a guessing game, writing four country names on the board and showing four (less obvious) places, one from each of the countries. Students work in teams to guess. Use full sentences when giving spoken feedback, e.g. *The Burj Khalifa is in the UAE.*

1 👤 Say: *I am from* (your country). *I am in* (the country you are teaching in). Ask students to repeat after you. Say: *I am* and write: *from* on the board. Do the same for *in*. Point at each one and ask students to say sentences with both prepositions, e.g. *I am in* (their country).

Focus on the photographs and the sentences. Students work individually, read the sentences and match the photographs. Go through answers as a class. Then students trace the words.

> **Answers**
>
> 2 b 3 a 4 d

2 👤 Write: *in* on the board. Write these words: *is it in it in*. Point at the first word you wrote (in) and elicit the pronunciation. Move your pen slowly across the words, encouraging students to shout *Stop!* when you get to the word *in*. Circle it twice.

Focus on the target words. Say: *Read and circle*. Students work individually and read and circle the words.

70 UNLOCK BASIC LITERACY TEACHER'S BOOK

DIFFERENT COUNTRIES UNIT 4

3 🔊 4.5 👤 Write: *in* and *from* on the board, in word shape boxes. Elicit sentences with each word, e.g. *It is in the UK. I'm from the UAE*. Write the sentences on the board if they are correct.

Students work individually, read and complete the sentences. Play the audio for students to listen and check. Go through answers as a class.

4 🔊 4.6 👤👥 Draw or show a simple picture of a well-known building, e.g. the Eiffel Tower. Say: *It is in New York*. Write a cross (✗) next to the sentence and elicit the correction (It is in Paris). Say: *It is in Paris. It is not in New York*, and then write it on the board. Read the sentences aloud, pointing at the words as you do so, but using the contracted forms (*It's, It isn't*) when speaking.

Focus on the sentences and the photographs in the book. Students work individually, read the sentences and match the photographs. Students compare their answers in pairs. Play the audio for students to listen. Go through answers as a class.

> **Answers**
> 2 a 3 c

5 👤 You can use Flashcards 4.2 to pre-teach this vocabulary set. Focus on the verb forms in the book. Make sure students understand that they first see an affirmative and then a negative verb form by pointing at *not* in each item. Students work individually, read and trace the words. Monitor and help as necessary.

NOTICE

Write: *It is* on the board. Erase the *i* in *is* and add an apostrophe. Draw a speech bubble and show how we use the contraction for speech.

Focus on the NOTICE box. Read the words aloud. Point out the verb form in each phrase. Focus on Exercise 4 and circle all the forms of the verb *be*.

Literacy tip

Contractions help represent the spoken form of the language in cases where a sound is dropped as a result of connecting two words (e.g. *He* and *is* – the *i* is dropped and replaced by an apostrophe), which shows where the letter was. Although they represent speech, they do often get used in writing, particularly in informal styles. In some academic contexts they are frowned upon, though many academics accept them. There is a parallel in Arabic, in which vowels may not be written, with small marks (diacritics) replacing them.

6 👤 Write: *They are from London.* on the board. Erase the *a* in *are* and elicit that there needs to be an apostrophe.

Focus on the sentences. Students work individually, read and complete the sentences. Go through answers as a class.

> **Answers**
> 2 is 3 are 4 are not

7 🔊 4.7 👤👥 Focus on the first photograph. Say: *Where is it? Is it in the UK?* Elicit the answer (It is not in the UK. It is in France.) and write it on the board. Say: *Read and listen*. Play the audio for students to listen and read. Say: *Write*. Students work individually, look at the photographs and the sentences and write the words. Students check answers in pairs. Write the full answers on the board.

> **Answers**
> 1 is 2 is not, is 3 is

👁 Common student errors

Grammar: Arabic L1 students often overuse the pronoun *it*, e.g. *The UK it is cold*. Arabic L1 students often include an additional *it* between the subject and the verb. The pronoun *it* in a sentence replaces the subject or object, but Arabic L1 students find it challenging to understand this rule. Whenever a student makes a mistake with the pronoun *it*, write it on the board, cross out the unnecessary pronoun and drill the correct form.

8 👤👥 Write the letters of the alphabet on the board (lowercase). Circle: *a*. Elicit the other vowels. If they don't remember, move your pen along the alphabet, hesitating over each letter, until you reach each vowel. Continue until all vowels are circled (a, e, i, o, u). Tell students they are very important in English.

Look at the picture of Iguazu Falls in the book and read the first sentence aloud. Focus on the underlined word *Mexico*. Students work individually and underline countries in the other sentences.

Point at the crossword. Complete the first line as a class. Students work individually and complete the rest of the crossword. Students compare their answers in pairs. Go through answers as a class.

> **Answers**
> 1 Brazil 2 Oman 3 Singapore 4 Greece 5 Mexico
> The country in the box: France

UNL*O*CK BASIC LITERACY TEACHER'S BOOK   71

9 ▪ Show a picture of a famous place or building, e.g. the Burj Khalifa. Write two sentences about it on the board, on one line with no first capital letters and no full stops, e.g.:
it is not in Singapore it is in the UAE
Write a cross (✗) next to the sentences. Elicit the mistakes (no first capital letter and no full stops). Elicit corrections and change the sentences on the board.

Focus on the sentences in the book. Students work individually, read and correct the sentences. Go through answers as a class.

> **Answers**
> 2 It is not in France. It is in the UK.
> 3 It is in Oman. It is not in Saudi Arabia.
> 4 It is in Japan. It is not in Singapore.

> **Optional activity**
> Write the names of some famous landmarks on individual strips of paper, e.g. *Big Ben*. Write matching sentences on other strips, e.g. *It is in London. It is not in Paris*. Give a place strip and a sentence strip (non-matching) to each student. Students walk around the class and read their sentences to each other. When they find a match, students hand the strips of paper to you and return to their seats. Continue until all the matching strips of paper are paired together.
> **Alternative to mingling:** Divide the class into groups. Give each group a set of matching strips, shuffled in a random order. Students match the places and sentences. The first group to match all of their strips of paper wins.

LISTENING AND READING 3

> **Learning objectives**
> - Read and write adjectives to describe cities – *new, old, expensive, cheap, beautiful, clean*
> - Write capital letters at the start of city names – *Doha*
> - Use capital letters and full stops in sentences about cities and countries
> - Write two sentences describing cities – *This is London, in the UK. It is cold and wet.*
> - Gain awareness of sound and spelling of letters *e, ee, ea*
>
> See p. 19 for suggestions on how to use these Learning objectives with your students.

> **Lead-in**
> Write: *Dubai, Doha, Istanbul, Riyadh* and *London* in a column on one side of the board. Write: *the UAE, Saudi Arabia, the UK, Qatar* and *Turkey* on the other side. Say the words aloud. Students match the cities to the countries, by either coming up to the board and drawing connecting lines or by saying them (Dubai – the UAE, Doha – Qatar, Istanbul – Turkey, Riyadh – Saudi Arabia, London – the UK). Say the words aloud again and ask students to repeat. Monitor students' pronunciation.

> **Vocabulary Pre-teaching / Review**
> You will need printable flashcards with the basic adjectives describing cities (Flashcards 4.3), which can be printed at esource.cambridge.org.
> Follow the procedure on p. 15.
> Write all the adjectives on the board (*new, old, expensive, cheap, beautiful, clean*). Students work in pairs, look at each adjective and think of a city they know that can be described by this word. Help students by providing them with an example from your country, e.g. *London is expensive*.

1 ◀)) 4.8 ▪ Write: *new* on the board and show the class something new, e.g. a new mobile phone or book. Say the word *new* for students to repeat.

Focus on the photographs and the adjectives. Say: *Listen and read*. Play the audio for students to listen and read the adjectives. Say: *Trace. Then write*. Students work individually, trace and then copy the words carefully. Monitor and help with handwriting.

> **◉ Common student errors**
> **Spelling:** The word *beautiful* is in the top 20 misspelled words by Arabic L1 students. This is the typical error: *beatiful*.
> Write on the board:
> beautiful   b _ _ _ t _ f _ l   b _ _ _ _ _ _ _ l
> Focus on the first word. Ask students to spell it. Then erase the word. Ask students to spell the word again and complete the first gap when they are successful. Then erase the word. Continue until students are able to write the whole word.

2 ◀)) 4.9 ▪▪▪ Draw the pattern *oOo* for *expensive* on board. Say: *old?* (no) *expensive?* (yes) Write: *expensive* on the board underneath the stress pattern.

Focus on the words in Exercise 1. Play the audio. Students work individually, listen, read and match the words to the stress patterns.

| DIFFERENT COUNTRIES | UNIT 4 |

Students compare their answers in pairs. Play the audio again for students to listen and repeat. Ask individual students to read all the words aloud.

> **Answers**
> O   2, 4, 6
> oOo   3
> Ooo   5

3 ◄) 4.10 Focus on the first photograph. Say: *What is Tokyo like? Is it cheap or expensive?* Elicit the answer (expensive). Students work individually, look at the photographs, read the sentences and choose the correct option. Play the audio for students to listen and check. Go through answers as a class.

> **Answers**
> 1 expensive 2 clean 3 beautiful

NOTICE

Write: *riyadh* on the board. Erase the *r* and write the capital letter *R*.

Focus on the NOTICE box. Read the city and then the sentence aloud. Point out the use of capital letter for cities. Focus on Exercise 3 and ask students to circle the capital letters in the cities.

---

4 Write: *This is* (your city without a capital), *in* (your country without a capital). Write two crosses (✗), one next to each mistake. Elicit the mistakes and correct them. Point out the use of a comma before the word *in*. Show students how to write capital letters *D*, *U* and *T* on the board.

Focus on the sentences. Students work individually, write the words with capitals and add the commas. Monitor and check that students use the correct strokes. Students work in pairs to compare their answers. Go through answers as a class.

> **Answers**
> 2 This is Doha, in Qatar.
> 3 This is Istanbul, in Turkey.
> 4 This is London, in the UK.

5 ◄) 4.11 Draw a word shape for *clean* on the board. Write: *clean* and *cheap* on the board and ask which one fits. Demonstrate writing it in the word shape on the board.

Focus on the words in the box and the sentences. Students write words in the word shapes. Monitor and help students with spelling and letter formation as necessary.

Play the audio for students to listen and check. Ask individual students to read the sentences aloud. Go through answers as a class.

> **Answers**
> 1 expensive 2 old, cheap 3 new, beautiful

WRITING CHALLENGE

6 Focus on the photograph of London and the model text. Point at the model text and ask a student to read it aloud. Focus on the rubric and read it aloud. Students work individually and write two sentences using adjectives to describe a city. Monitor and help as necessary. Check that students are writing in the correct position on the lines. Students swap notebooks and check each other's writing for correct language, spelling and punctuation.

Optional activity

Use students' sentences from the Writing challenge. Read out their sentences omitting the place names. Students guess the city that is being described. (Make sure they don't shout out their own answers.)

SOUND AND SPELLING *e, ee, ea*

Literacy tip

The sound /iː/ can be spelled in several ways. The spelling *ea* (cheap, clean) accounts for 25% of instances and the spelling *ee* (green, three) accounts for 26%. The sound is also frequently seen spelled as *e* in the high-frequency set of two-letter words (be, he, she, me).

As with much of English spelling, there are often exceptions to the patterns taught. With the *ea* spelling, common exceptions are *bread*, *head*, and *healthy* (all /e/). If a student notices this, give positive feedback for noticing and say simply that those words don't follow the pattern.

---

7 ◄) 4.12 Write: *the UA_* on the board. Point at the missing letter and elicit the country name (the UAE).

Focus on the photograph and the sentences. Play the audio for students to read and listen. Read the sentences aloud focusing on the sounds for spelling patterns *e*, *ee* and *ea*.

Students work individually and trace the letters. Write: *e, ea, ee* on the board. Pronounce the sound /iː/ and explain that these three spelling patterns can all have the same sound. Play the audio again for students to listen and repeat.

8 🔊 4.13 Copy on the board the headings in the table in the book. Say: *cheap*. Elicit that it goes in the first column. Say: *he* and elicit that it goes in the final column.

Play the audio for students to listen and read the words. Remind students how to write *e* and *a* with correct strokes. Students work individually and trace the letters. Monitor students' handwriting. Play the audio again for students to listen and repeat.

9 🔊 4.14 Focus on the pictures and the words. Say: *Read and listen.* Play the audio for students to listen and look at the words. Demonstrate how to match the words to the spelling patterns in Exercise 8 by pointing at item 1, *bean*, and then at *ea* in Exercise 8. Students work individually, read the words and match them to the spelling patterns, writing the words in the correct column. Play the audio again for students to listen and check. Go through answers as a class.

> **Answers**
> ea: bean, seat
> ee: peel, green
> e: me

10 🔊 4.15 Write: *She is in Greece.* on the board. Write the letters *e* and *ee* on the board. Point at the first spelling pattern you wrote (*e*) and circle the word *She*. Point at the second spelling pattern (*ee*) and circle the word *Greece*.

Focus on the words next to the photograph. Say: *Read and listen.* Play the audio for students to listen and read the words. Say: *Read and circle.* Students work individually, read the sentences and circle words that have the sound /iː/ spelled with *e*, *ee* or *ea*. Go through answers as a class. Chant each sentence as a class to help students memorize the sound/spelling relationships.

> **Answers**
> e: She
> ee: Greece
> ea: cheap, clean

LANGUAGE FOCUS

> **Learning objectives**
> - Use short questions, with and without contractions, to ask for information – *Who's this? What's this? Where's this?*
> - Revise spelling of short *a* and *e*, *ee* and *ea*
> - Write short questions – *Who is this? What is this? Where is this?*
>
> See p. 19 for suggestions on how to use these Learning objectives with your students.

> **Lead-in**
> Have some photographs of people, places and objects students will know (e.g. famous people, capital cities and makes of car). Hold one up and ask: *Who's/Where's/What's this?* Accept short answers. Repeat for all the photographs, changing the question word as appropriate. Elicit your three questions and write them on the board. Give the photographs to students and get them to ask the questions to each other or the whole class.

1 🔊 4.16 Focus on the photographs, the questions and the answers. Point at the completed example. Play the audio for students to listen and read. Students write the order in which they hear the dialogues. Go through answers as a class. Students read the texts again. Check that students understand the meaning of the texts. Encourage students to use dictionaries if necessary.

> **Answers**
> 1 Where's this? It's in Saudi Arabia.
> 3 What's this? It's a camel.

> **NOTICE**
> Focus on the NOTICE box. Read the questions aloud. Point out the use of a short verb form for speaking and a long verb form for writing. Write: *Who's this?* and *What's this?* on the board. Erase the apostrophe and *s* and elicit the full verb form to complete the sentences. Write: *is* in the gap in both sentences.

2 Write: *What is this?* on the board. Erase the *i* in *is* and replace it with an apostrophe.

Focus on the short verb form questions and the questions with the full verb form. Students work individually, read the questions and match them to the questions with full verb form. Go through answers as a class. Say: *Trace.* Students work individually and trace the question words.

> **Answers**
> 2 Who is this? 3 What is this?

DIFFERENT COUNTRIES   **UNIT 4**

3 **(4.17)** Write the name or show a picture of a place students will know, and say: *Where is this?* Write the answer on the board: *It is in …*

Focus on the questions and the answer options in the book. Students work individually, read the questions and the answers and choose the correct options. Students work in pairs and compare their answers. Play the audio for students to listen and check. Say: *where who what* aloud for students to repeat and practise pronunciation. Emphasize that *h* is totally silent.

> **Answers**
> 1 Where 2 Who 3 What

4 **(4.18)** Focus on the photographs and the boxes with questions and answers. Students work individually, read the questions slowly and match the answers. Students work in pairs and compare their answers. Play the audio for students to listen and check.

> **Answers**
> 1
> b This is my teacher.
> c This is his jeep.
> 2
> a This is on the beach.
> b This is my family.
> c This is the sea.

5 Write: *where is this* on the board. Circle the first *w* and the final *s*. Elicit the missing capital letter and the question mark and write them in, crossing out the first *w*.

Students work individually, read the questions and correct the mistakes. Go through answers as a class. Write another sentence answering each question (e.g. *It's in Mexico. This is my friend. This is my mobile phone.*), pointing out that another capital letter is needed after a question mark.

> **Answers**
> 2 Who is this? 3 What is this?

> **Optional activity**
> Write the four questions below on the board. Ask students not to look at their books. Write a cross (✗) next to each sentence to indicate a mistake. Ask students to work in pairs and find one mistake in each question. Elicit the answers and correct the sentences on the board.
> *Whoo is this?* (Who)
> *Whot is this?* (What)
> *Where is this.* (?)
> *Were is this?* (Where)

SOUND AND SPELLING REVIEW

6 **(4.19)** Focus on the words. Say: *Listen.* Play the audio for students to listen and read the words. Students work individually and trace the letters. Play the audio again for students to listen and repeat.

SPELLING CHALLENGE

7 Write: *t _ _ cher* on the board. Elicit: *ea* and complete the word on the board.

Ask students to cover Exercise 6. Students work individually and complete the words. Then they work in pairs and compare their spelling. Students uncover Exercise 6 and check their answers.

> **Answers**
> 2 d<u>e</u>sert 3 j<u>ee</u>p 4 b<u>ea</u>ch 5 f<u>a</u>mily 6 s<u>ea</u>

> **Common student errors**
> **Punctuation:** Arabic L1 students often use full stops instead of questions marks in *Wh-* questions, e.g. *What's this.* Whenever a student makes a mistake with the punctuation and replaces a question mark with a full stop, write it on the board, cross out the full stop and elicit the correct punctuation mark.

SOUND AND SPELLING *wh*

8 **(4.20)** Write: *where* on the board. Trace the letters *wh*. Ask students to look at the questions in the book. Play the audio for students to read and listen to the questions. Say: *Trace.* Students work individually and trace the letters *wh* in each question. Monitor students' handwriting.

9 **(4.21)** Focus on the pictures and the words. Check that students understand the meanings. Say: *Look and listen.* Play the audio. Say: *Trace.* Students work individually and trace the letters *wh*. Monitor students' handwriting. Students then say the words aloud.

UNL**O**CK BASIC LITERACY TEACHER'S BOOK   **75**

10 🔊 4.22 Focus on the question words and the gaps. Elicit how to say the question words aloud; play the audio from Exercise 8 again if required. Explain that the words are divided into two columns because even though they have the same spelling, the sounds are different (/w/ for *where* and *what* and /h/ for *who*). Say: *Look at 9* (pointing at the words in Exercise 9) *and match*. Students work individually, read and say the words and write them in the correct column. Play the audio for students to listen and check their answers. Play the audio again if required. Go through answers as a class.

> **Answers**
> where, what: whistle white wheel
> who: wholemeal

11 🔊 4.23 Focus on the photographs and the questions and answers. Say: *Listen and circle*. Play the audio. Students listen and circle the question word they hear. Say: *Match*. Students work individually, read the questions and match them to the answers. Play the audio again for students to listen and check. Go through answers as a class. Ask students to read the dialogues aloud focusing on the sounds in the question words.

> **Answers**
> 1 Where's, 3 2 What's, 1 3 Who's, 2

LISTENING FOCUS

Learning objectives
- Predict content before listening to a presentation
- Understand a short presentation about a city – *This is the desert.*
- Listen for detail

See p. 19 for suggestions on how to use these Learning objectives with your students.

Lead-in
Write the names of two cities on the board: *Doha* and *London*. Underneath write these sentences:

It is big. It is expensive. It is cold. It is wet.

Ask students to work in pairs, read the sentences and guess which city it is more likely to be about (London). Write: *London* next to the sentences. Students focus on the sentences that are not likely to be true for the second city (Doha) and change the adjective so it becomes true: *It is hot. It is dry.* etc. Write the new text and the word *Doha* next to it so that you have two completed descriptions, one for each city. Ask a student to read the description aloud. Correct students' pronunciation if required.

1 🔊 4.24 Focus on the photographs and the questions. Point at the options. Students work individually, read the questions, look at the photographs and circle the correct options. Say: *Listen and check*. Play the audio for students to listen and check their answers. Go through answers as a class.

> **Answers**
> 1 in class 2 Jeddah

2 🔊 4.25 Focus on the photographs and the sentences. Play the audio for students to read and listen. Students work individually, read the sentences again, look at the photographs and match. Ask a student to read out a sentence and say which photograph it is. Repeat for all three sentences.

> **Answers**
> 2 c 3 b

3 🔊 4.26 Focus on the sentences. Play the audio. Students work individually, listen and match the sentences with a description to the place. Play the audio again for students to listen and check. Ask a student to read out a sentence and say which description it matches. Repeat for all three sentences.

> **Answers**
> 1 It's big and hot.
> 2 It's beautiful and clean.
> 3 It's new. It's not old.

Optional activity
Alphabet categories: Follow the procedure on p. 17.
B (Brazil, Bahrain, beach, big, beautiful)
C (Canada, country, classroom, clean)
O (Oman, old)
S (Saudi Arabia, small)

DIFFERENT COUNTRIES   UNIT 4

⊙ KEY WORDS FOR LITERACY

Learning objectives

- Read, spell and pronounce key words for literacy – *what, who, when, where*
- Complete sentences with the key words for literacy

See p. 19 for suggestions on how to use these Learning objectives in your lessons.

1 👤 Write: *what* on the board. Write these words: *what who when what now*. Move the pen along the sentence and circle: *what* twice. Read the word aloud.

Focus on the words in bold. Say: *Read and circle*. Students work individually, look at the word and find it in the line of words. Monitor and help as necessary.

Optional activity

On a piece of paper, write: *what, who, when, where* all over it, randomly and multiple times. Make a copy for each pair of students. Students take it in turns to point out all the examples of each word as fast as possible – one student says a question word, their partner uses a pencil to point to all the examples of the question word they can see on the piece of paper. If they make a mistake, students stop and swap roles. Speed and accuracy are the aim of the activity. To make it more of a game, ask students to time each other; count how many words they can find in a set time, starting with 30 seconds, then speeding it up to 20/15/10.

2 👤 If required, remind students how to form *a, e, o* and *w, h, t, n, r* with correct strokes on the board. Students work individually, cover and complete the words. If necessary, prompt them to use something to cover the words on the left as they complete each one. Monitor and check that they are working from left to right. Encourage correct stroke direction and correct height and position of the individual letters.

3 🔊 4.27 👤 Hold up a pen. Write: _____ *is this? It is my pen.* Elicit: *what* and write it without a capital. Write a cross (✗) next to the word *what* and elicit the correction (What). Cross it out and write it again with the capital letter.

Say: *Read and write*. Students work individually and write the words with capital first letters to complete the questions. Monitor students' handwriting. Say: *Listen and check*. Play the audio for students to check their answers.

Answers
1 Where 2 What 3 When 4 Who

READING AND WRITING

Learning objectives

- Understand nouns as preparation for reading – *car, camera, Tokyo, Japan, Asia, students*
- Scan a text for nouns and adjectives
- Read and understand a text about a city – *Tokyo is a city in Japan. It is big and expensive.*
- Read for detail
- Complete a text about a city – *London is a city in England. It is big. It is not small.*

See p. 19 for suggestions on how to use these Learning objectives with your students.

Lead-in

Write these questions on the board:
Where is this? What is it like?
What is this? What is it like?
Who is this? What is _____ like?

Remind students of the adjectives they have studied (*old, big, expensive*, etc.). Write them on the board if they have difficulty remembering them. Students write down the name of a place, an object and a person. Students work in pairs, ask the three pairs of questions to find out the information and give an opinion using the adjectives they have studied. Monitor and help with vocabulary. Elicit and write a few examples on the board.

1 👥 Focus on the pictures and the words. Read the words aloud. Students work in pairs, look at the words and match them to the pictures. Write the words on the board and drill the pronunciation. Elicit why there is an *s* on *students* (plural form). Go through answers as a class.

Answers
1 b 2 a 3 d 4 e 5 f 6 c

2 🔊 4.28 👤 Say: *Japan. What's it like?* Write a few adjectives on the board (e.g. *big, small, clean, warm, cold*). Elicit answers using these adjectives, e.g. *It's clean*.

Focus on the words in the box. Demonstrate that scanning is looking quickly rather than reading carefully. Students work individually, scan the text, find the words and circle them. Play the audio for students to read and listen to the text.

UNLOCK BASIC LITERACY TEACHER'S BOOK   77

> **Answers**
>
> *Japan* is a country in *Asia*. Tokyo is a city in *Japan*. It is *big* and *expensive*. It is not boring. It is *interesting*. Nissan *cars* are from *Japan*. Canon and Sony *cameras* are from *Japan*. The Imperial Palace is in Tokyo. It is *big* and *old*. Ueno Park is in Tokyo. It is clean and *beautiful*. Tokyo University is in Tokyo. It is not new. It is *old*. *Students* study Japanese, Business and English.

3 🔊 4.29 👥 Focus on the sentences and the text in Exercise 2. Point at the first answer in the first line of the text and demonstrate tracing the word. Students work individually, read the sentences, refer back to the text in Exercise 2 and circle the correct option. Students compare their answers in pairs. Play the audio for students to listen and check. Go through answers as a class. Students work individually and trace the correct words.

> **Answers**
>
> 2 city 3 big 4 cars 5 Business

4 👤 Focus on the notes about London and the photograph. Say: *This is London, in the UK. This is London Eye. It is big and new.* Write: *this is london it is big* on the board. Write a cross (✗) next to the sentences. Elicit where the mistakes are. Write the correct sentences on the board (This is London. It is big.) Say: *Read and write.* Students work individually, read the model text, correct the lowercase letters and insert full stops. Write the correct model text on the board for students to check their answers.

> **Answers**
>
> The UK is a country. It is cold and wet. London is a city in the UK. It is interesting. It is not boring. The London Eye is in London. It is big and new.

5 👤 Focus on the notes. Students work individually and make notes about their own countries, city and places. Monitor students' handwriting. Elicit a few examples and write key words on the board.

6 👥 Ask students to look at the model text in Exercise 4 and their own notes in Exercise 5. Say: *Look and write.* Students work individually, use their notes and refer back to the model answer to complete a text about their country. Monitor and help as necessary. Check that students are writing in the correct position on the lines. Students swap notebooks and check each other's writing for correct language, spelling and punctuation.

> **Model answer**
>
> France is a country. It is big and beautiful. Paris is a city in France. It is old. It is not new. The Eiffel Tower is in Paris. It is big and beautiful.

Optional activity

Text reconstruction: Follow the procedure on p. 18.

Mexico City is a city in Mexico. It is big. The Palacio Postal is in Mexico City. It is big and beautiful.

Objectives review

See Teaching tips on p. 19 for ideas about using the Objectives review with your students.

WORDLIST

See Teaching tips on p. 21 for ideas about using the Wordlist on p. 142 with your students.

REVIEW TEST

See esource.cambridge.org for the Review test and ideas about how and when to administer the Review test.

5 WORK

LISTENING AND READING 1

> **Learning objectives**
> - Understand job names – *pilot, photographer, police officer, nurse, dentist, bank manager*
> - Read and understand sentences about people's jobs – *This is Ronesh. He is not a nurse. He is a dentist.*
> - Notice the article *a* in sentences – *He is a dentist.*
> - Write three sentences about a person's job – *This is Eduardo. He is not a dentist. He is a nurse.*
> - Gain awareness of sound and spelling of letters *f, ph, ff*
>
> See p. 19 for suggestions on how to use these Learning objectives with your students.

> **Lead-in**
> Write: *interesting, boring, easy* and *difficult* on the board. Underneath write: *doctor* and *teacher*. Ask students to choose one adjective only for each of the jobs. Students work in pairs and compare their ideas. Elicit all the answers from students and, as a class, choose one adjective that best describes each job.

> **Vocabulary Pre-teaching / Review**
> You will need printable flashcards with the job names (Flashcards 5.1), which can be printed at esource.cambridge.org.
>
> Follow the procedure on p. 15.
>
> Show a flashcard with a photograph to students. Elicit the name of the job in English. If students don't remember, say the word aloud. Write the first letter of the job on the board and elicit the next letter. Continue with all the letters until students spell the word aloud. Write the word on the board. Repeat the procedure with other jobs.

1 🔊 5.1 👤👥 Focus on the words to trace. Say: *Listen and read*. Play the audio. Say: *Trace*. Students work individually and trace the words. Focus on the photographs and the words. Students work individually, read the words and match the photographs. Students check answers in pairs. Go through answers as a class.

> **Answers**
> 2 c 3 a 4 f 5 d 6 e

2 🔊 5.1 👤 Focus on the photographs in Exercise 1. Focus on the stress patterns and the completed example. Point at the words in Exercise 1 and the stress patterns and say: *Match*. Students match the stress patterns. Play the audio for students to listen and check. Go through answers as a class.

> **Answers**
> O: 4
> Oo: 5
> OOoo: 6
> oOoo: 2
> oOooo: 3

SOUND AND SPELLING *f, ph, ff*

3 🔊 5.2 👤 Count students or objects, e.g. pencils, up to five. Say: *five* for students to repeat. Elicit the spelling of *five* and write it on the board. Circle the *f* and say the sound /f/. Hold up your phone and elicit: *phone*. Elicit the spelling and write it on the board next to *five*, circling the *ph*. Write: *f* and *ph* above the words and divide into columns.

Play the audio for students to listen and read the words. Write the first two words under the two on the board. They should be familiar, but deal with any problems of meaning by miming, showing photographs or using a dictionary. When you come to *officer*, start a new column and write it at the top. Students work individually and trace the letters. Monitor and help. Play the audio again for students to listen and repeat. Drill the pronunciation of the words on the board by getting students to read them out, together or individually. Do not clean the board yet.

4 🔊 5.3 👤👥 Focus on the photographs, questions and options. Say: *Read and underline*. Students work individually, read the questions and underline the correct answers. Students check answers in pairs. Play the audio for students to listen and check.

> **Answers**
> a No, he isn't. b Yes, he is. c No, she isn't.

UNLOCK BASIC LITERACY TEACHER'S BOOK

5 👥 Focus on the sentences and the photographs in Exercise 4. Students work individually, read the sentences and match them to the photographs. Students compare their answers in pairs. Remind students of letter formation for *i*, *s*, *n*, *o*, and *t*. Students work individually and trace the words. Monitor the handwriting.

> **Answers**
> 2 c 3 a

> **NOTICE**
>
> Say: *I am a teacher*, indicating yourself and writing the words on the board. Indicate the class and say: *You are students*. Write the words on the board. Circle: *a* in the first sentence and indicate *one*. Then circle the final *s* in *students* and indicate that there are many of them. Indicate one student and say: *He/She is a student*. Write the sentence on the board. Write: *1* above the singular sentences and a few plural numbers above the plural sentence.
> Focus on the NOTICE box. Ask a student to read the words and the sentence aloud.

6 🔊 5.4 👤 Write: *She is teacher.* on the board. Write a cross (✗) next to the sentence. Elicit the missing word (*a*) and write the correct sentence on the board (*She is a teacher.*). Read the sentence aloud, using contractions and weak form (schwa sound /ə/) of *a*.

Focus on the sentences and the completed example. Students work individually, read the sentences and write the missing article *a*. Play the audio for students to listen and check. Go through answers as a class.

> **Answers**
> 2 He is a photographer.
> 3 She is not a dentist.
> 4 He is not a nurse.

7 🔊 5.5 👤 Write: *Heisadentist.* on the board. Move the pen along the sentence and draw the first line after *He*. Move the pen again, encouraging students to shout *Stop!* at the word boundaries. Add lines between the words.

Focus on the half-completed example. Show how lines mark spaces between words. Students work individually through the sentences. Monitor and help as necessary. Play the audio for students to listen and repeat.

> **Answers**
> 1 He is a dentist.
> 2 She is not a nurse.
> 3 She is a bank manager.
> 4 He is not a police officer.

> **Literacy tip**
>
> The schwa sound /ə/ is the most common sound of vowels in English. The article *a* is generally unstressed and is pronounced as a schwa. It is hard for students to hear, and Arabic students especially have difficulty with the articles *a*, *an* and *the* due to interference from their own language, which doesn't use them in the same way or as frequently. A combination of these factors affects their literacy and grammar skills, as it is harder for them to process the sounds. Therefore, it is important to raise awareness of the fact that there is a word there, even if it is not easy to hear.

8 🔊 5.6 👤 Say: *police officer*. Ask students what words they heard and see if they can remember the spelling. Write their ideas on the board, then say the words again and show the correct words and spelling.

Play the audio for students to trace and write. Play the audio as many times as required. Go through answers as a class.

> **Answers**
> 1 police officer 2 dentist 3 bank manager 4 pilot
> 5 photographer 6 nurse

> **Optional activity**
>
> Dictation is a very useful activity for literacy, but it does not always have to be done in a traditional way. It can be done in a variety of other ways, each of which will make different demands on students' cognition. One easy way to enhance its value is to dictate the whole word while students listen but do not write, so that they have to remember the spelling for a few seconds. This will help them internalize the spelling. Tell students that they have to remember five words. Say these words, pausing after each word for a few seconds:
>
> *pilot*
> *teacher*
> *photographer*
> *nurse*
> *bank manager*
>
> After you have said all the words aloud, ask students to write them all on a piece of paper. Students compare their words and spelling in pairs. Elicit the correct words in order. Ask students to spell them aloud. Write the words on the board for students to check their spelling.

WORK UNIT 5

9 👤 Write: *She a teacher.* on the board. Write a cross (✗) next to the sentence. Say the sentence aloud and elicit where the mistake is. Write the correct sentence on the board. (*She is a teacher.*)

Focus on the sentences. Students work individually, read the sentences and find and correct the mistakes. Monitor and help as required. Go through answers as a class.

> **Answers**
> 2 He is <u>a</u> police officer.
> 3 She <u>is</u> a dentist.
> 4 He <u>is</u> not a bank manager.
> 5 She is not <u>a</u> nurse.

WRITING CHALLENGE

10 👤👥 Focus on the photograph of a nurse. Point at the photograph and say: *This is Eduardo. He is a nurse.* Ask a student to read out the model text. Focus on the rubric and read it aloud. Students work individually and write three sentences using names of jobs. Monitor and help as necessary. Check that students are writing in the correct position on the lines. Students swap notebooks and check each other's writing for correct language, spelling and punctuation.

LISTENING AND READING 2

Learning objectives

- Understand and write verbs to describe people's routines – *go to work, go to university, go to the library, go home, meet friends*
- Read about people's routines – *They go home at two o'clock.*
- Notice the preposition *at* with places of work or study
- Recognize the correct word order with present simple verbs
- Write three sentences about a person's routine – *My name is Tilly. I work at a bank. I go home at five-thirty.*

See p. 19 for suggestions on how to use these Learning objectives with your students.

Lead-in

Write word shapes for these words on the board:

university   ▪▪▌▪▪▪▪▪▌▌▄
library   ▌▌▌▪▪▪▄
home   ▌▪▪▄
friend   ▌▪▌▪▪▄
classes   ▪▌▪▪▪▪▪▄

Students work in pairs and think of words that fit the word shapes. If students find this challenging, include the first letter in the word shape. Continue adding letters until students guess the words. Ask students to spell them out. Write the correct words in the word shapes.

Vocabulary Pre-teaching / Review

You will need printable flashcards with the daily activities (Flashcards 5.2), which can be printed at esource.cambridge.org.

Follow the procedure on p. 15.

Draw a stick figure of yourself. Say: *This is me.*

Write on the board:

I go to work.
I go home.
I finish work.
I start work.

Ask students to put the activities in order. Write numbers next to each sentence: *I go to work 1, I start work 2, I finish work 3, I go home 4.*

Circle: *to* in the first sentence and show how there is no other *to* in any sentence. Write: *university* and see if students can guess if there is a *to* or not (Yes, there is.).

Literacy tip

Collocations – words which go together – are sources of many errors when writing (and speaking). Always point them out when reading. Students could make a collocation page in their notebooks. They need to understand that they are basically non-negotiable; it is just how English works. Ask for examples in their own language. For example, in Arabic, they use *bring* rather than *get* for a result of a test, e.g. *I bring 70%.* Try to show that this is just a matter of usage.

1 🔊 5.7 👤👥 Focus on the photographs and the collocations. Play the audio for students to read and listen to the collocations. Say: *Trace.* Demonstrate tracing the completed example. Students work individually, read and trace the collocations.

Focus on the photographs. Say: *Match.* Students work individually, read the collocations and match them to the photographs. Students compare their answers in pairs. Write the collocations on the board

UNL⌀CK BASIC LITERACY TEACHER'S BOOK   81

in two columns, with *to* (*go to work, go to university, go to the library*) and without *to* (*go home, meet friends, start work/classes, finish work/classes*). Check students' understanding by writing *to* between *go* and *home*, then crossing it out. Also point out *the* in *the library* and show that you don't use it with the other words.

> **Answers**
> 2 a 3 e 4 b 5 d 6 g 7 h 8 i 9 f

2 🔊 5.8 👤 Focus on the timetables and the photographs. Check understanding by asking simple questions, e.g. *What time does Sam meet friends?* Ask a student to read the sentences aloud. Repeat the first sentence aloud. Say: *Sam or Ali?* (Ali) Students work individually, refer to the timetable and photographs, read the sentence and tick the name. Play the audio for students to listen and check. Go through answers as a class.

> **Answers**
> 2 Sam 3 Sam 4 Ali 5 Ali

> **⊙ Common student errors**
>
> **Spelling:** The word *friend* is in the top 20 misspelled words by Arabic L1 students. This is the typical error: *frind*.
> Write on the board:
> d i n r f e
> Say: *friend* and ask students to look at the letters and put them in the correct order. Students compare their spelling in pairs. Write the word *friend* on the board. Erase the letters and the word after a few seconds and ask students to spell it again (without looking at their notes).

> **NOTICE**
>
> Focus on the NOTICE box. Read out the sentences with the weak form of *at* and *a*. Students repeat after you. Then students look at the sentences in Exercise 2 and circle: *at* and *a*.

3 👤 Focus on the photographs and sentence stems, then the expressions with *at*. Students work individually, read the sentence stems and match them to the expressions. Go through answers on the board. Circle: *at* with times twice (*at three o'clock, at one-thirty*) and use another colour to circle: *at* with places twice (*at university, at a bank*) Elicit more examples for each, e.g. *at school, at home, at five o'clock*.

> **Answers**
> 2 at one-thirty 3 at university 4 at a bank

> **NOTICE**
>
> Write: *We finish work.* on the board. Write: *meet friends I.* below. Write a cross (✗) next to the second sentence to indicate that the word order is wrong. Students match the structure of the second sentence to the first. Write the corrected second sentence under the first using the same colours as in the first (*I meet friends.*).
> Focus students on the NOTICE box. Ask a student to read the sentences aloud.

4 👤 Focus on the sentences and the NOTICE box. Point at the verbs in the NOTICE box and tell students to circle the verbs in the sentences in Exercise 4. Students work individually, read the sentences and circle the verbs. Go through answers as a class.

> **Answers**
> 2 start 3 study 4 meet 5 work

5 🔊 5.9 👤 Write: *nine* on the board. Write this sentence: *I go to work at nine o'clock.* Move your pen slowly across the sentence from left to right and encourage students to shout *Stop!* when you get to the word *nine*. Circle it.

Focus on the words in bold and sentences. Say: *Read and circle*. Students work individually, read and circle the words. Play the audio for students to read and listen to the sentences. Ask a student to read the sentences aloud.

6 👤 If required, remind students how to form *e, o* and *t, g, h, y* with correct strokes on the board. Ask students to work individually, cover and complete the words. If necessary, prompt them to use something to cover the words on the left as they complete each one. Monitor and check that they are working from left to right. Encourage correct stroke direction and correct height and position of the individual letters.

7 👤 Write: *start classes / at 8 o'clock. / We* on the board. Elicit the correct order for the words (*We start classes at 8 o'clock.*). Write the answer on the board.

Focus on the jumbled words in the book. Students work individually, look at the words and re-order them. Monitor and check students are using capitals and full stops correctly. Go through answers on the board; use different colours if possible to highlight the subject pronoun / verb pattern.

> **Answers**
> 2 We go home.
> 3 I study at university.
> 4 They meet friends.
> 5 We finish work at six o'clock.

WRITING CHALLENGE

8 Focus on the photograph. Point and say: *This is Tilly. She is a bank manager.* Ask a student to read out the model text. Focus on the rubric and read it aloud. Students work individually, complete the information and write three sentences. Monitor and help as necessary. Check that students are writing in the correct position on the lines. Students swap notebooks and check each other's writing for correct language, spelling and punctuation.

> **Optional activity**
> Ask students to write the sentences from the Writing challenge on strips of paper (with their name underneath). Collect and read them out, missing out the names. Students listen carefully to the sentences and guess who wrote each one. You could give points for this to make it into a simple communicative game.

LISTENING AND READING 3

> **Learning objectives**
> - Understand verbs with nouns to describe people's work – *meet people, take photographs, read emails, travel to different countries, write emails, help people*
> - Write verbs with correct vowels
> - Notice phrases with the verb *work* and preposition – *work in the city, work with people, work on a computer*
> - Notice the correct third person singular form for verbs in the present simple
> - Write three sentences about a person's routine – *Humaid is a police officer. He works in the city. He works with people.*
> - Gain awareness of sound and spelling of *s* in third person singular
>
> See p. 19 for suggestions on how to use these Learning objectives with your students.

> **Lead-in**
> Write these collocations on the board:
> *start classes*
> *finish classes*
> *go to the library*
> *meet friends*
> Ask students to look at the list and put the time for each activity that is correct for them. Students work in pairs and talk about the times they do these things. Ask students to find differences and similarities. Monitor and help students as necessary. Ask a few students to share their routines with the whole class.

> **Vocabulary Pre-teaching / Review**
> You will need printable flashcards with the work activities (Flashcards 5.3), which can be printed at esource.cambridge.org.
> Follow the procedure on p. 15.
> Teach students the word *photo(s)* with *photograph(s)* as a synonym.
> Write the verbs on one side of the board and the nouns on the other, in columns or mixed up in circles.
> Verbs: *take, read, write, help, meet, travel to*
> Nouns: *emails x2, people x2, photographs, different countries*
> Students work in pairs and match the verbs and nouns to make collocations. Go through answers as a class, connecting the verbs and nouns with lines on the board (*take photographs, read/write emails, help/meet people, travel to different countries*).

1 🔊 5.10 Focus on the photographs and the collocations. Students work individually and match the words to the photographs. Play the audio for students to listen to the words. Go through answers as a class. Ask a student to read the words aloud.

> **Answers**
> 2 a 3 b 4 f 5 c 6 d

> **◉ Common student errors**
> **Spelling:** The word *different* is in the top 20 misspelled words by Arabic L1 students. This is the typical error: *diffrent.*
> Write on the board:
> *different diffrent deffrient different diffrent different*
> Ask students to look at the first word in the line. Erase it after a few seconds. Ask students to look at the list of the same word but with correct and incorrect spellings of it. Ask students to find the words in the line with the correct spelling. Ask students to compare their answers in pairs. Circle the correct words (*different* x2) on the board.

> **Optional activity**
>
> **Team pelmanism:** Follow the procedure on p. 16. Use the collocations in Exercise 1.

2 👤 Draw a word shape for *take* on the board and write: *photographs* after it. Elicit: *take* and write it in the word shape. Write vowels *a, e, i, o, u* on the board, showing the correct formation.

Students work individually, read the collocations and complete the words. Monitor and help as necessary.

3 🔊 5.11 👤 Write the verbs from Exercise 2 on the board. Read the first part of the script aloud: *My name is Ross. I am a photographer. I take photographs. I meet people in the city.* Ask students to listen carefully and remember which verbs they heard. Repeat the text if required. Ask students to point at the verbs (meet, take).

Focus on the photographs in the book. Say: *Listen and match.* Ask students to read the sentences, listen and match the photographs. Go through answers on the board. Play the audio again if required.

> **Answers**
>
> a 2 b 3, 6 c 1, 4

> **NOTICE**
>
> Focus on the NOTICE box. Say: *I live in the city* (say whereabouts in the city). *I work with people* (say names of other teachers). *I work on a computer for two hours a day.* Emphasize the prepositions. Write the sentences on the board and point out the prepositions. Ask students to read the sentences aloud.

4 🔊 5.12 👤 Focus on the words in the box and the text. Read the words in the box aloud and point at the photograph. Students work individually, read the text and circle the words from the box. Play the audio for students to read and listen to the text.

> **NOTICE**
>
> Write: *I work.* on the board. Point at yourself. Write: *He work_.* Elicit: *s.* Repeat with *she*.
>
> Focus on the NOTICE box. Make sure students understand that *s* is only added to the verb for *he* and *she*, and it is singular, not plural. Ask a student to read the sentences aloud.

5 🔊 5.13 👤👥 Focus on the text about Saeed and the photograph. Students work individually, read the sentences and the text and underline the correct answers. Play the audio for students to listen and check. Students compare their answers in pairs. Students work individually and trace the words. Remind them of the correct strokes for some of the letters, e.g. *m, r, d, p, s.* Go through answers as a class. Play the audio again if required.

> **Answers**
>
> 1 works 2 writes 3 meets

6 🔊 5.14 👤 Write: *She works with people.* on the board. Circle: *She* and the third person *s* and draw a line to connect them.

Focus on the sentences in the book and the completed example. Students work individually, read the sentences and put the verbs in a correct form for the third person singular. Play the audio for students to listen and check. Go through answers as a class.

> **Answers**
>
> 2 travels 3 works 4 writes 5 works

SOUND AND SPELLING adding *s*

7 🔊 5.15 👤 Write: *help* on the board. Write: *He helps people.* Point at the first word you wrote (help) and elicit where it is in the sentence. Move your pen slowly across the sentence, encouraging students to shout *Stop!* when you get to the word *help*. Circle it in the sentence.

Focus on the words in bold and the sentences in the book. Say: *Read, listen and circle.* Play the audio. Students work individually, read, listen and circle the words. Go through answers as a class. Ask a student to read the sentences aloud.

8 🔊 5.16 👤👥 Focus on the spelling patterns in Exercise 8 and the words in Exercise 7. Point at the two completed examples. Students work individually, look at the words in Exercise 7 and write them in the column with the correct spelling pattern. Students compare answers in pairs. Go through answers as a class. Play the audio for students to listen and repeat.

> **Answers**
>
> + s: takes, helps + es: finishes *y* + ies: studies

WORK UNIT 5

9 🔊 5.17 Write stress patterns on the board as in Exercise 9. Say: *washes* and elicit that it goes under the second pattern. Say: *wash* and elicit that it goes under the first pattern.

Focus on the words in the box. Play the audio. Students work individually, listen to the words in the box and match them to the stress patterns. Go through answers as a class. Play the audio again for students to listen and repeat.

> **Answers**
> O: watch Oo: watches, finish Ooo: finishes

SPELLING CHALLENGE

10 🔊 5.18 Focus on the photographs and the verbs. Ask which verbs finish in *y* and *sh* or *ch*. Remind students about the spelling patterns in Exercise 8. Students work individually, read the verbs and complete the sentences. Play the audio for students to listen and check their answers. Write the correct answers on the board. Focus on Exercise 8. Say: *Look and write*. Students add the verbs from Exercise 8 to the list of verbs in Exercise 9 under the correct spelling pattern. Go through answers as a class.

> **Answers**
> 2 washes 3 flies 4 watches

LANGUAGE FOCUS

> **Learning objectives**
> - Read and write the months of the year – *January, February, March, April, May, June, July, August, September, October, November, December*
> - Notice and produce capital letters on months
> - Read and understand a planner with information about the academic year
> - Notice the preposition *in* with months
> - Identify word boundaries and capital letters in sentences
> - Gain awareness of sound and spelling of the letters *ou*
>
> See p. 19 for suggestions on how to use these Learning objectives with your students.

> **Lead-in**
> Write days of the week in the incorrect order on the board.
> Students work in pairs and put the days of the week in order (starting from Sunday or Monday, depending on which is the first day of the week in their country). Elicit the answers and write numbers above the words for students to check their answers.

> **Vocabulary Pre-teaching / Review**
> You will need printable flashcards with months (Flashcards 5.4), which can be printed at esource.cambridge.org.
> Follow the procedure on p. 15.
> Write: *1–12* on the board with the first letter of each month, in capitals, starting with *J* for January.
> Point at each letter and say the word for students to repeat. Repeat this procedure several times until students have remembered all the months. Elicit the spelling of each month as students say it. Ask which month is now. Say it for students to repeat.

1 🔊 5.19 Focus on the words in the book. Play the audio for students to listen and read. Students work individually and trace the letters. Monitor students' handwriting. Play the audio again for students to listen and repeat.

> **NOTICE**
> Write: *january* on the board. Write a cross (**X**) next to the word and elicit where the mistake is (capital *J* missing). Correct the mistake and write: *January*.
> Focus on the NOTICE box. Ask students to look back at Exercise 1 and underline all the capital letters in the months.

2 🔊 5.20 Draw on the board the five stress patterns in the book. Say: *March*. Students match it to the stress pattern. Write it under the first one (O).

Play the audio for students to listen and write. Students work individually and write the months in, looking at Exercise 1 for the spelling if required. Play the audio as many times as required. Write the answers on the board under the stress patterns. Play the audio again while students listen and repeat. Monitor and check students emphasize the stressed syllable in each month.

> **Answers**
> O: June, May
> Oo: April, August
> oOo: September, October, November, December
> oO: July
> Oooo: January, February

UNL*O*CK BASIC LITERACY TEACHER'S BOOK 85

3 Focus on the pictures and the phrases. Students work individually, read the phrases and match them to the pictures. Check that students understand the words *first*, *exam*, *holiday*, *summer*, *winter* and *January*. Encourage students to use a dictionary if required. Go through answers as a class.

> **Answers**
> 2 c 3 a 4 d

4 Focus on the academic planner. Ask a student to read all the information aloud. Students work individually, read the questions, look at the timetable and circle the correct options. Students check answers in pairs. Go through answers as a class.

> **Answers**
> 2 in March 3 in May 4 in June

> **NOTICE**
> Focus on the NOTICE box. Write three questions on the board: *When is the summer holiday? When is the (English) exam? When is your first day at university?* Elicit answers and ask students to give you the months for these events. Make sure they use *in* when answering.

> **Optional activity**
> Write the sentences below on strips of paper and get students to cut them up into individual words. Students mix the words up and then reassemble the sentences. To make this into a game, if appropriate, do it as a race between individuals or pairs. You could also ask them to reassemble different sentences, by changing the months.
> The Maths exam is in June.
> The summer holiday is in July.
> The winter holiday is in February.
> The first day of university is in September.

5 Focus on the sentences in the book. Point at the first sentence and elicit the lack of capitals. Correct the first one on the board. Students work individually, read the sentences and correct the mistakes. Go through answers as a class.

> **Answers**
> 2 The first day of university is in October.
> 3 The English exam is in May.
> 4 The History exam is in April.

6 5.21 Focus on the calendar. Students work individually, look at the calendar and complete the sentences. Monitor and check students' spelling, use of capitals and full stops, and letter formation. Play the audio for students to listen and check. Go through answers on the board.

> **Answers**
> 2 in November 3 in December

SOUND AND SPELLING *ou*

7 5.22 Focus on the sentence in the book. Play the audio for students to listen and read. Write the sentence on the board and circle the *ou* spelling pattern. Isolate the sounds, say each one and ask students to repeat. Students work individually and trace the letters. Play the audio again for students to listen and repeat.

8 5.23 Focus on the photographs and the words. Play the audio. Students work individually, read and match the words to the same sound. Play the audio again for students to listen and repeat. Focus on the *ou* sounds: /aʊ/ (*our*) /ɔː/ (*course*) /uː/ (*you*) /ʌ/ (*country*).

> **Answers**
> 2 four 3 group 4 young

9 5.24 Focus on the pictures and the words. Play the audio. Students work individually and write the words in the columns, matching the sounds. Students check answers in pairs. Go through answers as a class. Play the audio again for students to listen and repeat.

> **Answers**
> our: mouth, count, pound, shout
> course: your, fourteen
> you: youth
> country: double

WORK   UNIT 5

LISTENING FOCUS

Learning objectives

- Use photographs to predict information as preparation for listening
- Recognize sentence boundaries as preparation for listening
- Listen and understand people talking about jobs
- Practise fast reading and spelling of *with*, *first* and *people*

See p. 19 for suggestions on how to use these Learning objectives with your students.

Lead-in

Write these sentences on the board:
1 *She writes emails.*
2 *She helps people.*
3 *He studies English.*
4 *He takes photographs.*

Ask students to work in pairs and think of jobs that match the sentences (e.g. 1 bank manager, teacher; 2 nurse, doctor, dentist, police officer; 3 student; 4 photographer, police officer). Elicit their answers. Write all the jobs on the board.

1 Focus on the photographs and the words. Students work individually, look at the words and match them to the photographs. Go through answers as a class.

> **Answers**
> 2 c 3 a

2 (5.25) Focus on the photographs in Exercise 1. Point at the first photograph and say: *Is she a nurse? Is she a businesswoman?* (She is a businesswoman.)

Focus on the sentences in the book. Ask a student to read the sentences aloud. Say: *Listen and circle.* Play the audio for students to listen and circle. Students compare answers in pairs. Play the audio again if required. Go through answers as a class.

> **Answers**
> 2 No 3 No 4 Yes 5 No 6 Yes

3 Write: *katie is from the uk she is a nurse* on the board. Write a cross (✗) next to the sentences. Elicit where to write the full stops and the capital letters. Write the correct sentences on the board (Katie is from the UK. She is a nurse.)

Focus on the sentences in the book. Students work individually, read the sentences, find and correct the mistakes. Go through answers as a class.

> **Answers**
> 2 Peter works at night. He helps people.
> 3 They are teachers. They finish classes at two-thirty.

Optional activity

Collaborative vocabulary and spelling test: Follow the team spelling test procedure on pp. 16–17.

For this optional activity, prepare flashcards with all new vocabulary from this unit (Flashcards 5.1–5.4), which can be printed at esource.cambridge.org.

◉ KEY WORDS FOR LITERACY

Learning objectives

- Read, spell and pronounce key words for literacy – *with*, *we*, *work*, *write*
- Complete sentences with the key words for literacy

See p. 19 for suggestions on how to use these Learning objectives in your lessons.

◉ Common student errors

Spelling: The word *people* is in the top 20 misspelled words by Arabic L1 students. The typical errors include *pepole*, *peaple*, *peopel* and *peopl*.

Write on the board:
people
e p p o l e

Ask students to look at the word *people* and the letters. Erase the word. Say: *people*. Ask students to work together in pairs and use the letters to write the word *people* with the correct spelling. Elicit the spelling. Write the word on the board for students to check.

1 (5.26) Write: *with* on the board. Write: *She works with people.* Move your pen slowly across the sentence, encouraging students to shout *Stop!* when you get to the word *with*. Circle it.

Focus on the words in bold and the sentences in the book. Say: *Read and circle.* Students work individually, read and circle the words. Play the audio for students to read and listen to the sentences. Ask a student to read the sentences aloud.

UNLOCK BASIC LITERACY TEACHER'S BOOK   87

2 👤 Write: *with* on the board. Write these words: *when with what where with*. Point at the first word you wrote (with) and elicit the pronunciation. Move your pen slowly across the sentences, encouraging students to shout *Stop!* when you get to the word. Circle: *with* twice.

Focus on the words in bold in the book. Say: *Read and circle*. Students work individually, read and circle the words.

3 👤 Students work individually, cover and complete the words. If necessary, prompt them to use something to cover the words on the left as they complete each one. Monitor and check that they are working from left to right. Encourage correct stroke direction and correct height and position of the individual letters.

4 🔊 5.27 👤 Focus on the sentences and the gaps. Say: *Read and write*. Students work individually, read the sentences and complete the gaps with the missing words. Play the audio for students to listen and check. Go through answers as a class.

> **Answers**
> 1 write 2 with 3 work 4 We

READING AND WRITING

> **Learning objectives**
> - Understand verb-noun phrases in preparation for reading
> - Scan a text for information
> - Read for detail
> - Review the use of prepositions – *in, at, on, with*
> - Complete sentences about a friend – *This is Obaid. He is a student. He wants to be a pilot.*
>
> See p. 19 for suggestions on how to use these Learning objectives with your students.

Lead-in
Write: *Do they need English?* on the board. Say a few jobs aloud. Encourage students to listen and answer the question. Ask the question aloud. Draw a table on the board with a *Yes* column and a *No* column as below. Point at the question on the board again. Elicit students' answers and write their ideas on the board under each column.

	Yes	No
Teacher		
Nurse		
Pilot		
Doctor		
Bank manager		
Police officer		

1 🔊 5.28 👤👥 Focus on the photographs and the phrases. Students work individually and match the photographs to the phrases. Point at the poster. Students scan the poster for the phrases and circle them. Students compare answers in pairs. Play the audio for students to listen and check their answers.

> **Answers**
> 2 a 3 c

2 👤👥 Students read the sentence stems on the left in the book. Elicit any possible endings to the sentences that they can think of. Advise students to use the prepositions as clues for the type of information they need, e.g. *at* + a time. Students work individually, read the poster again and underline the information, then match the sentence halves. Students compare answers in pairs. Write the sentences on the board.

> **Answers**
> 2 three-thirty.
> 3 five o'clock.
> 4 room 11.
> 5 Mrs Hassan.
> 6 December.

WORK UNIT 5

3 🔊 5.29 👤 Write: *The classes are room 10.* on the board. Elicit the mistake (*in* is missing). Elicit the position of *in* and add it to the sentence (The classes are in room 10.).

Remind students how to write key letters, e.g. *a, t*. Focus on the words in the box. Students work individually, read and complete the sentences with the words from the box. Play the audio for students to listen and check their answers.

> **Answers**
> 2 He wants to be <u>a</u> police officer.
> 3 The English exam is <u>in</u> March.
> 4 She works <u>at</u> a bank.
> 5 He works <u>with</u> people.
> 6 He works <u>on</u> a computer.

4 👤👥 Focus on the photograph and the model text. Ask a student to read the text aloud. Write the following words on the board: *pilot, the university, eight o'clock, meets friends, in June*. Ask students to look at the words on the board and find and circle them in the model text. Elicit a few more ideas of what students can do in the evening (meet friends, go shopping, watch TV, play games, etc.).

Focus on the sentences to complete. Say: *Write about your friend*. Students work individually and complete the sentences using the model text. Monitor and help as necessary. Check that students are writing in the correct position on the lines. Students swap notebooks and check each other's writing for correct language, spelling and punctuation.

> **Model answer**
> This is Sarah. She is a student. She wants to be a teacher. She goes to classes at the university. She starts classes at eight o'clock in the morning. She goes shopping in the evening. The exams are in May.

> **Optional activity**
> Write these sentences on the board (they are not all correct):
> *They meets friends in the evening.*
> *He help people.*
> *She starts classes at nine o'clock.*
> *They work in a bank.*
> *He wants to be a doctor.*
> *She finishs classes at five-thirty.*
> Students work in pairs and find the three sentences which contain a mistake. Elicit which sentences are incorrect (1, 2, 6) and elicit the corrections. Write the correct sentences on the board. (They meet friends in the evening. He helps people. She finishes classes at five-thirty.)

> **Objectives review**
> See Teaching tips on p. 19 for ideas about using the Objectives review with your students.
>
> **WORDLIST**
> See Teaching tips on p. 21 for ideas about using the Wordlist on p. 142 with your students.
>
> **REVIEW TEST**
> See esource.cambridge.org for the Review test and ideas about how and when to administer the Review test.

6 FOOD AND HEALTH

LISTENING AND READING 1

Learning objectives

- Read and write words for food and drink – *drink, eat, juice, coffee, water, tea, bread, rice, cheese, salad, fish, meat, fruit, vegetables*
- Understand positive and negative forms of *eat* and *drink* in sentences
- Write the uncontracted verb forms in sentences
- Review sound and spelling patterns

See p. 19 for suggestions on how to use these Learning objectives with your students.

Lead-in

Write: *I drink. I eat.* on the board. Mime to show the meaning of the two verbs. Prepare a few identical sets of flashcards with food and drink photographs (Flashcards 6.1), which can be printed at esource.cambridge.org. Divide students into small groups. Students look at the photographs of food and drink and categorize the items under *I drink* or *I eat*. Go through students' answers as a class.

Vocabulary Pre-teaching / Review

You will need printable flashcards with words for food and drink (Flashcards 6.1), which can be printed at esource.cambridge.org.

Follow the procedure on p. 15.

Repeat the procedure from the Lead-in, but this time with flashcards with words (not photographs). Students look at the words and check if they remember what the English name stands for. Go through answers as a class.

1 🔊 6.1 Focus on the photographs and the words. Play the audio for students to listen and read the words. Check that students understand the meanings. Students work individually, read and trace the words. Then students write the words. Students check their answers in pairs. Play the audio again for students to listen and repeat.

2 🔊 6.2 Write the three stress patterns on the board. Say: *coffee* and elicit that it goes in the middle column. Repeat for *drink* (the first column).

Focus on the stress patterns in the book. Play the audio for students to listen. Students look at Exercise 1 and write the words in the correct column. Students compare their answers in pairs. Go through answers as a class. Students read the words aloud. Correct the pronunciation if required.

Answers
O: eat meat fish juice rice fruit cheese tea bread
Oo: salad water
Ooo: vegetables

Literacy tip

Make sure students do not look back for the spellings of words – it is important that they make the effort to recall them, which is a key to efficient memorization. Getting it wrong is fine, as they can erase and correct when they listen. If you give the spelling, the listening becomes ineffective.

SOUND AND SPELLING Review

3 🔊 6.3 Write: *big rice fish* on the board. Underline the letter *i* in *big*. Move the pen from left to right along the other two words (*rice, fish*) and underline the letter *i*. Say: /ɪ/ *big*. Then say: *rice, fish*. Repeat a few times. Students point at the word that has the same sound (/ɪ/) as the word *big* (*fish*). Circle: *fish*.

Focus on the words with the highlighted letters in the book. Students underline the same letters in the other words and circle the word that has the same sound. Play the audio for students to listen and check. Go through answers as a class.

Answers
2 co<u>ff</u>ee
3 r<u>i</u>ce
4 <u>br</u>ead
5 <u>fr</u>uit

4 🔊 6.4 If possible, bring a bottle of juice and a bottle of water to class. If it is not possible, use flashcards. Point at the water and say: *I drink water*. Point at the juice and say: *I don't drink juice* and make a negative gesture to show the meaning. Write the two sentences on the board. Circle: *do not* and again make a negative gesture.

90 UNLOCK BASIC LITERACY TEACHER'S BOOK

Play the audio for students to listen and read. Play the audio again for students to repeat. Ask a student to read the sentences aloud.

5 ◀) 6.5 Focus on the photographs. Read the names of the three people aloud. Say: *Listen and match*. Play the audio for students to listen and match the photographs. Play the audio again if required. Go through answers as a class.

> **Answers**
> Huda: 3
> Tariq: 1, 5
> Natasha: 2, 6

> **NOTICE**
>
> Write: *I don't drink coffee.* on the board. Say the sentence aloud. Erase *n't* and write: *not*. Make sure students understand they should use a short verb form for speaking and a long verb form for writing by saying: *Say I don't, write I do not.*
> Focus on the NOTICE box. Ask a student to read the sentences aloud.

6 Remind students of correct strokes for the letters *d*, *o*, *n* and *t* by writing them on the board. Focus on the sentences with short verb forms. Students work individually, read the sentences and complete the sentences with the full verb forms (do not). Go through answers as a class.

> **Optional activity**
>
> Students do a food survey. Prepare a list of food and drink vocabulary. Make copies and give one to each student. Students mingle and indicate food or drink items, one at a time, to other students. Students reply positively or negatively: *I eat* (fish) or *I don't eat* (fish). In stronger classes, students make a note of each response and report the results as a class. Write the results on the board, e.g. *Five students eat fish. Three students don't eat fish.*
> **Alternative to mingling:** If mingling is not appropriate in your context, students can work in small groups.

7 ◀) 6.6 Write: *eat rice. I* on the board. Elicit the correct sentence (I eat rice.). Write it on the board.

Students work individually, read the words in the book and put them in the correct order. Students then write the full sentences. Play the audio for students to listen and check their answers. Students say the sentences, using the contraction *don't* when they speak.

FOOD AND HEALTH — UNIT 6

> **Answers**
> 2 I eat fish.
> 3 I drink tea.
> 4 I do not eat bread.
> 5 I do not drink juice.

LISTENING AND READING 2

> **Learning objectives**
>
> - Read and write verb phrases for routine activities – *go to bed, have lunch, have dinner, walk to university, have breakfast, get up, drive to work*
> - Understand positive and negative forms of *eat* and *drink* with *he* and *she* in sentences
> - Identify and write the correct form of the present simple in sentences
> - Write two sentences about a friend – *Amna goes to university at eight o'clock. She finishes university at twelve o'clock.*
>
> See p. 19 for suggestions on how to use these Learning objectives with your students.

> **Lead-in**
>
> Tell the story of your day aloud, using the collocations below and giving the times.
> *I go to work at …*
> *I start classes at …*
> *I meet friends at …*
> *I go home at …*
> When you finish your story, ask students questions, e.g. *What time* (point at your watch or clock) *do I go to work?* If students don't recall, write the times out of order on the board and ask students to match. Go through answers as a class.

> **Vocabulary Pre-teaching / Review**
>
> You will need printable flashcards with verb phrases for routines (Flashcards 6.2), which can be printed at esource.cambridge.org.
> Follow the procedure on p. 15.
> Repeat the procedure from the Lead-in exercise, but this time with the collocations on the flashcards.

1 ◀) 6.7 Focus on the photographs and the words in the box. Students work individually, look at the photographs and use the word shapes to complete the phrases. Check that students understand the meanings. Students check their answers in pairs. Go through answers as a class. Play the audio for students to listen and repeat.

UNLOCK BASIC LITERACY TEACHER'S BOOK 91

> **Answers**
> 2 lunch 3 dinner 4 to university 5 breakfast 6 up
> 7 to work

2 🔊 6.8 👥 Focus on the text. Play the audio for students to listen and read. Check that students understand the meaning. Students work individually, read the text again and trace the words. Then students check their answers in pairs. Play the audio again for students to listen and repeat.

NOTICE

Write: *I get up at 8 o'clock. I don't get up at 8 o'clock.* on the board. Say the sentences aloud. Erase *n't* and write: *not*. Write: *He gets up at 8 o'clock.* Underline the letter *s* in *gets* and connect it with a line to the pronoun *He*. Write: *He doesn't get up at 8 o'clock.* Underline the word *doesn't* and connect it with a line to the pronoun *He*. Point at the verb *get* to show that there is no *s* in the main verb if a sentence is negative. Erase *n't* and write: *not*. Make sure students understand that they should use a short verb form for speaking and a long verb form for writing by saying: *Say* he doesn't *and write* he does not.
Focus on the NOTICE box. Ask a student to read the sentences aloud.

---

3 👤 Write: *He doesn't get up at six o'clock.* on the board. Erase *doesn't* and elicit the full verb form (*does not*). Write it on the board.

Focus on the sentences in speech bubbles in the book and the gapped sentences. Students work individually, read the speech bubbles and complete the gaps with full verb forms. Monitor students' handwriting. Go through answers as a class.

> **Answers**
> 2 do not 3 does not 4 does not

4 🔊 6.9 👤👥 Focus on Eissa's daily routine. Ask: *What time does he get up?* Elicit the full sentence *He gets up at 7:30.* Write it on the board and circle the *s* in *gets*. Connect the letter *s* with the pronoun *He*. Remind students as necessary how to write the letters, e.g. *g, f, t*. Students work individually, look at Eissa's routine and complete the sentences. Students compare their answers in pairs. Play the audio for students to listen and check. Go through answers as a class.

> **Answers**
> 3 does not go 4 has 5 does not finish 6 goes

5 🔊 6.10 👤 Write: *do* and the sentence *I do not eat fish.* on the board. Point at *do* and elicit the pronunciation. Move your pen slowly across the sentence, encouraging students to shout *Stop!* when you get to *do*. Circle it in the sentence.

Focus on the words in bold and the sentences in the book. Say: *Read and circle*. Students work individually, and read and circle the words. Play the audio for students to read and listen to the sentences. Ask a student to read the sentences aloud.

6 👤 Focus on the lines of words in the book. Students work individually, cover and complete the words. If necessary, prompt them to use something to cover the words on the left as they complete each one. Monitor and check that they are working from left to right. Encourage correct stroke direction and correct height and position of the individual letters.

WRITING CHALLENGE

7 👤👥 Focus on the photograph in the book. Point at the photograph and say: *This is Hind. She goes to university at eight o'clock.* Ask a student to read out the model text. Focus on the rubric and read it aloud. Students work individually and write two sentences using collocations and the correct verb form for the third person singular. Monitor and help as necessary. Check that students are writing in the correct position on the lines. Students swap notebooks and check each other's writing for correct language, spelling and punctuation.

Literacy tip

Beginners often ignore the sentence endings when reading, running the sentences together. This makes it hard for them to understand what they are reading. Reading aloud is a good way to address this. It reinforces the idea that punctuation is there for a purpose.

Optional activity

Aural dictation: Follow the procedure on p. 17.
1 *I don't drink coffee.*
2 *He eat meat.*
3 *She gets up at eight-thirty.*
4 *They doesn't drive to work.*
5 *They have breakfast at eight o'clock.*
6 *I eats fruit.*

FOOD AND HEALTH — UNIT 6

LISTENING AND READING 3

Learning objectives

- Read and write verb and noun phrases for healthy and unhealthy lifestyles – *green tea, go to bed late, red meat, fruit and vegetables, get up early, milk and sugar*
- Understand quantifiers in context – *a lot of, some, not a lot of*
- Identify word boundaries in sentences and identify the sentences in a text
- Write two sentences about people's habits – *A lot of people drink juice. Not a lot of people drink tea.*
- Gain awareness of sound and spelling of letters *ee, ea*

See p. 19 for suggestions on how to use these Learning objectives with your students.

Lead-in

Write: *eat drink* in two columns on the board. Elicit food and drink words without students looking in the book. Write the words on the board under the appropriate verb. Students spell them out for you to write.

Vocabulary Pre-teaching / Review

You will need printable flashcards with the verb and nouns that refer to healthy and unhealthy lifestyles (Flashcards 6.3), which can be printed at esource.cambridge.org.

Follow the procedure on p. 15.

Write: *healthy* and *unhealthy* on the board. Check students understand the meanings. Show flashcards illustrating different food and drink habits. Students say what is on the card and whether it is healthy or unhealthy. Write the correct word under the appropriate category.

1 ◀) 6.11 Focus on the photographs and the words. Play the audio for students to listen to the words. Make sure students understand these new words: *milk, sugar, early, late, red, fruit, with*. Students say the words aloud. Play the audio again if required.

2 ◀) 6.12 Elicit a popular drink in your country. Say: *Do you drink* (tea)? Students put their hands up. Count how many do and, if correct, say: *A lot of people drink tea*. Write it on the board. Repeat with an unpopular drink in your country and say, if correct: *Not a lot of people drink* (coffee). Write it underneath the first sentence, leaving a gap. Repeat for a drink that you know some of them drink. Say: *Some people drink* (juice). Write it in the middle.

Repeat each phrase on the board in order, asking students to raise their hands if they drink (tea/juice/coffee, etc.).

Focus on the words and phrases in the box and the information about the UK and Japan. Students complete the information using the word shapes and numbers to help them. Monitor and check for accuracy. Play the audio for students to listen and check. Go through answers as a class. Drill the pronunciation. Ask a student to read the answers aloud.

Answers

The UK
41%: to bed late
12%: green tea
Japan
9%: milk and sugar
38%: get up early
81%: fruit and vegetables

NOTICE

Focus on the NOTICE box. Point at the words and the dots representing amounts. Ask a student to read the phrases aloud. Check students understand the meaning by comparing the number of dots.

3 ◀) 6.13 Write: 40% on the board. Say: *a lot of, some, not a lot of* in a questioning tone. Elicit the correct answer (*some*).

Focus on the percentages and the options in the book. Students work individually, analyze the percentages and circle the correct option. Play the audio for students to listen and check. Go through answers as a class. Students work individually and write the correct options. Monitor their handwriting.

Answers

2 Not a lot of 3 A lot of 4 Some

◉ Common student errors

Confusable errors: Arabic L1 students often confuse the words *some* and *same*. They often make a mistake by replacing one with the other. This is because the only difference in spelling is one vowel (Arabic L1 students' biggest problem).

To practise the word *some*, which students see in this unit, write it on the board. Next to it, write: *same some same some some some same*. Move the pen along the line, encouraging students to shout *Stop!* when you reach the word *some*. Circle: *some* four times.

UNLOCK BASIC LITERACY TEACHER'S BOOK

4 🔊 6.14 Write: *Alotofpeopleeatfish.* on the board. Move the pen along the sentence and draw the first line after *A*. Move the pen again, encouraging students to shout *Stop!* at the word boundaries. Add lines between the words.

Focus on the first sentence in the book. Show how lines mark spaces between words. Students work individually through the other sentences. Monitor and help as necessary. Play the audio for students to listen and check. Go through answers as a class.

> **Answers**
> 1 Not a lot of people eat red meat.
> 2 Some people drink coffee with milk.
> 3 Some people drink green tea.
> 4 A lot of people in Spain eat fruit.

WRITING CHALLENGE

5 Focus on the photograph of a woman. Point at the photograph and say: *This is a woman in the UK.* Ask a student to read out the model text. Focus on the rubric and read it aloud. Students work individually and write two sentences. Monitor and help as necessary. Check that students are writing in the correct position on the lines. Students swap notebooks and check each other's writing for correct language, spelling and punctuation.

> **Optional activity**
> In small groups, students compile the information they wrote in the Writing challenge into a poster. They create a bar chart or graph to illustrate the information about drinking habits in their country. In stronger classes, groups present their posters to the class by indicating different parts of the chart or graph and saying short sentences, e.g. *A lot of people drink orange juice.*

SOUND AND SPELLING
ea, i, e, ee

6 🔊 6.15 Write: *We eat meat for dinner.* on the board and read aloud for students to repeat. Correct and then circle the vowel sounds. Say: /iː/ and write: *1* on the board, then say: /ɪ/ and write: *2* on the board. Point at *We* and elicit: *1* or *2* (1). Write it under *1*. Repeat for *eat*, *meat*, and *dinner*. Indicate that there is another spelling for /iː/. If possible, elicit: *ee* and write it on the board.

Focus on the sentences for tracing in the book. Play the audio for students to listen and read. Remind students of how to form the letters *e*, *a* and *i* correctly. Students work individually and trace the words. Play the audio for students to listen and say the sentences. Students then read the full sentences aloud.

> **Literacy tip**
> The spelling rules behind the choice of *ea* and *ee* are complex. However, it is interesting to note that, with regards to the /iː/ sound, the spelling *ea* (*cheap, clean*) accounts for 25% of instances and the spelling *ee* (*green, three*) accounts for 26%. The sound is also frequently seen spelled as *e* in the high-frequency set of two-letter words (*be, he, she, me*). Students need to learn and produce the correct spelling pattern in common words.
>
> There are a few words with odd spellings of the sound, *people* being the one that is most likely to be encountered at low levels. There are also some examples of common words with *ea* spelling but a different sound, e.g. *bread, breakfast*. These words need to be learned as exceptions.

7 🔊 6.16 Write: *eat cheese we drink* on the board. Say the words, emphasizing the vowel sounds. Elicit which word is different (*drink*). Erase it and write it below. Circle the vowels in each word. Say each word for students to repeat.

Focus on the words in the box. Students work individually and copy the words in the correct groups. Play the audio for students to listen and check. Students read the words. Monitor for correct vowel sounds.

> **Answers**
> 1 tea, me, coffee, he, green
> 2 fish, dinner

SPELLING CHALLENGE

8 🔊 6.17 Focus on the restaurant menu and the photographs. Say: *Listen and write.* Play the audio for students to listen and complete the words. Play the audio again if required. Go through answers as a class.

> **Answers**
> f<u>i</u>sh and ch<u>i</u>ps
> ch<u>ee</u>se
> gr<u>ee</u>n t<u>ea</u>

FOOD AND HEALTH | UNIT 6

LANGUAGE FOCUS

Learning objectives

- Read and write adjectives to describe how someone is – *fine, busy, tired, great, not well, hungry*
- Read and understand short dialogues about how people feel
- Understand descriptions with adjectives in context – *How are you? I'm fine.*
- Review pronoun referencing across sentences
- Gain awareness of consonant clusters in the end position of words

See p. 19 for suggestions on how to use these Learning objectives with your students.

Lead-in

Write the dialogue below in a random order on the board. Students work individually and reorder the lines to create a complete dialogue. Elicit the answers and write the dialogue in order on the board. Students work in pairs and say the dialogue aloud.

Hi
Hello
What's your name?
I'm Anna. What's your name?
I'm Sophie. How are you, Anna?
I'm cold!

Vocabulary Pre-teaching / Review

You will need printable flashcards with adjectives to describe how someone is (Flashcards 6.4), which can be printed at esource.cambridge.org.

Follow the procedure on p. 15.

Write these sentences on the board:

I want to go home!
I want to eat!
I want to go to the doctor!
I want to finish classes!

Students work in pairs, look at the sentences and think of adjectives to describe the person who said each sentence. Go through students' ideas on the board. (Possible answers: 1 busy, tired, 2 hungry, 3 not well, 4 busy, tired).

1 🔊 6.18 Focus on the words and the photographs. Play the audio for students to listen and read. Students work individually and trace the letters. Monitor students' handwriting.

Common student errors

Missing words: Arabic L1 students often forget about the pronoun *I*, especially at the beginning of a sentence. Students will start a sentence with a verb, e.g. *am not well*.

Teach students some phrases with *I'm* as if they're chunks of language (e.g. *I'm tired. I'm hungry.*) If students make a mistake and miss the pronoun *I*, write the wrong sentence on the board and elicit the correction.

2 🔊 6.19 Focus on the words in the box and the highlighted vowels in the numbered words. Say the sound each vowel makes (/æ/ /ɒ/ /e/ /ʌ/ /aɪ/). Students work individually, look at the words and match them by the sound the vowels make. Play the audio for students to listen and check. Drill the pronunciation. Students say the words aloud.

Answers

2 not 3 well 4 hungry 5 fine, tired

3 🔊 6.20 Ask a student: *How are you?* Accept any answer. The student repeats the question back to you. Answer: *I'm fine, thanks.* Repeat with another student, but this time answer: *I'm hungry* (with suitable gesture).

Focus on the words in the box. Read them aloud. Say: *Listen.* Play the audio for students to listen to the dialogues. Say: *Write.* Students work individually and write the missing words. Play the audio again for students to check. Demonstrate the dialogues with a student, with you taking one part. Then students read the dialogues in pairs. In stronger classes, students could try to say the dialogues from memory.

Answers

1 not bad, well 2 hungry, busy

NOTICE

Focus on the NOTICE box. Check students understand that *I'm not bad* means *I'm well* (even though we have the words *not* and *bad*, which may suggest a negative meaning). Ask a student to read the responses aloud.

4 🔊 6.21 Focus on the pictures and the sentences. Ask a student to read all the sentences aloud. Students work individually, read and match the sentences. Play the audio for students to listen and check their answers. Go through answers as a class.

UNLOCK BASIC LITERACY TEACHER'S BOOK   95

> **Answers**
> 1 d 2 a 3 b 4 c

5 👤👥 Write: *Jack is hungry. He wants to eat.* on the board. Circle: *Jack* and *He* and draw a line connecting them to make sure students understand that these sentences are about the same person. Elicit other pronouns using people in the class as examples (*they/she/he/I/we/you*).

Focus on the sentences in the book. Students work individually, read the sentences and circle the names and pronouns. Students compare their answers in pairs. Go through answers as a class.

> **Answers**
> 2 Julie and Shamsa, They
> 3 Lidia, She
> 4 Hussain, He

6 👤 Elicit all the subject pronouns and write them on the board (*I, you, he, she, it, we, they*). Then write them again with capital first letters and remind students when we use capitals (always with *I*, at the beginning of sentences).

Focus on the text in the book and ask: *What is it?* (an email). Point at the words in the box and say: *Read and write*. Students work individually, read the text and complete the sentences with the words in the box. Go through answers as a class.

> **Answers**
>
> From: eman@college.ac.ae
> Date: 17 June
>
> Hi Dalia,
> How are __you__ ?
> I am not bad. __I__ finish classes at three o'clock. Some students are busy. __They__ have a lot of classes. Our teacher is Mrs Locke. __She__ is great!
> Best wishes,
> Eman

> **Optional activity**
>
> Write a short text on the board about people in the class. Do not use pronouns in the text, e.g. *Alia is from Sharjah. Alia is a student at university. Alia has a friend, Hafsa. Alia and Hafsa study English. Alia and Hafsa drink tea.* Students replace as many of the names as possible with pronouns. In stronger classes, students write a similar text and swap with a partner. Their partner replaces some of the names with pronouns. (*Alia is from Sharjah. She is a student at university. She has a friend, Hafsa. Alia and Hafsa study English. They drink tea.*)

SOUND AND SPELLING
-nk -st -nch

7 🔊 6.22 👤 Focus on the sentence in the book. Play the audio for students to listen and read. Remind students how to form the letters *n, k, s, t, c* and *h* correctly. Students work individually and trace the letters. Play the audio for students to listen and repeat the sentence. Students focus on producing the correct sounds.

8 🔊 6.23 👤 Focus on the photographs and words. Use the photographs to check meaning. Play the audio for students to listen and read, then trace. Play the audio again. Students read words aloud, distinguishing clearly between the consonant clusters.

9 🔊 6.24 👤 Focus on the pictures and words and help students understand the meanings by looking at the pictures. Say: *Listen and write*. Play the audio for students to look at the pictures, listen and write the missing consonant clusters. Go through answers as a class.

> **Answers**
> 1 link, list 2 mink, mist 3 pink, pinch

10 🔊 6.25 👤👥 Focus on the words in Exercise 9. Say: *Listen and circle*. Students work individually, listen and circle the word they hear. Play the audio again if required. Students compare their answers in pairs. Go through answers as a class.

> **Answers**
> 1 link 2 mist 3 pinch

96 UNLOCK BASIC LITERACY TEACHER'S BOOK

FOOD AND HEALTH   UNIT 6

LISTENING FOCUS

Learning objectives

- Review spelling of vowels in vocabulary from the unit
- Predict content using photographs and background knowledge
- Listen for detail

See p. 19 for suggestions on how to use these Learning objectives with your students.

Lead-in

Revise vocabulary for daily activities. You will need printable flashcards with the daily routine vocabulary (Flashcards 5.2), which can be printed at esource.cambridge.org.

1 (6.26) Focus on the picture and survey about healthy eating. Play the audio for students to look and listen. Students work individually, read the words and complete the missing vowels. Go through answers as a class.

> **Answers**
> 2 m<u>ea</u>t 3 dr<u>i</u>nk 4 g<u>e</u>t 5 <u>u</u>niversity 6 l<u>a</u>te

2 (6.27) Focus on the picture. Elicit what is happening (a presentation at college). Focus on the completed example. Play the audio for students to listen and match the information to the correct phrase. Play the audio as many times as required. Go through answers as a class.

> **Answers**
> A lot of: 6
> Some: 4, 3
> Not a lot: 1, 5

3 (6.28) Tell students they are going to listen to a different presentation at college. Play the audio for students to listen and circle the correct options. Play as many times as required to allow students to check their answers. Go through answers as a class.

> **Answers**
> 2 Some 3 A lot of 4 A lot of 5 Not a lot of 6 Some

Optional activity

Write these phrases on small cards:
A lot of people
A lot of students
Some people
Some students
Not a lot of people
Not a lot of students

Make a number of copies of each card and put them in a box or a bag. Students take out a card in turn and say a true sentence using the phrase to begin their sentence. If their sentence is correct, give them a point. If it is not, elicit the correction from the class. This speaking game can be done in teams, pairs or individually. In stronger class, students could write their sentences and swap with a partner to check correct spelling.

⊙ KEY WORDS FOR LITERACY

Learning objectives

- Read, spell and pronounce key words for literacy – *of, some, lot, not*
- Complete sentences with the key words for literacy

See p. 19 for suggestions on how to use these Learning objectives in your lessons.

1 (6.29) Write: *of* and *Not a lot of students eat fish.* on the board. Move your pen slowly across the sentence, encouraging students to shout *Stop!* when you get to *of*. Circle it.

Focus on the words in bold and the sentences in the book. Say: *Read and circle*. Students work individually, read and circle the words. Play the audio for students to read and check. Ask a student to read the sentences aloud.

2 Write: *of* on the board. Write these words: *on of at of it*. Point at the first word you wrote (*of*) and elicit the pronunciation. Move your pen slowly across the sentences, encouraging students to shout *Stop!* when you get to *of*. Circle it twice.

Focus on the words in bold in the book. Say: *Read and circle*. Students work individually, read and circle the words.

3 Students work individually, cover and complete the words. If necessary, prompt them to use something to cover the words on the left as they complete each one. Monitor and check that they are working from left to right. Encourage correct stroke direction and correct height and position of the individual letters.

UNLOCK BASIC LITERACY TEACHER'S BOOK   97

4 🔊 6.30 👤 Focus on the gapped sentences. Students work individually, read the sentences and complete the gaps. Play the audio for students to listen and check their answers. Write the sentences on the board. Ask a student to read the sentences aloud.

> **Answers**
> 1 lot 2 Some 3 of 4 Not

READING AND WRITING

> **Learning objectives**
> - Predict information using pictures and background knowledge
> - Read to check predictions
> - Read for detail
> - Review *a lot of*, *not a lot of* and *some* in preparation for writing
> - Complete sentences about a friend – *My friend eats a lot of red meat. He eats some fish.*
>
> See p. 19 for suggestions on how to use these Learning objectives with your students.

> **Lead-in**
> You will need flashcards with foods and drinks (Flashcards 6.1), which can be printed at esource.cambridge.org. You need the cards with photographs.
>
> Ask students to write: *a lot of, not a lot of* and *some* in their notebooks, one under the other. Show students a card with a picture of food or drink and elicit the correct word. Write it on the board, asking students to spell it out for you. Students write it in their own notebook under the correct phrase (*a lot of, not a lot of* and *some*) so that it is true for them (referring to what they drink and eat). Repeat the procedure with a few more words. Students compare their answers in pairs.

1 🔊 6.31 👤 Write on the board a list of words for food and drinks from the text: *fruit, vegetables, bread, rice, red meat, sugar, cheese, fish*. Point to each word and say: *Is it healthy or unhealthy?* Elicit ideas from students.

Students look at the key to the chart in the book. Point at the three coloured boxes with white boxes next to them and ask students to predict what food and vegetables these colours may refer to. Elicit students' predictions as a class. Say: *Look and match*. Students use their predictions and match by writing the numbers 1–3 in the white boxes. Say: *Listen, read and check*. Play the audio. Students work individually, listen, read the text and check their answers. Go through answers as a class.

> **Answers**
> 1 35% fruit and vegetables
> 2 5% sugar
> 3 15% cheese

> ⊙ **Common student errors**
>
> **Confusable errors:** Arabic L1 students often confuse *a* and *an* or miss the articles/determiners from the sentences. For example, instead of *They eat a lot of bread*, Arabic L1 students are likely to say or write *They eat lot of bread*.
>
> To practise the use of articles, write the four sentences below on the board. Two are correct and two are incorrect. Students work in pairs and decide which sentences are incorrect. Students correct the mistakes (sentences 2 and 4) in their notebooks. Go through answers as a class.
> 1 Healthy people eat a lot of fruit and vegetables.
> 2 They do not eat a̲ lot of red meat.
> 3 They do not eat a lot of cheese.
> 4 They eat a̲ lot of fish.

2 👤👥 Focus on the text in Exercise 1 and the list of things healthy people eat. Students work individually, read the text again and complete the list by writing the missing words. Students compare their answers in pairs. Go through answers as a class.

> **Answers**
>
> Healthy people:
> . eat ___a lot of___ fruit and vegetables.
> . eat a lot of ___bread and rice___ .
> . do not eat ___a lot of___ red meat.
> . do not eat a lot of ___sugar___ .
> . eat ___some___ cheese.
> . eat some ___fish___ .

FOOD AND HEALTH | UNIT 6

3 🔊 6.32 👤 Focus on the text. Indicate the heading and elicit what the text is about (unhealthy eating). Indicate the photograph and elicit who the text is about (Rashid). Write: *He drinks ___ lot of juice with sugar.* on the board and elicit the missing word (a). Students work individually, read the text and then complete the exercise by writing the missing words. Play the audio for students to read and check. Write the answers on the board.

> **Answers**
>
> He <u>does not eat a lot of</u> fruit and vegetables. He <u>drinks a lot of</u> juice with sugar. He <u>does</u> not <u>drink a lot of</u> green tea. He <u>eats some</u> cheese.

> **Optional activity**
>
> Conduct a class survey. Write: *Do you eat a lot of _____?* Each student writes one question in their notebook with a food of their choice. Students ask their questions to the whole class and note how many people say *yes*. After all students have asked their questions, ask them to report back using the language they have learned, e.g. *A lot of people eat rice.* If students have access to computers, they could make a simple pie chart, either individually or compiling all of the information as a class. To finish, if appropriate, ask the class to decide if they are healthy or unhealthy in their eating habits.

4 🔊 6.33 👤 Write: *She does not eats cheese.* on the board. Write a cross (✗) next to the sentence and elicit where the mistake is (incorrect *s* in *eats*). Correct it on the board.

Focus on the sentences in the book. Students work individually, read and correct the sentences. Play the audio for students to listen and check. Go through answers as a class.

> **Answers**
>
> 2 He do<u>es</u> not eat cheese.
> 3 She does not <u>drink</u> milk.

5 👤👥 Tell students about the eating and drinking habits of a friend of yours. Use the same vocabulary and structures as in the model text, e.g. *Sally drinks a lot of coffee in Starbucks!*

Focus on the text in Exercise 3. Elicit some sentences, e.g. *Omar does not eat cheese.* Students work individually, read the gapped text, comparing it with the case study. Students put the name of the friend (if appropriate) and then complete the fact file with foods and drinks. Monitor and help with more vocabulary if necessary, to encourage genuine, communicative writing. Students compare their texts in pairs. Check students' writing.

> **Model answer**
>
> My friend eats a lot of fruit and vegetables. She eats some bread. She does not eat red meat. She drinks a lot of green tea. She drinks some coffee. She does not drink juice.

> **Objectives review**
>
> See Teaching tips on p. 19 for ideas about using the Objectives review with your students.
>
> **WORDLIST**
> See Teaching tips on p. 21 for ideas about using the Wordlist on p. 142 with your students.
>
> **REVIEW TEST**
> See esource.cambridge.org for the Review test and ideas about how and when to administer the Review test.

7 PLACES

LISTENING AND READING 1

Learning objectives

- Read and understand words for places – *a park, a hospital, a train station, a beach, a shopping centre, an office building, an airport*
- Read and understand descriptions of where people live – *I live near an office building and a hospital.*
- Use *a* and *an* correctly
- Write three sentences about where you live – *I live near a shopping centre and a hospital. There are some good restaurants. There is an interesting market.*
- Gain awareness of sound and spelling of letters *-rt, -rk*

See p. 19 for suggestions on how to use these Learning objectives in your lessons.

Lead-in

You will need one or more sets of the alphabet flashcards (Flashcards 0.2), enough to give five cards to each group of three students. Take out the Xs and the Zs.

Write the letter *c* on the board and say: *something in the university, c* /k/. Elicit at least one idea (e.g. *computer, chair, classroom*). In weaker classes, point at the objects that start with *c*. Divide students into groups of three and give each group five flashcards. Groups think of something in the university that begins with each letter they have and write it down. The group that finishes first is the winner. Monitor and help as necessary. When a group finishes, check their list.

Vocabulary Pre-teaching / Review

You will need printable flashcards for places (Flashcards 7.1), which can be printed at esource.cambridge.org.

Follow the procedure on p. 15.

Use one of the flashcard activities on pp. 16–17 to test students' recall of the set.

1 ◀)) 7.1 Focus on the photographs and the words. Play the audio for students to listen and read. Students work individually and trace the words. Monitor and encourage correct stroke direction.

Play the audio again for students to listen and repeat. Monitor and help with any pronunciation difficulties.

2 ◀)) 7.2 Draw on the board the two stress patterns in the book. Say: *shopping*, clearly stressing the first syllable and counting the syllables on your fingers. Elicit that *shopping* matches pattern 1. Write the word under the correct pattern.

Play the audio while students listen and match the stress patterns to the words in the book. Go through answers as a class.

> **Answers**
> 1 airport 2 hospital 1 building

Optional activity

Students add six more words, three for each of the stress patterns in Exercise 2.

Two countries (e.g. pattern 1: *Japan*, pattern 2: *Mexico*)

Two foods (e.g. pattern 1: *salad*, pattern 2: *vegetables*)

Two adjectives (e.g. pattern 1: *boring*, pattern 2: *beautiful*)

3 Focus on the four photographs above the first text. Ask: *What is her name? Where is she from? What is this?*

Focus on the text and the words in the box. Say: *I live in Dubai. I live near an …* Elicit the words *office building* and write them on the board. Students work individually to complete the word shapes. Monitor and encourage correct stroke direction. Repeat the procedure with the second text and set of photographs.

> **Answers**
> Nadia: office building, shopping centre, hospital
> Andy: park, train station, airport

---

100 UNLOCK BASIC LITERACY TEACHER'S BOOK

PLACES UNIT 7

NOTICE

Focus on the NOTICE box. Write the vowels *a, e, i, o, u* on the board. Ask: *What is the first letter in* park? (p) Point at the vowels on the board. Ask: *Is it here?* (no) Point at the article *a* before *park*. Say: *a park*. Repeat for *beach*. Then ask: *What is the first letter in* airport? (a) Point at the vowels on the board. Ask: *Is it here?* (yes) Point at the article *an* before *airport*. Say: *an airport*. Repeat the procedure with *office*. Check that students understand that *a/an* means *one*. Ask: *How many parks?* (1) *How many airports?* (1) Drill the pronunciation of the phrases in the NOTICE box.

4 ◀) 7.3 👤 Focus on the texts in Exercise 3. Students work individually, read the texts again and circle the articles. Play the audio for students to listen and read. Monitor and check that students have circled all the articles. Go through answers as a class.

Answers
Nadia: I live in Dubai. I live near <u>an</u> office building and <u>a</u> shopping centre. I do not live near <u>a</u> hospital.
Andy: I live in London. I live near <u>a</u> park and <u>a</u> train station. I do not live near <u>an</u> airport.

Literacy tip
There is an exception to the rule of using *an* before vowels. With words beginning with *u* where it is pronounced /j/ , e.g. *university*. In this case, we use *a* rather than *an*. If students notice, point it out, using the following procedure:

Write: *university* on the board and underline the first letter. Say: *a university*. Exaggerate the /j/ sound. Indicate, by cupping your ear, that it is the sound that is important. Write: *a university* and *a yacht* on the board and model the articles and pronunciation again.

5 ◀) 7.4 👤 Write on the board: *I live / and / near / a beach / a park*. Elicit the correct order for the words (*I live near a beach and a park. / I live near a park and a beach.*).

Focus on the jumbled sentences. Students work individually and write the sentences with the words in the correct order. Monitor and help as necessary. Play the audio for students to listen and check. Go through answers as a class.

Answers
2 I live near a hospital and an airport.
3 I do not live near a shopping centre.
4 I do not live near an office building.

SOUND AND SPELLING *-rt, -rk*

6 ◀) 7.5 👤 Write: *radio, country, park* and *teacher* on the board. Focus on the words. Ask: *Which letter is in all of the words?* (r) Underline *r*. Model the phoneme /r/ and then say the first word: *radio*. Ask: *Can you hear /r/?* (yes) Help students to understand the question by cupping your ear and using culturally appropriate gestures to indicate *yes or no*. Repeat the procedure with each of the words: *country* (yes), *park* (no), *teacher* (no). Say the words again. Students listen and repeat the words. Correct any errors with the phonemes /r/, /ɑː/ or /ə/ by modelling the sounds and then the words for students to repeat.

Focus on the sentence in the book. Play the audio for students to listen and read. Then point out the letters for tracing. Students work individually and trace the letters.

⊙ Common student errors
For Arabic L1 students, it is confusing to have a silent letter like the *r* in *park* which is not pronounced. This leads to spelling errors. It is important to focus on silent letters in spelling patterns and the way they affect sound. In the sentence *The park is near the airport*, *r* changes the vowel sound, rather than being individually pronounced.

7 ◀) 7.6 👤 Focus on the photographs. Play the audio and point to each photograph, encouraging students to do the same. Then point at each line and ask: *What letters are the same?* (1 rk, 2 rt). Students work individually and trace the letters. Play the audio again for students to listen and repeat.

8 ◀) 7.7 👤 Focus on the headings above the two columns of words. Point out the same letters in each word in each column. Focus on the new words (*fort, part, cork*), point to these and try to elicit their pronunciation. Play the audio. Encourage students to follow the text by pointing at each word as they hear it. Students work individually and trace the letters. Play the audio again for students to listen and repeat.

9 ◀) 7.8 👤 Write a familiar minimal pair on the board, e.g. *bear* and *pear*. Say: *pear*. Elicit which word you should circle. Play the audio for students to listen and circle the words they hear. Go through answers as a class. Play the audio for each item again to reinforce the answers.

Answers
1 fork 2 part 3 court

UNLOCK BASIC LITERACY TEACHER'S BOOK 101

SPELLING CHALLENGE

10 🔊 7.9 👤👥 Write: *starat* on the board. Ask: *What word is this?* (start) *What's wrong?* Elicit the correct spelling. Erase the word and write: *start*. Ask a student to read the first sentence. Continue by asking other students to read incomplete sentences 2–4. For each sentence, elicit what the missing word is. Students complete the sentences with the correctly spelled words. Check that students are writing in the correct position on the lines. Students work in pairs and compare answers. Play the audio for students to listen and check.

> **Answers**
> 2 park 3 airport 4 work

LISTENING AND READING 2

> **Learning objectives**
> - Read and understand words for places – *a restaurant, a factory, a hotel, a house, a shop*
> - Review short vowels, *ea*, *o_e* and *ou* sound/spelling patterns
> - Use *There is* and *There are* correctly – *There is a shop. There are some hotels.*
> - Read and write the correct plural endings *-ies* and *-es* – *factories, beaches*
> - Write three sentences about your city – *There is a university. There are some factories. There are a lot of hotels.*
>
> See p. 19 for suggestions on how to use these Learning objectives in your lessons.

> **Lead-in**
> You will need printable flashcards for places (Flashcards 7.2), which can be printed at esource.cambridge.org. You need the sides with photographs only.
>
> Hold up one card. Elicit the vocabulary item, e.g. *a hospital*. Make sure students give you the article as well as the noun. Hold up two cards together. Elicit the vocabulary items, e.g. *a hospital, an airport*. Say: *a hospital, an airport*. Say again for students to repeat. Divide the class into two teams. Hold up the cards, two at a time. Students knock on the desk if they can remember the names of the items. Award a point for each correct answer. Deduct a mark for incorrect articles or long pauses. The first team to get five points is the winner.

> **Vocabulary Pre-teaching / Review**
> You will need printable flashcards for places (Flashcards 7.2), which can be printed at esource.cambridge.org.
>
> Follow the procedure on p. 15.
>
> Write each word (with its article) on the board. Above them write: *I live in … I live near … I don't live near …* Say: *I live in a house. I live near a shop and a restaurant. I don't live near a factory.* Conduct a chain sentences activity. Demonstrate the activity. Say: *I live in a house.* Then move to a new spot, as if you are the next person to speak, and say: *I live in a house. I live near a shop.* Then move to a new spot again and say: *I live in a house. I live near a shop and a restaurant.* Move back to your original spot and start the chain again. Encourage a student to continue the chain, and then find a volunteer to continue after that. Keep the chain going as long as possible.

1 🔊 7.10 👤👥 Focus on the photographs and the words in the box. Students work individually to complete the word shapes. Monitor and encourage correct stroke direction. When most students are finished, tell them to swap books and check each other's writing for correctly filled boxes and the height of the individual letters. Play the audio for students to listen and check. While the audio is playing write the answers on the board. Students look at the words on the board and check their answers.

> **Answers**
> 2 a factory 3 a hotel 4 a shop 5 a house

> ⊙ **Common student errors**
> **Spelling**: The word *restaurant* is in the top 10 misspelled words by Arabic L1 students. This is the typical error: *resturant*.
> Write on the board:
> restaurant rest_ _ rant rest _ _ _ ant res _ _ _ _ ant
> Focus on the first word. Ask students to spell it out. Then erase the word. Ask students to spell the word out again and complete the first gap with *au* when they are successful. Then erase the word. Continue like this with all of the words until students can spell the word unassisted.

SOUND AND SPELLING Review

2 🔊 7.11 👤 Write: *bag hotel factory* on the board. Point at *a* in *bag* and ask students which of the other words match (*factory*). Point at *a* in *factory*. Then say each word.

102 UNLOCK BASIC LITERACY TEACHER'S BOOK

PLACES UNIT 7

Focus on the list of words and the highlighted letters in the book. Point out the completed example. Students match and write the numbers in the boxes. Play the audio for students to listen and check. Go through answers as a class.

> Answers
>
> 2 a restaurant, i centre
> 3 d shop, f hospital, h shopping j office
> 4 g beach
> 5 c hotel
> 6 e house

3 ◀) 7.12 Focus on the text and options. Play the audio for students to listen and read. Play the audio again for students to listen and circle the correct options. Go through answers as a class. Students work individually to trace the words. Monitor and encourage correct stroke direction.

> Answers
>
> Muscat is a city in Oman. There is a beach. There are some hotels near the beach. There are a lot of restaurants and shops. There is an airport near the city. There is a factory.

NOTICE

Focus on the NOTICE box. Ask a student to read the sentences aloud. Write: *There _ _ _ restaurant. There _ _ _ some restaurant_.* on the board. Elicit the answers: *is a, are, s*. Drill other examples of the sentences, starting with those in the box.

4 ◀) 7.13 Write: *Therearealotofhotels.* on the board. Move your pen along the sentence, encouraging students to shout *Stop!* at the word boundaries. Add vertical lines between the words.

Focus on the sentences in the book. Students work individually to complete the exercise. Monitor and help as necessary. Play the audio for students to listen and check. Go through answers as a class.

> Answers
>
> 1 There are a lot of hotels.
> 2 There is a factory and an airport.
> 3 There are some factories and shops.
> 4 There is an airport near the city.
> 5 There are a lot of beaches and two universities.

NOTICE

Focus on the NOTICE box. Write: *a beach* on the board. Underline the final two letters that affect the spelling of the plural of *beach*. Write on the board: *some beach_ _*.
Students look again at the NOTICE box and tell you the spelling of the plural form (beach<u>es</u>). Model the pronunciation: *beach beaches* and ask students to repeat. Repeat the procedure for *university*.

5 ◀) 7.14 Point out the letters to trace at the end of each word. Students work individually and trace the letters. Spell out *beach* on your fingers: *b-e-a-c-h*. Then ask a student to spell out *beaches*. Repeat with *university* and *factory*. Play the audio for students to listen and repeat the words.

Optional activity

Write the name of your city on the board. Underneath write: *How many?* and some places in the city (see examples below). Try to include two things that there is only one of in your city (perhaps an airport or a beach). Ask: *How many (shops) in (your city)?* Elicit: *a lot of*. Write this next to the word. Now ask students to work individually and write how many there are of each thing, e.g.

How many?

1 shops (a lot of), 2 shopping centres (one), 3 beaches (one), 4 airports (one), 5 factories (two), 6 restaurants (a lot of)

Allow students two minutes for this. Demonstrate the activity with a student. Say: *There are a lot of shops*. Elicit: *Yes. There are a lot of shops*. Continue until you find a *No* answer and the student says something different from you. Students work in pairs and compare their ideas. Share any differences of opinion.

6 Focus on the words in bold. Students look and circle the correct words. Go through answers as a class. Elicit how many examples there are of each word (live 3, a 3, an 2, there 2).

7 Focus on the word shapes. Students complete the words. Monitor and check that they are working from left to right. Encourage correct stroke direction and correct height and position of the individual letters.

8 ◀) 7.15 Read the first sentence aloud, pausing at the gap. Elicit the missing word (live). Students work individually and complete the exercise. Play the audio for students to check their answers. Go through answers as a class.

> Answers
>
> 1 live 2 an 3 There 4 a

WRITING CHALLENGE

9 Ask a student to read out the model text. Focus on the rubric and read it aloud. Students work individually to write two sentences. Monitor and help as necessary. Check that students are writing in the correct position on the lines. Students swap notebooks and check each other's writing for correct language, spelling and punctuation.

LISTENING AND READING 3

Learning objectives

- Read and write adjectives with nouns for places – *tall buildings, old streets, beautiful beaches, a busy square, an interesting market, a famous stadium*
- Read and understand descriptions of places – *There is a famous stadium.*
- Write sentences about places with the adjective in the correct position – *There are a lot of busy streets.*
- Write three sentences about a city – *There are some old streets and buildings. There is an interesting market. There is a busy square.*

See p. 19 for suggestions on how to use these Learning objectives in your lessons.

Lead-in

Write two categories on the board: *Places, Adjectives*. Call out a letter of the alphabet. Students think of a place and an adjective which begin with that letter. Only use letters with examples which have been included in the course so far (however, accept any valid words students give you), e.g.

B (*Brazil, Bahrain, beach, bank, building, big, beautiful, boring, busy*)
C (*country, Canada, classroom, cheap, cold, clean*)
H (*hospital, hot, hungry, healthy*)
I (*India, interesting*)
O (*office building, Oman, old*)
S (*Saudi Arabia, shopping centre, shop, station, small*)

Write the pairs of words on the board. When you have worked through all the letters, elicit sentences with the pairs of words on the board, e.g. *Brazil is big. Canada is not cheap. Our classroom is cold.* You can do this activity as a whole class or as a competitive game.

Vocabulary Pre-teaching / Review

You will need printable flashcards for places (Flashcards 7.3), which can be printed at esource.cambridge.org.

Follow the procedure on p. 15.

Write all the words from the cards in two categories on the board (*Places* and *Adjectives*) in a random order. (Places: *street, market, square, beaches, stadium, buildings*; Adjectives: *tall, famous, busy, beautiful, old*). Hold up a flashcard. Elicit the word. Ask: *Is there an (old street) in (your city's name)?* If *yes*, ask: *What's its name?* Elicit the name. Continue until all the cards have been used.

1 ◀)) 7.16 Focus on the photographs and the words for tracing. Students look, read and match the words. Play the audio for students to listen and check. Students work individually and trace the words. Monitor and encourage correct stroke direction.

> **Answers**
> a 3 b 6 d 5 e 2 f 4

2 ◀)) 7.17 Draw the three stress patterns on the board. Say: *tall,* clearly stressing the syllable and counting the syllable on your fingers. Elicit that *tall* matches pattern 1. Write the word under the correct pattern. Continue with *famous* (pattern 2) and *stadium* (pattern 3).

Play the audio for students to listen and look. Students then copy the words in each column. Drill the words row by row.

3 ◀)) 7.18 You will need a map of the world. Focus on the first sentence in each speech bubble. Read them aloud. (*I live in Dublin. I live in Singapore.*) Ask: *Where is Singapore? Where is Dublin?* Ask a student to show you on the map. Focus on the photographs and the speech bubbles. Point out the completed example. Students work individually, read and match the texts to the photographs. Play the audio for students to listen and check. Go through answers as a class.

> **Answers**
> 1 b, e, f 2 c, d

4 ◀)) 7.19 Focus on the text and the words in the box. Read: *I live in Manchester. It is an …* Elicit the words: *interesting city.* Students work individually and complete the word shapes. Monitor and encourage correct stroke direction. Play the audio for students to listen and check. Go through answers as a class.

PLACES   UNIT 7

> **Answers**
> It is an <u>interesting</u> city. There are a lot of <u>new buildings</u>. There are two <u>famous stadiums</u>. There is an <u>old library</u>.

> **NOTICE**
> Write these words on the board: *interesting / an / city*. Focus on the NOTICE box. Read the first sentence: *It is an interesting city*. Focus back on the board. Elicit the correct order for the words (an interesting city). Repeat for *new / library / a; buildings / a lot of / beautiful; squares / old / some*. Drill the sentences in the NOTICE box.

5 (◀) 7.20 👤 Write: *It is a city.* on the board. Then write: *new* to the left of the sentence. Move your pen across the sentence in the book from left to right encouraging students to shout *Stop!* when you get to the correct space for *new*. Write a small arrow under the line and the word above the line.

Students work individually and insert the words to the left. Monitor and check that students are copying the words correctly. Play the audio for students to listen and check their answers.

> **Answers**
> 2 There is a <u>busy</u> square.
> 3 There are some <u>tall</u> buildings.
> 4 There are a lot of <u>old</u> houses.
> 5 There is a <u>famous</u> stadium.

WRITING CHALLENGE

6 👤👥 Focus on the photograph of Barcelona. Ask: *Where is Barcelona?* (Spain) Ask a student to read out the model text. Focus on the rubric and read it aloud. Focus students on the notes with blank lines. Students work in pairs. They choose a city and write it in the city name gap. Read through the adjectives. Tell students to write a different place in the city on each line. Students work in pairs and complete the notes.

Monitor and help as necessary. Check that students are writing in the correct position on the line. Students swap notebooks and check each other's writing for correct language, spelling and punctuation.

> **Optional activity**
> Get students to change one or two facts about their cities in their texts. Demonstrate the activity using the model text about Barcelona.
> *There are a lot of new streets and buildings.*
> *There is a boring market.*
> *There is a busy library.*
> Students listen and tell you what is different. Students work in the same or different pairs. They read out the text with the new information and the other student listens and corrects the different information.

LANGUAGE FOCUS

> **Learning objectives**
> - Read and write prepositions for describing where places are – *on the left/right / on New Street, near the park, next to the houses, between the bank and the stadium*
> - Read and understand descriptions of where places are – *The bank is next to the shopping centre.*
> - Write sentences describing where places are – *The houses are near the park.*
> - Understand directions to places – *The library is on the right.*
> - Gain awareness of sound and spelling of letters *st, tr, str*
>
> See p. 19 for suggestions on how to use these Learning objectives in your lessons.

> **Lead-in**
> Write the names of two well-known streets in the centre of your city or town. Elicit more examples from students. Write these across the top of the board. Ask students about one street: *What buildings and places are on (street name)?* Write students' ideas in a list under the street name.
>
> Students work in pairs and discuss the rest of the streets. Monitor and help students with any vocabulary they do not know, e.g. *zoo, palace*. Take note of any interesting new vocabulary you hear.
>
> Write sentences on the board with the new vocabulary, e.g. *There is a palace on (street name)*. Encourage students to guess what each word means. Alternatively, students can use a dictionary. Students could also name the building, e.g. *Al Alam Palace is on Al Saidaya Street*.

UNL🔒CK BASIC LITERACY TEACHER'S BOOK

Vocabulary Pre-teaching / Review

You will need printable flashcards for directions (Flashcards 7.4), which can be printed at esource.cambridge.org.

Follow the procedure on p. 15.

Write on the board the phrases in two columns as below. Ask students to work in pairs and match the phrases. Elicit the answers and draw lines on the board to match the words (next to the house, on the left, between the restaurant and the train station). Ask a student to read them aloud.

next to	the left
on	the restaurant and the train station
between	the house

1 (🔊 7.21) Focus on the pictures and the phrases. Play the audio for students to listen and read. Write: *on the right* on the board and then demonstrate tracing the word *on* pointing out the correct place to start on the letter *o*. Students work individually. Monitor and encourage correct stroke direction.

Point to the words *on the right* in the book. Say: *on the right* and point to each word as you say it. Play the audio again. Students listen and repeat the words.

2 (🔊 7.22) Write the example sentence on the board with no spaces: *ThehousesareonAshStreet.* Move your pen along the sentence, encouraging students to shout *Stop!* where the first word ends. Add a vertical line at that point. Continue moving your pen until all the correct word boundaries have been marked. Students work individually to complete the exercise. Monitor and help as necessary. Play the audio for students to listen and check.

Focus on the map and on Ash Street and the houses. Point out the completed example. Students work in pairs and match the sentences to the boxes on the map. Go through answers as a class.

Answers

1 The houses are on Ash Street.
2 The train station is near the park.
3 The library is on the right.
4 The stadium is on the left.
5 The university is next to the bank.
6 The shop is between the hotel and the restaurant.

Optional activity

Students draw a simple map using the vocabulary of places in cities. Use the map in Exercise 2 as an example. Demonstrate the next part of the activity by describing part of the map in Exercise 2 to students. Encourage them to draw what they hear. Students work in pairs, Student A and Student B. Student As keep their map hidden and describe it using the target language. Student Bs listen and draw the map Student As describe. When they finish, Student As show their map to Student Bs to check. Then students swap roles.

NOTICE

Write: *on / Baker Street / is* on the board. Focus on the NOTICE box. Read the first sentence aloud. Focus back on the board. Elicit the correct order for the words (is on Baker Street). Repeat for *the right / is / on*; *the bank / the park / between / and / is*; *the library / next to / are*. Explain by pointing at the words on the board to show that the preposition (between, on, next to) always comes after *be* and before the noun. Students underline *be* in each sentence in the NOTICE box. Drill the sentences in the NOTICE box.

3 (🔊 7.23) Write: *The hotel is the restaurant and the shops.* on the board. Then write: *between* to the left of the sentence, as in the book, and look confused. Move your pen across the sentence, encouraging students to shout *Stop!* when you get to the correct space between words. Draw a small arrow under the line and the word above the line. (The hotel is <u>between</u> the restaurant and the shops.)

PLACES   UNIT 7

Focus on the prepositions and the sentences in the book. Students work individually and correct the sentences. Monitor and check that students are copying the words correctly. Play the audio for students to listen and check their answers.

> **Answers**
>
> 2 The hotel is <u>between</u> the restaurant and the shops.
> 3 The park is <u>next to</u> the university.
> 4 The airport is <u>near</u> the stadium.
> 5 The shops are <u>on</u> the right.

4 (7.24) Focus on the completed example in the book. Ask a student to read the sentence. Students work individually and write the sentences with the words in the correct order. Monitor and help as necessary. Play the audio for students to listen and check. Go through answers as a class.

> **Answers**
>
> 2 The market is near the shops.
> 3 The office buildings are on the left.
> 4 The university is between the bank and the park.
> 5 The shopping centre is on Renton Street.

SOUND AND SPELLING *st, tr, str*

5 (7.25) Say the three sounds /st/, /tr/ and /str/ and ask students to repeat. Write: *st* on the board and say the sound /st/ again. Elicit the spellings of the other sounds and write them on the board. Write: *train*, *stop* and *straight* on the board and ask students to match them to the sounds (/st/: stop; /tr/: train; /str/: straight). Focus on the photographs and the words. Play the audio for students to listen and read. Students work individually and trace the letters. Play the audio again for students to listen and repeat.

6 (7.26) Focus on the sentence in the book. Play the audio for students to listen and read. Students work individually and trace the letters. Play the audio again for students to listen and repeat.

7 (7.27) Focus on the photographs. Play the audio and point to each photograph, encouraging students to do the same. Then point at each line and ask: *What letters are the same?* (1 st, 2 tr, 3 str). Students work individually and trace the letters. Play the audio again for students to listen and repeat.

SPELLING CHALLENGE

8 (7.28) Write: *tirain* on the board. Ask: *What word is this?* (train) *What's wrong?* Elicit the correct spelling. Erase the word and write: *train*. Students write the correctly spelled words on the lines. Students work in pairs and compare answers. Play the audio for students to listen and check. Go through answers as a class.

> **Answers**
>
> 2 station 3 street 4 student

> **◉ Common student errors**
>
> Consonant clusters such as those in the words in this lesson can be problematic for Arabic L1 students as they are much more restricted in Arabic. As a result, students often make mistakes with intrusive vowels (e.g. *tirain* for *train*).
>
> Raise students' awareness of consonant clusters in new vocabulary sets by circling them and sounding and spelling them out. You could also contrast the sounds of clusters with the sounds of the same letters around vowels. Aural discrimination between *tr* and *tir*, *st* and *sit*, *str* and *sitar*, can help build student awareness of the sound/spelling relationships.

LISTENING FOCUS

> **Learning objectives**
>
> - Use pictures to predict information
> - Listen for general understanding
> - Listen for detail
> - Review sound and spelling patterns with two letters for one or two sounds
>
> See p. 19 for suggestions on how to use these Learning objectives in your lessons.

> **Lead-in**
>
> Write the names of a local shopping centre and market across the top of the board. Elicit adjectives to describe them. If necessary, help by asking questions: *Is it old? Is it busy?* etc. Write students' ideas in a list under the place names.

1 (7.29) Focus on the place names. Read them aloud (Tsukiji /tsʊkiːdʒiː/ fish market; Dubai Mall). Play the audio. Tell students to listen and number the place names 1 and 2.

> **Answers**
>
> Tsukiji fish market 2
> Dubai Mall 1

2 🔊 7.30 👥 Focus on the photographs. Ask: *What is this place?* about each picture and elicit: *a market* and *a shopping centre*. Ask: *What is this market like?* Elicit some adjectives. Repeat for the shopping centre. Focus on the words in the box. Ask them to guess which three words go with each place and write them on the lines under the photographs. Students work in pairs and complete the activity. Play the audio for students to listen and check. Go through answers as a class.

> **Answers**
> 1 shopping centre, big, new
> 2 market, busy, famous

3 🔊 7.29 👤 Focus on the notes and the options in the book. Play the audio for students to listen and circle the correct answers. Go through answers as a class.

> **Answers**
>
> **DUBAI MALL**
> - big and new
> - a lot of shops with cameras, computers, **(bags)**/ **books**, and mobile phones
> - restaurants from different **cities** /**(countries)** some cheap
> - tall **(building)**/ **bank**
>
> **TSUJIKI FISH MARKET**
> - in Tokyo
> - starts at **4:00** /**(5:00)** o'clock
> - a lot of **big** /**(small)** shops
> - some restaurants
> - eat fish
> - drink **coffee** /**(green tea)**

> **Optional activity**
>
> You will need a short and simple text such as the one below to share with your students.
>
> *This is Covent Garden. It's a famous market in London. It starts at 10 o'clock in the morning. There are a lot of small and big shops. There are some restaurants. The market is busy. It's a great place.*
>
> Tell students you are going to talk about a place. Write: *What, Where* and *What … like?* on the board. Elicit questions from students: *What is it? Where is it? What is it like?* Don't answer the questions. Write them on the board.
>
> Ask students to make notes to answer the questions. Tell them not to worry about spelling and grammar. Read the text aloud twice. Then ask students to share their notes with you. Reconstruct your text on the board as students share different parts of their notes with you.

SOUND AND SPELLING Review

4 🔊 7.31 👤 Write: *sh phone shop* on the board. Point at *sh* and ask students which word matches (*shop*). Point at the *sh* in *shop* and say: *sh /ʃ/ shop*.

Review sound-spelling patterns *sh, ch, ph, th, gr* and *dr*. Focus on the pairs of letters numbered 1–6. Ask individual students to spell out the highlighted letters and say each sound. Demonstrate with *sh*: *sh /ʃ/*. Make sure they understand that *gr* and *dr* make two sounds (/gr/ /dr/), but the rest are just one sound (/ʃ/ /tʃ/ /f/ /ð/).

Focus on the words in the box. Students match and write the words on the lines. Play the audio for students to listen and check. Go through answers as a class. Play the audio again for students to listen and repeat.

> **Answers**
> 1 /ʃ/ fish
> 2 /tʃ/ cheap
> 3 /f/ phone
> 4 /ð/ there with
> 5 /gr/ green great
> 6 /dr/ drink

👁 KEY WORDS FOR LITERACY

> **Learning objectives**
> - Read, spell and pronounce key words for literacy – *new, old, between, to*
> - Complete sentences with the key words for literacy
>
> See p. 19 for suggestions on how to use these Learning objectives in your lessons.

1 🔊 7.32 👤 Write: *old* on the board. Write this sentence: *Tsukiji fish market is old.* Move your pen slowly across the sentence, encouraging students to shout *Stop!* when you get to *old*. Circle it.

Focus on the words in bold in the book. Students work individually and read and circle the words. Play the audio for students to listen and check.

2 👤 Focus on the words in bold in the book. Students work individually and read and circle. Go through answers as a class. Ask how many examples there are of each word and then confirm their position by reading out the line of words.

108 UNLOCK BASIC LITERACY TEACHER'S BOOK

PLACES   UNIT 7

3 👤 Students look at the words and then cover and complete them. If necessary, prompt them to use something to cover the words on the left as they complete each one. Monitor and check that they are working from left to right. Encourage correct stroke direction and correct height and position of the individual letters.

4 (🔊 7.33) 👤 Read the first sentence aloud: *The university is next ____ the stadium.* Point at the first sentence in the book and elicit the missing word (to). Play the audio for students to listen and write. Students work individually and complete the sentences. Play the audio again for students to check their answers. Go through answers on the board.

| Answers
| 1 to 2 new 3 between 4 old

READING AND WRITING

Learning objectives
- Skim to identify section headings and topics
- Read for detail
- Correct sentences describing a place
- Write about a famous place in the students' country

See p. 19 for suggestions on how to use these Learning objectives in your lessons.

Lead-in
Write the word *university* in a circle at the centre of the board. Draw lines coming out from the circle in a spidergram shape. Elicit words related to the topic of *university*, (e.g. *students, teachers, class*) Write the words at the top of the lines. Elicit more words and add them to the spidergram. If students are stuck for ideas, give clues, e.g. pick up a book and say: *the place with a lot of books* (library).

Tell students they are going to read about a new university.

1 (🔊 7.34) 👤 Focus students on the three words in the box. Point out gaps 1–3 in the text. Students look at the three texts, but do not read them. Students look for the words in the box and match the headings as quickly as possible. Play the audio for students to listen and check their answers.

| Answers
| 1 university 2 students 3 teachers

Literacy tip
If you speak the students' L1, explain that it is always helpful to try to get an idea of what a text is about by skimming, before reading for detail. Having a general idea makes it much easier to understand the text when reading carefully.

As a teacher, whenever you use a text with headings, you can remove them to create a matching activity. It is also worth pointing out that headings (like notes and bullet points) usually don't have full stops.

2 👤 Focus on the sentences and the completed example. Students work individually and tick or cross each sentence. Encourage students to read each sentence one at a time and then find the information, rather than reading the whole text first.

Go through answers as a class, asking students to show you the sentences in which they found the information for each answer. Ask them to write corrections for the wrong sentences.

| Answers
| 2 ✓
| 3 ✗ (There are big buildings.)
| 4 ✓
| 5 ✓
| 6 ✗ (The students study IT, Business, Maths and English.)
| 7 ✗ (There are cheap shops.)
| 8 ✗ (There are 150 teachers.)
| 9 ✓
| 10 ✗ (The houses are near the classrooms.)

3 (🔊 7.35) 👤 Write: *The university is the park next to.* on the board. Read the sentence aloud and look confused. Move your pen along the sentence, encouraging students to shout *Stop!* where the mistake is. Circle the words: *the park next to*. Elicit the correction from students (next to the park).

Point out the completed example in the book. Students work individually to find and correct the mistakes. Monitor and, if necessary, explain that there are different types of errors in the sentences (spelling, word order, grammar). Check that students are writing in the correct position on the lines. Play the audio for students to check their answers. Elicit complete correct answers and write them on the board.

UNLOCK BASIC LITERACY TEACHER'S BOOK   109

> **Answers**
>
> 2 There <u>are</u> some good restaurants.
> 3 There are a lot of beautiful <u>beaches</u>.
> 4 There are some <u>old buildings</u>.
> 5 The train <u>station</u> is near the bank.
> 6 There is <u>an</u> interesting market.

4 Write: *famous* on the board and say it. Say the name of a famous person students will know.

Focus on the photograph of the Burj Al Arab. Ask: *What is this building?* (a hotel) *Where is it?* (in Dubai) *Is it near the beach?* (yes). Ask a student to read out the model text. Focus on the rubric and read it aloud. Elicit ideas for famous places in the students' country and write them on the board. Ask: *What is each place?* Write the type of place, e.g. *hotel, park, hospital, market*.

Ask students to choose a famous place from the list on the board and complete the first sentence in the notebook.

Students work individually and write three more sentences. Monitor and help as necessary. Check that students are writing in the correct position on the lines. Students swap notebooks and check each other's writing for correct language, spelling and punctuation.

> **Model answer**
>
> Kings Cross is a famous train station in London. There is a new building. There are a lot of shops. There are some expensive restaurants.

> **Literacy tip**
>
> As students are now writing more freely, it is less mechanical and the content is more personalized. In order to help them see writing as communicative, encourage students to read each other's work and find positive things to say about it (you could teach expressions like *This is interesting* and *This is new*, or they could do it in their own language, rather than only focusing on errors). However, at these early literacy stages, accuracy is very important, so make sure you give clear feedback on errors made on things they have studied, e.g. punctuation and capitalization.

> **Optional activity**
>
> To check students' spelling skills, give a short test of some of the words taught in this unit. Read out these words:
>
> 1 *park*, 2 *hospital*, 3 *airport*, 4 *restaurant*, 5 *house*, 6 *market*, 7 *square*, 8 *building*
>
> Students listen and write the words in their notebooks. Students swap notebooks. Go through answers as a class. Students check each other's writing for correct spelling and use of capital letters.

> **Objectives review**
>
> See Teaching tips on p. 19 for ideas about using the Objectives review with your students.
>
> **WORDLIST**
> See Teaching tips on p. 21 for ideas about using the Wordlist on p. 143 with your students.
>
> **REVIEW TEST**
> See esource.cambridge.org for the Review test and ideas about how and when to administer the Review test.

8 SPENDING

LISTENING AND READING 1

Learning objectives

- Read and understand words for things that people own – *a tablet, a newspaper, a bank card, a smartphone, a T-shirt, a video game, a watch, a laptop*
- Read and understand descriptions of what people own – *He doesn't have a lot of T-shirts.*
- Write three sentences to describe what your friend owns – *Suhail has two laptops. He has a lot of T-shirts. He doesn't have a watch.*
- Complete descriptions of what people own – *I have two watches.*
- Learn about stress patters for words describing things that people own

See p. 19 for suggestions on how to use these Learning objectives in your lessons.

Lead-in

Write the scrambled letters below on the board for students to reorder the letters to make words. Make sure students understand that all words are common objects. Students work in pairs, reorder the letters and write the words. Elicit answers as a class and write them on the board.

mpuertco (computer)

mareca (camera)

agb (bag)

dictnaiory (dictionary)

Vocabulary Pre-teaching / Review

You will need printable flashcards with words for things that people own (Flashcards 8.1), which can be printed at esource.cambridge.org.

Follow the procedure on p. 15.

Say the words below aloud to all students. Students listen carefully and quickly find the object in their bags (if they have them) or somewhere in the classroom and show them to you. Continue until at least a few objects are found and presented to the class.

tablet, watch, mobile phone, bank card, smartphone

1 ◀) 8.1 Focus on the photographs and the words. Play the audio for students to listen and read the words. Elicit why the article *a* is in each word (all nouns start with consonants, all are singular). Students work individually and trace the words. Monitor and check correct stroke direction. Write the words on the board. Play the audio again for students to listen and repeat. Insist on correct vowel sounds. Erase the vowels and elicit them back onto the board to check spelling.

2 ◀) 8.2 Focus on the words in the box. Students cover all the words in Exercise 1. Students work individually and read and complete the words. Play the audio for students to listen and check. Go through answers as a class.

Answers

2 watch 3 tablet 4 laptop 5 video game 6 T-shirt
7 smartphone 8 newspaper

3 ◀) 8.3 Draw a circle representing the first stress pattern in the book on the board. Write: *watch, game, laptop, card* on the board. Tap on the circle while you say the words aloud, tapping twice when it gets to *laptop*. Write a tick next to all of the words apart from the word *laptop*, which requires a cross.

Say: *Listen and write*. Play the audio for students to listen and write ticks and crosses. Play the audio again for students to check their answers. Write the words on the board under the correct stress patterns.

Answers

1 watch ✓ game ✓ laptop ✗ card ✓
2 T-shirt ✓ newspaper ✗ tablet ✓ laptop ✓
3 video ✓ smartphone ✗ newspaper ✓

NOTICE

Focus on the NOTICE box. Allow students a minute to read through the information. Point out the use of the plural in the question and the quantity and corresponding singular or plural noun in the answer. Ask two students to read the texts aloud. One student reads the questions and one reads the answers.

Optional activity

Mingle: Follow the procedure on p. 18.

How many _____ do you have?

I have (number) _____. I don't have _____.

Alternative to mingling: Students work in small groups and ask and answer questions about objects they own.

4 🔊 8.4 👤👥 Focus on the pictures, the words in the boxes and the mini-dialogues. Students work individually and complete the dialogues. Students compare their answers in pairs. Play the audio for students to listen and check. Go through answers as a class.

> **Answers**
> 1 How many T-shirts do you <u>have</u>?
>   I have <u>a lot of</u> T-shirts.
> 2 How many <u>watches</u> do <u>you</u> have?
>   I have one <u>watch</u>.
> 3 How <u>many</u> video games <u>do</u> you have?
>   I do not have a lot of video <u>games</u>.

5 🔊 8.5 👤👥 Follow the procedure from Exercise 4, above. This time students complete longer questions and sentences. Go through answers as a class.

> **Answers**
> 2 I <u>have one tablet</u>.
> 3 How many laptops <u>do you have</u>?
> 4 <u>How many T-shirts do you have</u>?

NOTICE

Focus on the NOTICE box. Allow students a minute to read through the information. Review the features of the questions (in the previous NOTICE box) and then focus on the verb forms and how the third person differs. Write: *How many English books ___ you have?* on the board. Point at *you* and elicit from students which auxiliary verb should be used (do). Write it on the board. Write the number *0* next to the question. Say the sentence aloud pointing at the number *0* and elicit the full answer from students (I do not have an English book.). Write: *How many English books ___ he have?* on the board. Point at *he* and elicit from students which auxiliary verb should be used with he (does). Write it on the board. Write the number *0* next to the question. Elicit the full answer (He does not have an English book.). Ask students to read the questions and answers in the NOTICE box aloud.

6 🔊 8.6 👤 Write: *I ___ (have/has) a lot of bank cards.* Point at *I* and elicit the correct answer (have). Write it on the board.

Play the audio for students to listen and circle the correct words. Go through answers on the board. Students work individually and write the words, copying all the letters carefully. Monitor and help with letter strokes as necessary. Make sure students understand that in positive sentences they should use *have* with *do* or *does*, and *has* with *he/she*.

> **Answers**
> 2 do 3 have 4 does 5 have 6 have

7 🔊 8.7 👤 Write: *She not does have a tablet* on the board. Write a cross twice next to the sentence. Make sure students understand that there are two mistakes (word order and a full stop missing). Move your pen along the sentence from left to right, encouraging students to shout *Stop!* when you get to a mistake. Elicit the corrections and write the correct sentence on the board (She <u>does not</u> have a tablet<u>.</u>).

Focus on the sentences in the book. Students work individually, read and correct the sentences. Then they write a missing full stop or a question mark. Play the audio for students to listen and check. Go through answers as a class.

> **Answers**
> 1 I do <u>not have</u> a watch.
> 2 How many <u>T-shirts do you</u> have<u>?</u>
> 3 How many bank cards do <u>you have?</u>
> 4 She does <u>not have</u> a tablet<u>.</u>

WRITING CHALLENGE

8 👤👥 Focus on the photographs. Ask a student to read out the model text. Focus on the rubric and read it aloud. Students work individually and write three sentences using the correct verb form for the third person singular. Monitor and help as necessary. Check that students are writing in the correct position on the lines. Students swap notebooks and check each other's writing for correct language, spelling and punctuation.

SPENDING   UNIT 8

LISTENING AND READING 2

Learning objectives

- Read and understand vocabulary describing periods of time – *a week, a month, a day, a year*
- Read and understand frequency expressions – *once/twice a day/week/month/year*
- Read and understand sentences with frequency expressions – *She buys a smartphone once a year.*
- Write sentences using frequency expressions – *He buys a newspaper once a day.*
- Write three sentences about what your friend spends money on – *Omar buys a newspaper once a day. He buys coffee twice a day. He buys a smartphone once a year.*

See p. 19 for suggestions on how to use these Learning objectives in your lessons.

Lead-in

Revise the days of the week and months with students. Write all the months out of order in one column and all the days of the week out of order in another column. Students work in pairs and put both columns in order. Go through answers as a class.

Vocabulary Pre-teaching / Review

You will need printable flashcards with the frequency expressions (Flashcards 8.3), which can be printed at esource.cambridge.org.

Follow the procedure on p. 15.

Draw the timetable below on the board. Write: *once a day, once a week, twice a week* on the board. Ask three questions about different subjects in the timetable and ask students to answer using the words on the board. Ask: *How often do you have English class?* (once a day) *How often do you have Business class?* (twice a week) *How often do you have Japanese class?* (once a week)

Sunday	Monday	Tuesday	Wednesday	Thursday
10:00–12:00 English	10:00–12:00 English	10:00–12:00 English	10:00–12:00 English	10:00–12:00 English
2:00–4:00 Business		2:00–4:00 Business		2:00–4:00 Japanese

1 8.8 You can use Flashcards 8.2 to pre-teach this vocabulary set. Focus on the words. Students work individually, read the words and match. Play the audio for students to listen. Go through answers as a class.

Answers
3 Monday 4 SMTWTFS 2 September 1 2017

2 8.9 Focus on the calendars and the words. Check students understand that the phrases are in the order of frequency (from *twice a day* to *once a year*). Students work individually and trace the words. Monitor students' handwriting. Play the audio for students to listen to the phrases.

NOTICE
Focus on the NOTICE box. Ask a student to read the expressions aloud. Point out the use of the article *a* with *once, twice*.

3 8.10 Focus on the calendars and the word shapes. Students work individually, look at the calendars and complete the word shapes with frequency expressions. Monitor students' handwriting. Play the audio for students to listen and check. Go through answers as a class.

Answers
2 a year 3 twice a 4 once a

4 8.11 Focus on the expressions in the box and the three stress patterns. Check students understand that all the expressions in the box have the same stress pattern. Play the audio for students to listen and repeat. Students work individually and circle the correct stress pattern. Elicit the answer as a class.

Answer
They all match pattern 2.

Literacy tip
It is vital that you follow up work such as this by making sure students use the correct stress pattern when they use the expressions in any other activity. As well as enabling them to form correct habits, it will also help them develop an ear for stress, which will be beneficial for both speaking and listening. If you only focus on stress in the actual exercise, they may see it as an empty exercise rather than an important part of how the English language works.

UNLOCK BASIC LITERACY TEACHER'S BOOK   113

> **Optional activity**
>
> **Mingle:** Follow the procedure on p. 18.
>
> *How often do you* (buy coffee / buy a newspaper)?
>
> **Alternative to mingling:** Students work in small groups and ask and answer questions.

5 Focus on the calendars and the sentences. Point at the first calendar and ask a student to read the sentence aloud. Elicit if it represents what is on the calendar (no). Students put a cross next to the first sentence. Elicit the correct sentence: *He buys lunch once a week*. Students work individually and follow the procedure for the other sentences. Students compare their answers in pairs. Go through answers as a class.

> **Answers**
>
> 1 ✗ – once a week 2 ✓ 3 wrong – twice a year
> 4 wrong – every day

> **NOTICE**
>
> Focus on the NOTICE box. Ask a student to read the sentences aloud. Point out the use of the article *a* with *once* and *twice* and no article for the expression *every day*. Students look at Exercise 5 and circle the expressions in the sentences.

6 (◄)) 8.12 Focus on the gapped sentences. Ask a student to read the sentences aloud. Play the audio for students to listen and write the correct expressions. Students compare their answers in pairs. Play the audio again for students to listen and check. Go through answers as a class.

> **Answers**
>
> 1 once a day
> 2 once a week
> 3 twice a week
> 4 once a year

7 (◄)) 8.13 Write the example sentence on the board with no spaces: *TheybuyanewTVonceayear*. Move your pen along the sentence, encouraging students to shout *Stop!* at the word boundaries. Add vertical lines between the words.

Focus on the sentences in the book. Students work individually to complete the exercise. Monitor and help as necessary. Play the audio for students to listen and check. Go through answers as a class.

> **Answers**
>
> 1 They buy a new TV once a year.
> 2 I buy a coffee once a day.
> 3 He meets friends twice a month.
> 4 She eats fish twice a week.

> **Common student errors**
>
> **Spelling:** Arabic L1 students often miss the last letter *e* on words such as *once*, *twice*, *people* and *please*. To practise the spelling of words that finish with *e*, do the exercise below.
>
> Write these words on the board:
>
> once onc onece once onec
>
> twic twice twaic twiec twice
>
> Students analyze each word and choose the words with correct spelling (*once* x2, *twice* x2). Students spell the words aloud for you to write them on the board.

8 (◄)) 8.14 Write: *once* on the board. Write this sentence: *He buys a mobile phone once a year*. Point at the first word you wrote (once) and elicit the pronunciation. Move your pen slowly across the sentence, encouraging students to shout *Stop!* when you get to the word. Circle: *once* in the sentence.

Focus on the words in bold and the sentences in the book. Say: *Read and circle*. Students work individually, read and circle the words. Play the audio for students to read and listen to the sentences. Ask a student to read the sentences aloud.

9 Students work individually, cover and complete the words. If necessary, prompt them to use something to cover the words on the left as they complete each one. Monitor and check that they are working from left to right. Encourage correct stroke direction and correct height and position of the individual letters.

10 (◄)) 8.15 Focus on the gapped sentences and the words in the box. Students work individually, read the sentences and complete the gaps. Play the audio for students to listen and check their answers. Go through answers as a class. Ask a student to read the sentences aloud.

> **Answers**
>
> 2 month 3 once

11 🔊 8.16 👤 Write: *He / a tablet / once a year. / buys* on the board. Point at the chunks of language to make sure students understand that they need to reorder the words to make a sentence. Elicit the correct answer and write it on the board (*He buys a tablet once a year.*).

Students work individually and reorder the words to create sentences. Play the audio for students to listen and check. Go through answers as a class.

> **Answers**
> 1 I buy a smartphone once a year.
> 2 He buys a video game twice a month.
> 3 She buys a T-shirt once a month.

LISTENING AND READING 3

Learning objectives

- Read and understand verb-noun phrases for shopping – *go shopping, spend money, buy clothes, buy shoes, pay with cash, pay by card*
- Read and understand places to buy things – *internet, market, shopping centre*
- Identify prepositions *on* and *at* when referring to shopping places – *on the internet, at the shopping centre, at the market*
- Write three sentences about shopping – *I buy clothes once a week. I buy clothes at the shopping centre. I buy shoes on the internet.*
- Recognize sound and spelling patterns – *ay, a_e, ai*

See p. 19 for suggestions on how to use these Learning objectives in your lessons.

Lead-in

Write: *once/twice a day/week/month/year* on the board. Write the following expressions underneath:

buy coffee
buy lunch
buy a mobile phone
buy a newspaper

Ask: *How often do you buy coffee?* Elicit different answers from students. Encourage students to use the frequency expressions on the board. Write: *How often do you buy coffee?* on the board next to the phrase *buy coffee*. Students work in pairs, use the phrases on the board to ask their partners about their spending habits. Monitor and help as necessary. Write a few students' ideas on the board, next to the phrases.

Vocabulary Pre-teaching / Review

You will need printable flashcards with verb-noun phrases for shopping (Flashcards 8.4), which can be printed at esource.cambridge.org.

Follow the procedure on p. 15.

Write two columns as below on the board, one with verbs and one with nouns:

go	shoes
buy	with cash
pay	money
spend	shopping

Point at the verbs and the nouns. Demonstrate matching the verbs to the nouns to create verb-noun phrases for shopping by pointing at *go* and *shopping*. Elicit: *go shopping*. Students work in pairs. They do not write anything at this stage, just say the answers aloud. Elicit the correct answers and draw lines connecting the words (*go shopping, buy shoes, pay by cash, spend money*).

1 🔊 8.17 👤 Focus on the photographs and the words in the box. Play the audio for students to listen and look. Students work individually, read and complete the words. Use the photographs to check understanding and encourage the use of a dictionary if required. Students write the whole verb-noun phrase. Monitor and check students' handwriting.

> **Answers**
> 2 money 3 clothes 4 shoes 5 cash 6 card

2 🔊 8.18 👤 Focus on the photographs and the phrases. Students work individually, look and match the phrases to the photographs. Encourage the use of a dictionary to check meaning if required. Play the audio for students to listen and check their answers.

> **Answers**
> a 2 b 3 c 1

3 🔊 8.19 👤 Students look at the photographs and the mini-dialogues. Say: *Listen and read*. Play the audio for students to read and listen to the dialogues. If necessary, remind students how to form some or all of the letters on the board. Students work individually and trace the words. Circle: *How often / Where / Do* and the question marks. Connect each one with *once a week / on the internet / Yes*. Play the audio again for students to listen and repeat.

UNL*O*CK BASIC LITERACY TEACHER'S BOOK **115**

NOTICE

Focus on the NOTICE box. Ask two students to read the questions and answers aloud as a dialogue. Point out the words in red. Write all three questions on the board. Point out the auxiliary verb *do* in each question. Point out question words in the first two questions. Elicit whether there is a question word in the third (no). Make sure students understand that if there is no question word and the question starts with an auxiliary verb, the answer is always *yes* or *no*. Write the answers on the board (once a day, at the market, Yes, I do. / No, I don't.).

◉ Common student errors

Word order errors: In questions, Arabic L1 students often struggle with word order. For example, Arabic L1 students are likely to say or write: *Do pay you with cash?* instead of *Do you pay with cash?*, or *Where do buy you new shoes?* instead of *Where do you buy new shoes?*

To practise word order in questions, do the exercise below.

Write sentence parts below out of order on the board. Students work in pairs and unscramble the sentences. Elicit the answers and write them on the board (Do you pay with cash? Do you pay by card? Where do you buy new shoes?).

with cash / do / pay / you
pay / you / do / by card
buy / do / you / where / shoes / new

WRITING CHALLENGE

4 👤👥 Focus on the questions and the answers in the model text. Ask a student to read out the model text. Focus on the rubric and read it aloud. Students work individually, read the questions in the model text and write three sentences by answering the questions. Monitor and help as necessary. Check that students are writing in the correct position on the lines. Students swap notebooks and check each other's writing for correct language, spelling and punctuation.

Optional activity

Aural dictation: Follow the procedure on p. 17.
1 How often do you buy clothes?
2 Do you buy clothes at the shopping centre?
3 Where do you buy shoes?

SOUND AND SPELLING
ay, a_e, ai

5 🔊 8.20 👤 Write the first sentence: *I buy a newspaper every day.* on the board. Read it aloud, then ask students to read it out. Circle the highlighted letters as in the book. Say: /eɪ/ /ə/ newspaper and /eɪ/ day. Then say the whole sentence again for students to repeat.

Play the audio for students to listen and read. Remind students how to form the letters *e, y, a* and *i* correctly. Students work individually and trace the letters. Play the audio for students to listen and repeat. Ask students to read the full sentences aloud, focusing on producing the correct sounds.

6 🔊 8.21 👤👥 Focus on the photographs and words, and check that students understand the meanings by looking at the photographs. Play the audio for students to listen and read. Students work individually and trace the letters. Play the audio again for students to listen and repeat. Students read each group of words aloud focusing on producing the sound correctly.

SPELLING CHALLENGE

7 🔊 8.22 👤👥 Focus on the gapped sentences and the words with spelling mistakes. Say: *Look and correct.* Students work individually, read the sentences, think about the word that is missing and correct the spelling mistake. Play the audio for students to listen and check. Students compare their answers in pairs. Go through answers as a class.

Answers
2 games 3 train 4 pay 5 newspaper

LANGUAGE FOCUS

Learning objectives

- Read and understand words, symbols and shortened forms for different currencies – £ pounds, $ dollars, € euros
- Read and write prices in different currencies
- Read, understand and write high numbers in words – hundred, thousand, million
- Write statements about the price of items – *It is 150 euros.*
- Recognize and practise the spelling of words ending with *-nd* and *-ng*

See p. 19 for suggestions on how to use these Learning objectives in your lessons.

SPENDING UNIT 8

Lead-in
Revise all the numbers taught in previous units. You will need printable flashcards with numbers (Flashcards 0.1, 0.4 and 2.3), which can be printed at esource.cambridge.org.

Vocabulary Pre-teaching / Review
You will need printable flashcards with currencies (Flashcards 8.5), which can be printed at esource.cambridge.org.

Follow the procedure on p. 15.

Write two columns as below on the board: one with currency words and one with currency short forms.

£5	thirty euros
$20	thirteen euros
€13	five pounds
€30	twelve dollars
$12	fifty pounds
£50	twenty dollars

Point at the columns and make sure students understand that they need to match the prices to descriptions. Students work in pairs. Students do not write anything at this stage, just say the answers aloud. Elicit the correct answers and draw lines connecting the words (£5 – five pounds, $20 – twenty dollars, €13 – thirteen euros, €30 – thirty euros, $12 – twelve dollars, £50 – fifty pounds).

1 (◆) 8.23 Focus on the country names and the currencies. Play the audio for students to listen and look. Students work individually, read and match each country to its currency. Students compare their answers in pairs. Go through answers as a class.

> **Answers**
> dollars 4 euros 3 riyals 1 dirhams 2

⊙ Common student errors

Spelling: The word *dollars* is in the top 20 misspelled words by Arabic and Turkish L1 students. This is the typical error: *dolars*.

To focus students on this word, include the exercise below in your lesson.

Write the following on the board:

dollars dolars dollars dolars dolllars dollars

Move your pen slowly across the words, encouraging students to shout *Stop!* when you get to the word with the correct spelling. Circle: *dollars* three times.

2 Focus on the currency symbols. Students match the symbols to the currencies, in pairs or small groups. Go through answers as a class.

> **Answers**
> 1 euros 2 dollars 3 pounds

3 (◆) 8.24 You can use Flashcards 8.6 to pre-teach this vocabulary set. Focus on the numerals and the written amounts. Students work individually, read and trace the words. Monitor and check students' handwriting. If necessary, check students understand higher numbers by referring back to the numerals. Play the audio for students to listen and repeat. Ask individual students to read the amounts aloud.

4 (◆) 8.25 Point at the numerals and the written numbers. Ask a student to read the completed example aloud. Students work individually, look at the numerals and match them to their written forms. Students compare their answers in pairs. Play the audio for students to listen and check.

> **Answers**
> 2,005,000 – two million five thousand
> 9,633 – nine thousand six hundred and thirty-three

Literacy tip
The use of commas in numbers (e.g. *1,500*) is not universal. Check in the country where you are teaching what system they use. If it differs from English, you will need to point this out.

In English, plurals of *hundred/thousand/million* are not used when the number is given, e.g. *five hundred*. However, if the number isn't specific, plurals are used, e.g. *Millions of people watch this programme*.

NOTICE
Focus on the NOTICE box. Ask a student to read the text aloud. Point out the word *and* in red. Point out that *and* is used after *hundred* and *thousand* in numbers of three digits or more.

5 (◆) 8.26 Focus on the numbers and the word shapes. Remind students about the NOTICE feature and the use of *and*. Students work individually, look at the numbers and complete the written form. Monitor students' handwriting. Play the audio for students to listen and check.

UNLOCK BASIC LITERACY TEACHER'S BOOK

> **Answers**
> 1 nine hundred and fifty
> 2 six thousand one hundred and forty-five
> 3 five million four thousand

6 Focus on the questions and read them aloud. Write: *How much is it?* on the board. Point at the answers with prices in the book and point at the question on the board again to demonstrate that we use this question to ask about prices. Students work individually and match the questions to the answers. Go through answers as a class.

> **Answers**
> 1 It is 25 riyals.
> 2 It is 950 dollars.

7 (8.27) Write: *How much is this book?* on the board. Write: *12 euros* and *20 euros* on the board. Say: *It is 12 euros.* Students listen to the sentence and point at the correct answer (12 euros). Circle the number *12*.

Focus on the questions and options in the book. Say: *Listen, read and circle.* Play the audio for students to listen, read and circle the numbers they hear. Students compare their answers in pairs. Go through answers on the board. Play the audio again for students to listen and write the whole sentence. Play the audio again if required. Go through answers as a class.

> **Answers**
> 2 It is 125 dollars.
> 3 It is 2 pounds.
> 4 It is 320 euros.

Optional activity

Classroom messages: Follow the procedure on p. 18.
three million six thousand
seven thousand five hundred
two hundred and fifty-two

SOUND AND SPELLING nd, ng

8 (8.28) Write the first sentence on the board. Read it aloud, then get students to read it out. Circle the consonant cluster *ng* (/ŋ/) in the word *shopping* and say the word aloud. Play the audio for students to listen and read. Remind students how to form the letters *n*, *g* and *d* correctly. Students work individually and trace the words. Play the audio for students to listen and repeat the sentences. Then get students to read the full sentences aloud, focusing on producing the correct sounds (/ŋ/ /nd/).

9 (8.29) Focus on the photographs and words, and check that students understand the meanings by looking at the photographs. Play the audio for students to listen and read.

10 (8.30) Ask students to look at the words in Exercise 9. Play the audio for students to listen and circle the words they hear. Play the audio again if required. Go through answers as a class.

> **Answers**
> 1 hand 2 wing 3 band

LISTENING FOCUS

> **Learning objectives**
> - Predict content as preparation for listening
> - Listen for main ideas
> - Listen for detail
>
> See p. 19 for suggestions on how to use these Learning objectives with your students.

> **Lead-in**
>
> Bring in a newspaper, a book, a smartphone and a bank card. Ask: *How often do you buy a newspaper?* If possible, elicit an answer from a student at random. Otherwise, write the question on the board and ask a student to read it to you. Answer the question, e.g. *I buy a newspaper every day.* Write your answer on the board. Point to the expression *every day*. Ask a student the question again. Continue by asking the class about the remaining three items.

1 (8.31) Focus on the options to tick. Check that students understand all the topics. Play the audio. Students listen to the audio, focus on the main ideas and tick the topic of the discussion.

> **Answer**
> money

SPENDING **UNIT 8**

2 🔊 8.32 👥 Focus on the sentences and the options. Students work individually and read the sentences. Say: *Listen, read and circle.* Play the audio for students to listen, read the sentences and circle the options they hear. Students compare their answers in pairs. Play the audio again for students to listen and check.

> **Answers**
> 1 day 2 dirhams 3 books 4 month 5 smartphone
> 6 month 7 by card 8 at the shopping centre

3 🔊 8.33 👥 Students look at the numbers in the box. In stronger classes, ask a student to read the numbers aloud. Say: *Listen and write.* Play the audio for students to listen to the sentences and complete them using the numbers in the box. Students compare their answers in pairs. Go through answers as a class.

> **Answers**
> 1 20 2 150 3 2,500

> **Optional activity**
> Write these gapped sentences and options on the board:
> *I spend _____ on newspapers once a day.*
> *I spend _____ on books once a month.*
> *I pay with cash / by card once a day.*
> *I buy new shoes on the internet / at the shopping centre.*
> Students work individually and complete the sentences so that they are true for them (they do not have to be exact when it comes to the amount of money). Students work in pairs and talk about their spending habits. Elicit a few answers from students and write them on the board.

👁 KEY WORDS FOR LITERACY

> **Learning objectives**
> - Read, spell and pronounce key words for literacy – *buy, by, have, and*
> - Complete sentences with the key words for literacy

1 🔊 8.34 Write: *by* on the board. Write this sentence: *He pays by card.* Point at the first word you wrote (*by*) and elicit the pronunciation. Move your pen slowly across the sentence from left to right, encouraging students to shout *Stop!* when you get to *by*. Circle it in the sentence.

Focus on the words in bold and the sentences. Say: *Read and circle.* Students work individually, read and circle the words. Play the audio for students to listen and check. Ask a student to read the sentences aloud.

2 Write: *by* on the board. Write these words: *by buy bye by.* Point at the first word you wrote (*by*) and elicit the pronunciation. Move your pen slowly across the sentences, encouraging students to shout *Stop!* when you get to *by*. Circle it twice.

Focus on the words in bold in the book. Say: *Read and circle.* Students work individually, read and circle the words.

3 Students work individually, cover and complete the words. If necessary, prompt them to use something to cover the words on the left as they complete each one. Monitor and check that they are working from left to right. Encourage correct stroke direction and correct height and position of the individual letters.

4 🔊 8.35 Focus on the gapped sentences. Play the audio for students to listen and complete the gaps. Play the audio again for students to listen and check their answers. Go through answers on the board. Ask a student to read the sentences aloud.

> **Answers**
> 1 buy 2 by 3 have 4 and

READING AND WRITING

> **Learning objectives**
> - Review vocabulary from previous lessons as preparation for reading
> - Read and understand main ideas in a text about spending
> - Read for detail
> - Complete sentences about a friend's spending habits – *Ali has a lot of video games. He buys video games once a month. He spends 300 dirhams on one video game. He pays by card.*
>
> See p. 19 for suggestions on how to use these Learning objectives with your students.

> **Lead-in**
> Draw a pie chart (circle) on the board. Write: *100%* in the centre of it. Write: *How much do people in your country spend on: food, clothes and shoes, university, house?* Students work in pairs and think about how much people spend on each category. Encourage them to draw pie charts representing percentages of spending. Elicit a few ideas from the class and a draw a pie chart that represents the majority of the class's ideas.

1 (8.36) Focus on the photographs, the words in the box and the word shapes. Ask a student to read the words aloud. Use the photographs to check understanding of meaning if required. Students work individually, match and write the words. Monitor and check students' handwriting. Play the audio for students to listen and repeat.

> **Answers**
> 2 school 3 clothes 4 shoes 5 health

2 (8.37) Read aloud the title of the text. Point at the country words in the box, the chart and the missing headings in the text. Say: *Look, read and add*. Students work individually, look at the chart, read the text and complete the headings with the words from the box. Play the audio for students to listen and check. Go through answers as a class.

> **Answers**
> 1 Brazil 2 Philippines 3 Jordan

3 (8.37) Focus on the text in Exercise 2 and the gapped sentences in Exercise 3. Students work individually, read the text and complete the sentences with the missing information. Students compare their answers in pairs. Play the audio again to listen and check. Go through answers as a class, asking students to point at the places in the text where they found the missing information.

> **Answers**
> 1 8 2 food and drink 3 health 4 houses
> 5 36 6 clothes and shoes

4 Tell students about a friend of yours. Use the same vocabulary and structures as in the model text: *Sally has a lot of English books. She buys English books every week.* etc.

Focus on the sentences about Ali in the model text in the book. Ask a student to read the sentences aloud. Students work individually, read the text and write about a friend. Students compare their texts in pairs. Monitor students' writing.

> **Model answer**
> My friend has a lot of books. My friend buys books once a week. My friend spends 100 pounds on books. My friend pays by card.

> **Optional activity**
>
> **Aural gap fill:** Follow the procedure on p. 17 with sentences below.
> She buys new shoes (at) the shopping centre.
> He buys a newspaper (once) a week.
> Anna pays with (cash).
> I buy new clothes (on) the internet.

> **Objectives review**
> See Teaching tips on p. 19 for ideas about using the Objectives review with your students.
>
> **WORDLIST**
> See Teaching tips on p. 21 for ideas about using the Wordlist on p. 143 with your students.
>
> **REVIEW TEST**
> See esource.cambridge.org for the Review test and ideas about how and when to administer the Review test.

9 TECHNOLOGY

LISTENING AND READING 1

Learning objectives

- Read and understand words for technology items – *a blog, a website, an app, a USB drive, GPS, a webinar*
- Read and understand verb-noun collocations for technology items – *write a blog, read a website, buy an app, have a USB drive, use GPS, watch a webinar, learn English online, play video games*
- Read and understand descriptions of how often people use technology – *I often play video games.*
- Produce correct work order for sentences with adverbs of frequency – *She never uses GPS.*
- Write four sentences to describe how you use technology – *I always use GPS. I never use a USB drive. I often look at English websites. I sometimes listen to webinars.*

See p. 19 for suggestions on how to use these Learning objectives in your lessons.

Lead-in

Write the words below with gaps on the board:

_ n t _ r n _ t
v _ d _ _ g _ m _
m _ b _ l _ p h _ n _
l _ p t _ p
_ m _ _ l

Students work in pairs and discuss which letters complete the gaps to create technology words. Ask students not to write anything, just think of the options. Go through answers as a class (internet, video games, mobile phone, laptop, email). Write the letters in the gaps on the board. Students read the words aloud.

Vocabulary Pre-teaching / Review

You will need printable flashcards with items related to technology (Flashcards 9.1), which can be printed at esource.cambridge.org.

Follow the procedure on p. 15.

Write the questions below on the board. Next to the questions, write: *Yes, I do. / No, I don't.*

Do you write a blog?
Do you learn English online?
Do you listen to webinars in English?
Do you play video games?
Do you use GPS?

Students work in pairs and ask each other the questions. Encourage them to answer using the short answers on the board. Monitor and listen to what students say. Discuss the questions with the whole class.

1 🔊 9.1 👤 Focus on the photographs and the words in the box. Students work individually, look at the photographs and write the words in the word shapes. Play the audio for students to listen and check. Write the words on the board. Ask a student to read them aloud.

> **Answers**
>
> 2 buy an app 3 look at a website 4 use GPS
> 5 use a USB drive 6 watch a webinar
> 7 learn English online 8 play video games

SOUND AND SPELLING Review

2 🔊 9.2 👤👥 Write the vowels *a, e, i, o, u* on the board. Remind students how to write the letters if necessary. Write: *game, use* and *video* on the board. Students read the words aloud. Correct their pronunciation if required. Move your pen slowly across the words, encouraging students to shout *Stop!* when you get to a vowel. Circle all the vowels in the words (g(a)m(e), (u)s(e), v(i)d(e)(o)).

Point at the words in the box in the book. Say: *Match and write.* Students work individually, read the words in the box and match them to the words with the same sound. Students compare their answers in pairs. Play the audio for students to listen and check their answers. Students then read the words aloud, focusing on the sounds (1 /ɪ/ 2 /æ/ 3 /e/ 4 /eɪ/ 5 /aɪ/ 6 /ɒ/ 7 /uː/). Go through answers as a class.

> **Answers**
>
> 2 app /æ/ 3 webinar /e/ 4 game /eɪ/
> 5 write, website /aɪ/ 6 blog /ɒ/ 7 use /uː/

3 🔊 9.3 👤 Focus on the pictures of the two women and the texts. Say: *Listen and read.* Play the audio for students to read and listen to the text. Check that students understand the meaning of the texts. Point at the technology items and the names to choose from. Say: *Read* *and tick the name.* Students work individually, read the text again and tick the name the item refers to. Go through answers as a class. Play the audio again if required.

> **Answers**
>
> 1 Khadijah   2 Hana   3 Khadijah   4 Khadijah

> **NOTICE**
>
> Focus on the NOTICE box. Read through the information there as a class. Point at the use of articles *a* and *an* for singular objects and the use of *s* when creating plural nouns. Ask a student to read the phrases aloud.

4 Write: *never sometimes often usually always* on the board. Read the words aloud. Write: *0%* above the words *never* and *100%* above the word *always*. Read the words aloud again for students to listen and repeat.

Students work individually, look at the scale in the book and complete the words. Monitor students' handwriting.

> **NOTICE**
>
> Focus on the NOTICE box. Read through the information there as a class. Write: *I learn always English online.* on the board. Write a cross next to the sentence. Move your pen along the sentence, encouraging students to shout *Stop!* when you get to the mistake. Elicit the correction and write it next to the original sentence (*I always learn English online.*).

> **Common student errors**
>
> **Spelling**: Arabic L1 students often misspell the word *sometimes*. This is the typical error: *some times*.
>
> To focus students on this word, include the exercise below in your lesson.
>
> Write these sentences on the board:
>
> *She sometimes drinks tea.*
>
> *He some times reads blogs.*
>
> *I some times learn English online.*
>
> *They sometimes have English in room 10.*
>
> Students work in pairs and analyze each sentence. Tell them to choose the two with correct spelling (1 and 4). Erase the incorrect sentences from the board.

5 9.4 Write: *never* on the board. Write this sentence: *They never study English online.* Move your pen slowly across the sentence, encouraging students to shout *Stop!* when you get to *never*. Circle it in the sentence.

Focus on the words in bold and the sentences in the book. Say: *Read and circle.* Students work individually, read and circle the words. Play the audio for students to listen and check. Ask a student to read the sentences aloud.

6 9.5 Write: *uses / GPS. / never / She* on the board. Elicit the correct order of words to create a sentence. Write the sentence on the board (*She never uses GPS.*).

Students work individually, read the words and put them in order to create sentences. Students compare their answers in pairs. Play the audio for students to listen and check. Go through answers as a class.

> **Answers**
>
> 2 He usually buys apps.
> 3 I never use a USB drive.
> 4 She always looks at websites.

> **Optional activity**
>
> Play a variation on team pelmanism (see p. 16). Make a set of cards with activities (*read blog, learn English online, write a blog, read a website, use GPS, use a USB drive, play a video game*). Copy one set for each pair of students. Make another set of adverbs (*never, sometimes, often, usually, always*), with two copies for each pair. If possible, copy them on different-coloured paper.
>
> Students work in teams. Activity cards should be face down in a pile, and adverb cards face down scattered on the desk. One student picks up an activity card and says a sentence, e.g. *I sometimes use GPS.* Then they turn over one of the adverb cards. If the word on it matches what the student said, they keep the adverb card. If not, they turn the card with the adverb over again and the next student tries. The winner is the student with the most adverb cards at the end.

WRITING CHALLENGE

7 Focus on the adverbs of frequency. Ask a student to read the model text aloud. Focus on the rubric and read it aloud. Point at the photographs. Students work individually and write four sentences using the adverbs of frequency and the photographs. Monitor and help as necessary. Check that students are writing in the correct position on the lines. Students swap notebooks and check each other's writing for correct language, spelling and punctuation.

TECHNOLOGY UNIT 9

LISTENING AND READING 2

Learning objectives

- Read and understand words describing everyday objects – *a chair, glasses, a fridge, a watch, a smart chair, smart glasses, a smart fridge, a smart watch*
- Read and understand sentences with *can* and *cannot* about ability and possibility – *It can send messages. It cannot go online.*
- Understand the contraction *can't* and write the full form *cannot*
- Learn how to link sentences with *but* – *It can send messages, but it cannot take photographs.*
- Write two sentences to describe what a smart TV can or cannot do – *It cannot cook. It can play a webinar, but it cannot take photographs.*

See p. 19 for suggestions on how to use these Learning objectives in your lessons.

Lead-in

Write these words in two columns:

write	a car
speak	GPS
drive	an email
shop	online
use	Japanese

Students work in pairs and match the words to create collocations. Ask students not to write anything, just think of the options. Go through answers as a class (write an email / Japanese, speak Japanese, drive a car, shop online, use GPS / a car / an email / Japanese). Draw lines linking the words. Students read the phrases aloud.

Vocabulary Pre-teaching / Review

You will need printable flashcards with words and phrases for technology (Flashcards 9.2), which can be printed at esource.cambridge.org.

Follow the procedure on p. 15.

Follow the procedure from the Lead-in exercise, but this time with the words below (collocations: *send messages/photographs/food, cook food, go online, use GPS/messages/photographs/food, take photographs/messages/food*).

send	online
cook	messages
go	photographs
use	food
take	GPS

1 🔊 9.6 👤 Focus on the pictures and the words in the box. Students work individually, look at the pictures and write the words in the word shapes to complete phrases. Play the audio for students to listen and check. Go through answers as a class. Ask a student to read them aloud.

> **Answers**
> 2 send 3 cook 4 go 5 take 6 use 7 use

2 🔊 9.7 👤 Draw the three stress patterns on the board. Sound out the stress patterns using neutral sounds, e.g. DUH-duh-DUH for OoO. Face students and say: *cook*, clearly stressing the word and counting the syllable on your fingers. Elicit that *cook* matches with pattern 1. Write the word under the correct pattern.

Play the audio for students to listen and match the words to the stress patterns. Play the audio again for students to listen and repeat. Go through answers as a class.

> **Answers**
> cook 1 take photographs 3 send messages 3
> go online 2

3 🔊 9.8 👤👥 Focus on the photographs, the texts about smart objects and the phrases with ticks and crosses. Say: *Listen and read.* Play the audio for students to read and listen to both texts. Say: *Read and match.* Students work individually, read the texts again and match the phrases with ticks and crosses to the texts. Students compare their answers in pairs. Play the audio again if required. Go through answers as a class.

> **Answers**
> Malia 2 Jeff 1 4

NOTICE

Focus on the NOTICE box. Read through the information there as a class. Write: *It can send messages.* on the board. Write a tick next to the sentence. Write: *It can't cook food.* Write a cross next to the sentence. Erase *can't* from the second sentence and write: *cannot*. Say: *Say* can't, *write* cannot. Ask a student to read the sentences in the NOTICE box aloud.

UNL⦿CK BASIC LITERACY TEACHER'S BOOK

Literacy tip

Can is the only modal verb which becomes one word in the negative form: *cannot*. Negative modal verbs are generally stressed when speaking, unlike positive modal verbs, and this is how we distinguish them in speech.

4 Write: *It can't go online.* on the board. Erase *can't* and elicit from students what else you can insert in its place (*cannot*). Write: *cannot* on the board.

Students work individually, read the sentences with the short verb form *can't* and change them to the full verb form *cannot*. Monitor students' handwriting.

Answers
2 cannot
3 cannot

5 9.9 Write: *Itcangoonline,butitcannottak ephotographs.* on the board. Move the pen along the sentence and draw the first line after *It*. Move the pen again, encouraging students to shout *Stop!* at the word boundaries. Add lines between the words.

Focus on the first sentence in the book. Show how lines mark spaces between words. Students work individually through the sentences. Monitor and help as necessary. Play the audio for students to listen and check. Write the sentences with spaces on the board for students to check their answers.

Answers
1 It can send messages, but it cannot take photographs.
2 It can play TV, but it cannot go online.
3 It cannot send messages, but it can take photographs.

NOTICE

Focus on the NOTICE box. Read through the information there as a class. Point at the comma and *but* in the sentence. Make sure students understand how to use it to link two sentences (one affirmative and one negative). Tell students to look at Exercise 5 and circle a comma and *but* in each sentence.

6 9.10 Focus on the completed example. Ask a student to read it aloud. Students work individually, read the chunks of language and put these in order to create sentences. Check students understand *play TV* by showing a video on a smartphone or a laptop. Write the answers on the board for students to check.

Answers
2 It can send messages about food, but it cannot cook.
3 It can play TV, but it cannot go online.

⊙ Common student errors

Spelling: Arabic L1 students often fail to capitalize the word *TV*. This is the typical error: *tv*.

To focus students on this word, include the exercise below in your lesson.

Write these sentences on the board:
1 *It can play TV.*
2 *It cannot play tv online.*

Students work in pairs and analyze each sentence. Tell them that only one is correct (1). Erase the incorrect sentence from the board.

Optional activity

Students write two things their mobile phone can do (e.g. go online, take photographs) and one thing it cannot do (e.g. use a USB drive). Students work in pairs and say the things to each other (just the things, not the full sentences). Their partner guesses which two they can do and which one they cannot do.

WRITING CHALLENGE

7 Ask a student to read out the model text. Focus on the rubric and read it aloud. Point at the pictures with crosses and a tick. Students work individually and write two sentences using *can/cannot* and the pictures. Monitor and help as necessary. Check that students are writing in the correct position on the lines. Students swap notebooks and check each other's writing for correct language, spelling and punctuation.

TECHNOLOGY　　UNIT 9

LISTENING AND READING 3

Learning objectives

- Read and write singular and plural nouns for people – *people, a man, men, a woman, women, a girl, a boy, a child, children, an adult*
- Read and write frequency expressions – *every second, every minute, every hour, every day, every year*
- Read and understand sentences about how often people use technology – *A lot of people go online every second.*
- Recognize the sound and spelling pattern for words starting with *bl*, *pl* and *gl*

See p. 19 for suggestions on how to use these Learning objectives in your lessons.

Lead-in

Revise all subject pronouns using photographs of people (or indicating students in the class if appropriate in your context). Start with *I, he* and *she*. Move on to *we, you, they*. Write all the subject pronouns on the board.

Vocabulary Pre-teaching / Review

You will need printable flashcards with singular and plural nouns for people (Flashcards 9.3), which can be printed at esource.cambridge.org.

Follow the procedure on p. 15.

Do not show the flashcards any more. Write the words below with gaps on the board. Students work in pairs and think of a vowel that can complete each word. Elicit the answers and complete the gaps with the missing vowels (person, woman, men/man, girl, boy, child, adult).

p _ r s o n
w _ m a n
m _ n
g _ r l
b _ y
c h _ l d
a d _ l t

1 (9.11) Focus on the photographs and the words to trace. Play the audio for students to listen and read. Students work individually, read and then trace the words. Make sure students understand the meanings. Monitor and check students' handwriting. Play the audio again for students to listen and repeat.

2 (9.12) Focus on the words in the box. Students work individually, look at the singular nouns and complete the plural noun forms using the word shapes. Play the audio for students to listen and check. Write both singular and plural words on the board. Ask a student to read them aloud.

Answers
2 women 3 girls 4 boys 5 children 6 adults 7 people

3 (9.13) Say: *Listen and write*. Say: *person, p-e-r-s-o-n* for students to listen and write. Repeat the procedure with the word *people*. Ask student to compare their spelling in pairs. Write both words on the board.

Play the audio for students to listen and write the words. Write the words with the correct spelling on the board.

Answers
2 children 3 men 4 women

4 (9.14) Students look at the pictures and the words. Play the audio for students to read and listen to the words. Check that students understand the meanings. Students work individually and trace the words. Monitor their handwriting. Play the audio again for students to listen and repeat. Ask a student to read the phrases aloud.

5 Focus on the text with facts about technology, the pictures and the frequency expressions. Point out the completed example. Students work individually, read the text and match the expressions to the pictures. Students compare their answers in pairs. Go through answers as a class.

Answers
1 d 2 e 4 c 5 a

NOTICE

Focus on the NOTICE box. Ask a student to read the sentences aloud. Point at the position of *every* in each sentence. Ask students to look at the text in Exercise 5 and underline *every*.

UNLOCK BASIC LITERACY TEACHER'S BOOK **125**

> **Optional activity**
>
> Write a few sentences with *every*: *Some adults send messages every day. A lot of boys and girls play video games every day. People send 16 million messages every minute.* Make copies of your sentences for each pair or small group of students. Cut each sentence into chunks and mix the pieces of paper up. Students make as many sentences as they can using the chunks. Ask them to write their sentences on a piece of paper. This can be a timed competition, if appropriate in your context, with students receiving points for each correct sentence. The winner is the person or a group with the most points.

SOUND AND SPELLING *bl, pl, gl*

6 9.15 Write the first sentence on the board: *He writes a blog*. Read it aloud, then get students to read it out. Circle: *bl* (/bl/) in the word *blog* and say the word aloud.

Play the audio for students to listen and read. Remind students of how to form the letters *l*, *b*, *p* and *g* correctly. Students work individually and trace the words. Play the audio again for students to listen and repeat. Students read the full sentences aloud, focusing on producing the correct sounds (/bl/ /pl/ /gl/).

7 9.16 Focus on the pictures and words and check that students understand the meanings. Play the audio for students to listen and read, then ask them to trace the letters. Play the audio again for students to listen and repeat. Students read each group of words aloud focusing on producing the sounds correctly.

8 9.17 Focus on the pictures and words and check that students understand the meanings by indicating the pictures. Play the audio for students to listen and read.

9 9.18 Students look at the words in Exercise 8. Play the audio for students to listen and circle the words they hear. Play the audio again if required. Go through answers as a class.

> **Answers**
>
> 1 glue 2 blank 3 plum

SPELLING CHALLENGE

10 9.19 Focus on the words with spelling mistakes. Say: *Look and correct*. Students work individually and correct the spelling mistakes. Play the audio for students to listen and check. Students compare their answers in pairs. Go through answers as a class.

> **Answers**
>
> 2 He has smart <u>glasses</u>.
> 3 I sometimes write a <u>blog</u>.

LANGUAGE FOCUS

> **Learning objectives**
>
> - Read and understand a question and answer about people's opinions – *What do you think of my smartphone? I think it's good.*
> - Write a question and answer about your opinions – *What do you think of my smartphone? I think it is good.*
> - Read and understand people's opinions in context
> - Write phrases to agree and disagree – *I agree. I disagree. I don't think so. I think so too.*
> - Recognize and practise the spelling of words ending with *-dge* and *-tch*
>
> See p. 19 for suggestions on how to use these Learning objectives in your lessons.

> **Lead-in**
>
> Revise all the adjectives taught in previous units. You will need printable flashcards with adjectives (Flashcards 3.3, 4.1 and 4.3), which can be printed at esource.cambridge.org.
>
> Follow the procedure on p. 15.
>
> Ask students to choose and write three adjectives on a piece of paper. Tell them not to show these to other students. Students work in pairs and start spelling each adjective letter by letter to their partners. Students listen, write each letter and try to guess what the word is. If they don't know after one letter, they ask for the next one until they guess the word or write the complete adjective. Monitor students' spelling.

TECHNOLOGY   UNIT 9

> **Vocabulary Pre-teaching / Review**
>
> Write these sentences on the board:
> *I think it's interesting.*
> *I think it's difficult.*
> *I think it's boring.*
> *I think it's expensive.*
> *I think it's great.*
>
> Ask students these questions:
> *What do you think of my new smartphone?*
> *What do you think of Maths?*
> *What do you think of this English book?*
> *What do you think of my watch?*
>
> Say the questions aloud, one by one (if you can, prepare and show the objects you are asking about). Students listen to your questions and choose an answer from the board. Students say their answer aloud. In stronger classes, you could collate student responses on the board. Elicit sentences by writing the following on the board: ____ *students think Maths is difficult.* ____ *students think Maths is great.*

1 ◀) 9.20 Focus on the photographs and the adjectives. Play the audio for students to listen and read. Students work individually and match the adjectives to the photographs. Students compare their answers in pairs. Go through answers as a class. Students trace the words.

> **Answers**
> a 2 b 4 c 1 d 3

2 ◀) 9.21 Focus on the pictures, the questions and the responses. Students work individually, read the questions and match them to the correct responses. Students compare their answers in pairs. Play the audio for students to listen and check.

> **Answers**
> a 3 b 1 c 2

> ◉ **Common student errors**
>
> **Confusable words:** Arabic L1 students often confuse the words *think* and *thing*. Arabic L1 students are likely to replace one word with the other, which results in problems with clarity.
>
> To focus students on *think*, include the exercise below in your lesson.
>
> Write these words on the board:
> *think think thing thank thing think*
>
> Move your pen along the line of words, encouraging students to shout *Stop!* when you reach the word *think*. Circle it three times.

> **NOTICE**
>
> Focus on the NOTICE box. Ask one student to read the dialogue aloud with you. Point at the words and letters in red in the questions and the answers (*it is, they are*) and write them on the board. Point at *watch* and ask: *How many?* (1). Point at *it is*. Draw a line connecting *watch* and *it*. Point at *video games* and ask: *How many?* (2+). Point at *they are*. Draw a line connecting *video games* and *they are*. Ask students to underline examples of *it is* and *they are* in Exercise 2.

3 ◀) 9.22 Write: *Whatdoyouthinkofmyphone?* on the board. Move the pen along the sentence and draw the first line after *What*. Move the pen again, encouraging students to shout *Stop!* at the word boundaries. Add lines between the words.

Focus on the first sentence in the book. Show how lines mark spaces between words. Students work individually through the other sentences. Monitor and help as necessary. Play the audio for students to listen and check. Write the sentences with spaces on the board for students to check their answers.

> **Answers**
> 1 **A:** What do you think of my laptop?
>   **B:** I think it is interesting.
> 2 **A:** What do you think of smartwatches?
>   **B:** I think they are expensive.
> 3 **A:** What do you think of this website?
>   **B:** I think it is great.

4 ◀) 9.23 Students close their books. Play the audio for students to listen to the dialogues. Ask students what they remember.

Students open their books. Play the audio again for students to listen and read the dialogues. Point at the words in the box. Students work individually and write the words from the box in the gaps. Go through answers as a class.

> **Answers**
> 1 boring, photographs 2 tablet, TV, video games

UNL**O**CK BASIC LITERACY TEACHER'S BOOK   **127**

5 👥 Students look at the dialogues in Exercise 4 and the opinion expressions in Exercise 5. Say: *Read Exercise 4 and underline*. Students work individually, look at the expressions, find the same one in the dialogues and underline it. Students compare the phrases they have underlined in pairs. Say: *Match*. Students work individually, read the expressions with opinions and match them to the smiley or frowning face. Go through answers as a class.

> **Answers**
> 2 b   3 a   4 b

Optional activity

Give students different items (bags, pencils, shoes, books, mobile phones, etc.) or, if appropriate, ask them to use their own things they have in the class. Write: *What do you think of my …?* on the board. Ask the question about one of your own possessions. Elicit and write possible answers on the board, e.g. *I think it's great*. Students work in pairs, ask each other questions about different items and offer opinions. Monitor and note any mistakes. Go over the mistakes as a class once all conversations are finished.

NOTICE

Write: *I don't think so.* on the board. Erase *don't* and elicit the full form (do not). Write the correct answer on the board.

Focus on the NOTICE box. Read through the information there as a class. Point at the speaking and writing icons for students to differentiate between the verb forms used. Ask a student to read the text aloud.

---

6 👤 Write: *I think it's good.* on the board. Erase *it's* and elicit the full form (it is). Write the correct answer on the board.

Students work individually, read the gapped sentences and write the full forms. Go through answers as a class.

> **Answers**
> 1 is   2 do not

SOUND AND SPELLING *dge, tch*

7 🔊 9.24 👤 Write the first sentence on the board. Read it aloud, then get students to read it out. Circle: *dge* /dʒ/ in the word *fridge* and say the word aloud.

Play the audio for students to listen and read. Remind students of how to form the letters *d, g, c, h, t* and *e* correctly. Students work individually and trace the letters. Play the audio for students to listen and repeat. Students read the full sentences aloud, focusing on producing the correct sounds (/dʒ/ /tʃ/).

8 🔊 9.25 👤 Focus on the photographs and words and check that students understand the meanings. Play the audio for students to listen and read, then let them trace the letters. Play the audio again for students to listen and repeat. Students read each pair of words aloud, focusing on producing the sounds correctly (/dʒ/ /tʃ/).

9 🔊 9.26 👥 Students look at the gapped sentences. Say: *Listen and read*. Play the audio for students to read and listen to the sentences. Say: *Write*. Students work individually and write the missing letters. Students compare their answers in pairs. Write the sentences on the board. Ask students to read the sentences aloud.

> **Answers**
> 1 ma<u>tch</u>   2 he<u>dge</u>, bri<u>dge</u>   3 ju<u>dge</u>, sti<u>tch</u>

SPELLING CHALLENGE

10 🔊 9.27 👥 Focus on the words with spelling mistakes. Say: *Look and correct*. Students work individually and correct the spelling mistakes. Play the audio for students to listen and check. Students compare their answers in pairs. Go through answers as a class.

> **Answers**
> 1 fridge   2 watch

TECHNOLOGY   UNIT 9

LISTENING FOCUS

Learning objectives
- Use visuals to understand gist
- Listen for main ideas
- Listen for key information

See p. 19 for suggestions on how to use these Learning objectives with your students.

Lead-in
Revise all the singular and plural nouns for people. You will need printable flashcards (Flashcards 9.3–9.4), which can be printed at esource.cambridge.org.
Write these words in two columns on the board:

a man	women
a woman	children
a child	men
an adult	people
a person	adults

Ask students to work in pairs and match the singular forms to the plural forms. Check the answers as a class by drawing lines and connecting the words (a man – men; a woman – women; a child – children; an adult – adults; a person – people).

1 9.28 Play the audio for students to listen. Ask questions to elicit what students remember: *How many people are there?* (3) *Is there a man?* (yes) *Is there a woman?* (no) *Are there any children?* (no)

Focus on the incomplete sentence and the options. Say: *Listen and complete.* Play the audio for students to listen and choose the correct topic.

Answer
2 smartphones

2 9.29 Focus on the sentences and the names. Say: *Listen and tick.* Play the audio for students to listen and select the name of a person who says the sentence. Students compare their answers in pairs. Go through answers as a class.

Answers
1 Badar 2 Saud 3 Saud 4 Badar

3 9.29 Ask a student to read all the phrases aloud. Point at the options and say: *Listen and circle.* Play the audio again for students to listen and circle the name. Play the audio as many times as required. Go through answers as a class.

Answers
2 Saud 3 Saud 4 Teacher

4 9.30 Focus on the sentences and options. Ask a student to read all the sentences aloud. Say: *Listen and circle.* Play the audio for students to listen, read the sentences and circle the correct options. Play the audio again if required. Students compare their answers in pairs. Go through answers as a class.

Answers
2 bad 3 difficult 4 interesting 5 great

Optional activity
Collaborative vocabulary and spelling test: Follow the procedure on pp. 16–17 with the words below.
person, people, child, children, boy, girl, woman, women, man, men, adult, adults

⊙ KEY WORDS FOR LITERACY

Learning objectives
- Read, spell and pronounce key words for literacy – *can, never, often, always*
- Complete sentences with the key words for literacy

See p. 19 for suggestions on how to use these Learning objectives with your students.

1 9.31 Write: *can* on the board. Write this sentence: *She can go online.* Point at the first word you wrote (can) and elicit the pronunciation. Move your pen slowly across the sentence, encouraging students to shout *Stop!* when you get to *can*. Circle it in the sentence.

Focus on the words in bold and the sentences in the book. Say: *Read and circle.* Students work individually, read and circle the words. Play the audio for students to read and listen to the sentences. Ask a student to read the sentences aloud.

2 👤 Write: can on the board. Write these words: *man can can't can pan*. Point at the first word you wrote (can) and elicit the pronunciation. Move your pen slowly across the words, encouraging students to shout *Stop!* when you get to *can*. Circle it twice.

Focus on the words in bold. Say: *Read and circle*. Students work individually, read and circle the words.

3 👤 Students work individually, cover and complete the words. If necessary, prompt them to use something to cover the words on the left as they complete each one. Monitor and check that they are working from left to right. Encourage correct stroke direction and correct height and position of the individual letters.

4 (🔊 9.32) 👤 Focus on the gapped sentences. Say: *Listen and write*. Play the audio for students to listen and write the words. Play the audio again for students to listen and check their answers. Write the correct sentences on the board. Ask a student to read the sentences aloud.

| Answers
| 1 sister often 2 and women 3 always listen
| 4 it can

READING AND WRITING

Learning objectives
- Read and understand main ideas in a text about smartphones
- Read for detail
- Differentiate between *and* and *but* in sentences
- Write three sentences about your smartphone or tablet – *I use my tablet every day. It can go online. It cannot take photographs.*

See p. 19 for suggestions on how to use these Learning objectives with your students.

Lead-in
Write these activities on the board:

watch TV in the evening

use a smartphone

use GPS

take photographs on the smartphone

look at English websites

Ask students to work in pairs and think about people in their countries. Students think about what percentage of people do the activities. Students do not have to say the word *percent*, they can just use the numbers. Encourage students to use the phrase *I think*, e.g. *watch TV in the evening? I think 80(%)*. Elicit students' ideas and write the most common numbers on the board next to the activities.

1 (🔊 9.33) 👤👥 Focus on the article. Students read the title and the three options for paragraph 1 aloud. Say: *Look* (pointing at the three options for each paragraph), *read* (pointing at the text) *and circle* (pointing at the options again). Students work individually, read the text and circle the correct options. Students compare their answers in pairs. Go through answers as a class. Play the audio for students to read and listen to the text.

| Answers
| 2 Adults 3 Children

2 👤👥 Focus on the gapped sentences and the article in Exercise 1. Students work individually, read the sentences and complete the gaps. In weaker classes, write the answers out of order on the board so that students can match them to the sentences. Students compare their answers in pairs. Write the sentences on the board.

| Answers
| 1 day 2 use 3 smartphone 4 watch 5 photographs
| 6 every

NOTICE
Focus on the NOTICE box. Read through the box with students. Read through the information there as a class. Point at the words *and* and *but* in bold. Point at *can* and *cannot* to explain the difference between using *and* and *but* when linking sentences. Make sure students understand that we link two affirmative sentences with *and*, and contradictory sentences with a comma and *but*.

TECHNOLOGY UNIT 9

3 Write: *It can go online but it cannot take photographs* on the board. Write a full stop (.) and a comma (,) on the board. Elicit from students where you should insert these two punctuation symbols. Write them in the sentences (It can go online, but it cannot take photographs.).

Students work individually, read the sentences in the book and insert the full stops and commas. Go through answers as a class. Ask a student to read the sentences aloud.

> **Answers**
> 1 A lot of people go online on their smartphones, but not a lot of adults watch TV.
> 2 Some people look at websites and they write blogs.

> **Literacy tip**
> When writing texts on lined paper, students at this level often put a comma at the beginning of a line, rather than at the end of the previous line. To help them see that this is wrong, teach them that it is 'attached' to the previous word and cannot be separated.

4 Write: *I can go online. I can take photographs.* on the board. Write: *and* next to the second sentence. Elicit from students how to join these sentences using *and*. Write the correct answer on the board (I can go online and I can take photographs.). Repeat the procedure with *I can go online. I cannot take photographs.* and *but* (I can go online, but I cannot take photographs.).

Students work individually, read the sentences and join them using *and* or *but*. Students compare their answers in pairs. Write the joined sentences on the board.

> **Answers**
> 1 It can send messages and it can have a USB drive.
> 2 It can go online, but it cannot cook.

5 Focus on the notes with a tick and a cross and the sentences in the model text. Ask a student to read the sentences aloud. Students work individually and complete the notes with their ideas about smartphones or tablets. Students then use their notes and the model text to write about their smartphones or tablets. Students compare their texts in pairs.

> **Model answer**
> I use my smartphone every day. It can play webinars. It cannot play TV.

> **Optional activity**
> **Classroom messages:** Follow the procedure on p. 18 with the sentences below.
> *It can go online, but it can't take photographs.*
> *It can send you messages, but it can't cook your food.*
> *I can look at websites and I can write a blog.*

> **Objectives review**
> See Teaching tips on p. 19 for ideas about using the Objectives review with your students.
>
> **WORDLIST**
> See Teaching tips on p. 21 for ideas about using the Wordlist on p. 143 with your students.
>
> **REVIEW TEST**
> See esource.cambridge.org for the Review test and ideas about how and when to administer the Review test.

10 FREE TIME AND FASHION

LISTENING AND READING 1

Learning objectives

- Read and understand phrases for free time activities – *go for a walk, talk on the phone, bake cakes, go to the park, have a picnic, visit friends and family, do exercise, go shopping*
- Read and understand a description of a person's free time activities – *I often bake cakes. I also go to the park.*
- Use *also* correctly in a sentence – *I also talk on the phone.*
- Use prepositions *on, for, to* and *at* correctly in a sentence
- Write four sentences about free time – *In my free time, I go shopping. I also go to the park. I sometimes do exercise at home. I also bake cakes.*

See p. 19 for suggestions on how to use these Learning objectives in your lessons.

Lead-in

Write these free time activities on the board:

use the internet, cook, play video games, learn a new language, watch TV, read books, visit different countries

Underneath the activities, write: *never, always, usually, sometimes* and *often*. Say: *Look at the free time activities. What do you do in your free time?* Students work in pairs, look at the activities and say how often they do these things in their free time. Monitor students' discussions and note any mistakes you hear. Go over the mistakes as a class once all discussions are finished.

Vocabulary Pre-teaching / Review

You will need printable flashcards with words for free time activities (Flashcards 10.1), which can be printed at esource.cambridge.org.

Follow the procedure on p. 15.

Write the questions below on the board. Next to the questions, write: *Yes, I do.* and *No, I don't.*

Do you go for a walk in your free time?
Do you bake cakes in your free time?
Do you have a picnic in your free time?
Do you do exercise in your free time?
Do you talk on the phone in your free time?
Do you visit friends and family in your free time?
Do you go shopping in your free time?

Students work in pairs and ask each other questions. Encourage them to answer using the short answers on the board. Monitor and listen to what students say. Discuss the questions with the whole class.

1 🔊 **10.1** Focus on the photographs and the phrases to trace. Play the audio for students to listen and read. Students work individually and trace the words. Say: *Match*. Students read the free time activities and match them to the pictures. Go through answers as a class. Write the phrases on the board. Ask a student to read them aloud.

> **Answers**
> a 2 b 3 d 4 e 7 f 8 g 6 h 5

2 🔊 **10.2** Focus on the phrases in Exercise 1 and the stress patterns. Read all the stress bubbles using neutral sounds, e.g. DUH-DUH (OO), DUH-DUH-duh (OOo). Students work individually, look at the phrases and match them to the stress patterns. Play the audio for students to listen and check. Go through answers as a class. Ask a student to read the phrases aloud.

> **Answers**
> a 2 bake cakes
> b 8 go shopping
> c 3 have a picnic
> d 4 do exercise
> e 7 visit friends and family
> f 1 go for a walk, 5 talk on the phone, 6 go to the park

132 UNLOCK BASIC LITERACY TEACHER'S BOOK

FREE TIME AND FASHION — UNIT 10

> **Optional activity**
>
> Write all free time activities from Exercise 1 on the board. Tell students what you do in your free time, including four of these expressions and using the present simple, e.g. *I sometimes visit friends and family. I go shopping. I often watch TV. I usually talk on the phone.* Students listen carefully and tick the activities in Exercise 1 that you mention. Check that they tick the correct activities. In stronger classes, students can do the same exercise in pairs.

3 (10.3) Students look at the text and the list of free time activities. Students work individually, read the text and decide if the activity is mentioned in the text or not. Students tick the activities that are mentioned. Students compare their answers in pairs. Play the audio for students to listen and check. Go through answers as a class.

> **Answers**
> 1 ✓   3 ✓   4 ✓   6 ✓   8 ✓

4 (10.4) Write: *also* on the board. Write: *They also go to the park.* Point at the first word you wrote (*also*) and elicit the pronunciation. Move your pen slowly across the sentence, encouraging students to shout *Stop!* when you get to *also*. Circle it in the sentence.

Focus on the words in bold and the sentences in the book. Say: *Read and circle*. Students work individually, read and circle the words. Play the audio for students to listen and check. Ask a student to read the sentences aloud.

5 Write: *also* on the board. Write: *on also and so also*. Point at the first word you wrote (*also*) and elicit the pronunciation. Move your pen slowly across the words, encouraging students to shout *Stop!* when you get to *also*. Circle it twice.

Focus on the words in bold in the book. Say: *Read and circle*. Students work individually, read and circle the words.

> **NOTICE**
>
> Focus on the NOTICE box. Read through the information as a class. Point at the prepositions. Students look at the text in Exercise 3 and circle all the prepositions.

6 (10.5) Write: *I talk at the phone with my family.* Write a cross next to the sentence. Move your pen along the sentence, encouraging students to shout *Stop!* at the mistake (wrong preposition – *at*). Cross it out and write the correct word (*on*). Ask a student to read the correct sentence aloud.

Students work individually, read the sentences in the book and circle the mistakes with prepositions. They write the correct prepositions next to the sentences. Play the audio for students to listen and check. Go through answers as a class.

> **Answers**
> 2 to for   3 for at   4 on to   5 at on

> **NOTICE**
>
> Focus on the NOTICE box. Read through the information as a class. Point at the use of *and* and *also* when joining two positive sentences to show agreement between them. Explain that the only difference is in the way we form the sentences: *and* joins sentences to make one; *also* keeps two sentences separate. Students look at the text in Exercise 3 and underline all instances of *also* and *and*.

7 (10.6) Focus on the completed example. Ask a student to read it aloud. Students work individually, read the chunks of language and put these in order to create sentences. Play the audio for students to listen and check. Go through answers as a class.

> **Answers**
> 2 I also go shopping.
> 3 I also have a picnic.
> 4 I also go for a walk.

WRITING CHALLENGE

8 Focus on the list of free time activities for Salma. Ask a student to read out the model text. Focus on the rubric and read it aloud. Students work individually and write four free time activities they enjoy. They use their notes to write four sentences. If possible, students should use *also* in some of their sentences. Monitor and help as necessary. Check that students are writing in the correct position on the lines. Students swap notebooks and check each other's writing for correct language, spelling and punctuation.

LISTENING AND READING 2

Learning objectives

- Read and understand verbs for free time activities – *sleep, draw, chat, wait*
- Review verb-noun phrases for free time activities – *go shopping, take photographs, watch TV, write a blog, drive a car, learn new languages, travel to different countries, buy clothes*
- Read and understand sentences with *like* + *-ing* to describe what people like doing – *She likes cooking.*
- Spell verbs with *-ing* correctly
- Write four sentences to describe free time activities a friend likes doing – *Shadi likes chatting with friends. He also likes sleeping. He does not like waiting. He does not like talking on the phone.*

See p. 19 for suggestions on how to use these Learning objectives in your lessons.

Lead-in

Revise all the free time activities taught in the previous lesson. You will need printable flashcards with free time activities (Flashcards 10.1), which can be printed at esource.cambridge.org.

Draw a smiley and a sad face on the board with the phrases below.

go for a walk, bake cakes, have a picnic, do exercise, talk on the phone, go to the park, visit friends and family, go shopping

Ask students to work in pairs and decide on activities that they both like and do not like doing. Students write the words under the smiley or sad faces in their notebooks. Compare answers as a class.

Vocabulary Pre-teaching / Review

You will need printable flashcards with *wait, sleep, draw, chat online* (Flashcards 10.2), which can be printed at esource.cambridge.org.

Follow the procedure on p. 15.

Expand on the new vocabulary by asking students to create phrases. Write the words below in two columns on the board.

wait	pictures
sleep	online
draw	a lot
chat	for friends

Students work in pairs and match the words to create phrases. Make sure students match in such a way that each verb is used only once. Elicit students' ideas and draw lines to create phrases (wait for friends, sleep a lot, draw pictures, chat online). Ask students if they can create any other phrases (wait a lot, draw a lot, draw for friends, chat a lot).

1 🔊 10.7 Focus on the pictures and the words. Students work individually, look at the pictures and trace the words. Play the audio for students to listen and repeat. Ask a student to read the words aloud.

> ### 👁 Common student errors
> **Missing words:** Arabic L1 students often miss the preposition *for* in the phrase *wait for somebody*. This is the typical error: *wait friends*.
>
> To focus students on this word, include the exercise below in your lesson.
>
> Write these sentences on the board:
> 1 *He often waits his friends.*
> 2 *He often waits for his friends.*
>
> Students work in pairs and analyze each sentence. Tell them that only one is correct (2). Erase the incorrect sentence from the board.

2 🔊 10.8 The aim of this exercise is to revise all free time activities from previous units. Point at the completed example. Students work individually, look at the photographs, the words in the box and complete the phrases. Play the audio for students to listen and check. Go through answers as a class. Ask a student to read the phrases aloud.

> ### Answers
> 2 <u>go</u> shopping 3 <u>take</u> photographs 4 <u>watch</u> TV
> 5 <u>write</u> a blog 6 <u>learn</u> new languages
> 7 <u>travel</u> to different countries 8 <u>buy</u> new clothes

SOUND AND SPELLING Review

3 🔊 10.9 Write the vowels *a, e, i, o* on the board. Remind students how to write the letters if required. Write: *bake, take* and *write* on the board. Students read these words aloud. Correct their pronunciation if required. Move your pen slowly across the words, encouraging students to shout *Stop!* when you get to a vowel. Circle all the vowels in the words. Point to *e* at the end of each of the words, cup your ear and ask: *Can you hear* e? (no). Say the words aloud a few times. Elicit from students which word has a different sound (write /aɪ/).

Point at the words in the box. Say: *Match and write.* Students work individually, read the words in the box and match them to the words with the same sound. Students compare their answers in pairs. Play the audio for students to

FREE TIME AND FASHION UNIT 10

listen and check their answers. Students then read the words aloud, focusing on the vowel sounds (languages, travel /æ/; take /eɪ/; drive, write /aɪ/; go /əʊ/). Go through answers as a class.

| Answers
| 1 travel 2 take 3 drive, write 4 go

4 ◀) 10.10 Focus on the dialogue and the pictures. Say: *Listen and read*. Play the audio for students to read and listen to the dialogue. Focus on the photographs with boxes and say: *Write T for Tariq or O for Omar*. Point out the completed example. Students work individually, read the dialogue again, look at the pictures and decide who does each activity. Students compare their answers in pairs. Play the audio again if required. Go through answers as a class.

| Answers
| 2 O 3 O 4 T 5 O 6 T

> **NOTICE**
>
> Focus on the NOTICE box. Read through the information with students. Point at the use of the verb *like* in negative and affirmative sentences for different subject pronouns. Remind students about using short verb forms for speaking and full verb forms for writing.

SOUND AND SPELLING -ing

5 Write: *watch, bake, chat* on the board. Write: *-ing* next to the words. Say: *I like watching TV. I like baking. I like chatting with friends.* pointing at each verb on the board as you say its -ing form. Add -ing to the three verbs on the board. Write: *watch + -ing watching*. Then write: *bake + -ing bakeing* and *chat + -ing chatting*. Point at the three spelling patterns.

Students work individually, read the verbs and write them with -ing, following the spelling patterns. Write the correct answers on the board.

> **Literacy tip**
>
> In general, verbs ending in *consonant + one vowel + consonant* (CVC) need to double the final consonant to make the -ing form, e.g. *chat → chatting*. Not doing so would affect the sound of the vowel in most words. It is worth showing this rule on the board so students can see when to double the consonant. Write the alphabet on the board divided into consonants and vowels. Write the words *chat* and *travel* on the board. Spell each word out, pointing at the letters in the two alphabet groups to show how the last three letters switch from group to group. Write *CVC* under the last three letters in each word. It is important that students start to realize that English spelling is highly rule-based, even though most rules have a few exceptions.

6 Focus on the photographs, the gapped sentences and the completed example. Students work individually, read the sentences, look at the photographs with ticks and crosses, and complete the gaps. Students compare their answers in pairs. Write the sentences on the board. Ask a student to read the sentences aloud.

| Answers
| 2 likes travelling
| 3 don't like chatting
| 4 doesn't like taking

WRITING CHALLENGE

7 Focus on the photograph, the notes and the model text. Ask a student to read the model aloud. Focus on the empty notes box with ticks and crosses. Students work individually and write about their friend. Students then use their notes and the model text to write four sentences about their friend. Monitor students' handwriting and help with any grammar or spelling problems.

> **Optional activity**
>
> Ask students to write four more sentences, but this time about their own likes and dislikes. Then ask them to swap with another student and change the sentences into the third person. Check that students use correct grammar and spelling. Finish by getting students to read the sentences about their partner aloud.

UNLOCK BASIC LITERACY TEACHER'S BOOK 135

LISTENING AND READING 3

Learning objectives

- Read and write words for clothes – *to wear, a coat, a jacket, a dress, a shirt, a scarf, a hat, trousers*
- Read and understand sentences about clothes – *These are my new shoes. This is my dress.*
- Understand the difference between *these* and *this* with plural and singular nouns – *These are my trousers. This is my coat.*
- Review consonant sound and spelling relations

See p. 19 for suggestions on how to use these Learning objectives in your lessons.

Lead-in

Encourage students to discuss the topic of clothes and fashion. Write the questions below on the board.

How often do you buy new shoes?
How often do you buy new clothes?
Where do you buy new shoes?
Where do you buy new clothes?
Do you like buying clothes and shoes?

Students work in pairs and ask and answer the questions. In weaker classes, write adverbs of frequency (*never, always, sometimes,* etc.) and shopping places (*market, online, shopping centre*) on the board for students to match to the questions. Discuss the questions as a class.

Vocabulary Pre-teaching / Review

You will need printable flashcards with clothes (Flashcards 10.3), which can be printed at esource.cambridge.org.

Follow the procedure on p. 15.

Say: *a jacket, a hat, trousers, a coat, a shirt*. Students listen carefully and remember the words you say. Hold up each flashcard with a picture of an item of clothing one by one. Students say *yes* if you said this word aloud. Elicit the five pieces of clothing you said and write them on the board.

1 🔊 10.11 Focus on the photographs and the words. Make sure students understand the meanings. Play the audio for students to listen and read. Students work individually, trace and then write the words. Monitor students' handwriting. Play the audio again for students to listen and repeat.

Optional activity

For this activity, you will need flashcards with clothes (Flashcards 10.3), which can be printed at esource.cambridge.org. You need the sides with photographs.

Draw the crossword below on the board but without any letters in it. Show students flashcards in this order: shirt, dress, coat, shoes, jacket, T-shirt, scarf. Elicit the words and insert them into the crossword one by one. Students spell the words for you. Students say the clothes word running vertically in the crossword (trousers). You could ask students after each horizontal word whether they can guess the mystery clothing item running vertically.

S	H	I	R	T			
			D	R	E	S	S
			C	O	A	T	
				U			
				S	H	O	E	S
J	A	C	K	E	T		
T-	S	H	I	R	T		
				S	C	A	R	F

2 🔊 10.12 Focus on the photographs and the words in the box. Students work individually, look at the photographs and complete the word shapes. Play the audio for students to listen and check. Students work individually and trace the words. Monitor students' handwriting.

Answers
1 scarf 2 T-shirt, jeans 3 shoes

3 🔊 10.13 Play the audio. Elicit the pieces of clothing mentioned and write them on the board (coat, scarf, shoes).

Play the audio again for students to read and listen to the dialogue. Students work individually, read the sentences, refer back to the dialogue and complete the gaps with the words in the box. Go through answers as a class.

Answers
1 beautiful 2 Turkey, expensive 3 the USA, old

FREE TIME AND FASHION — UNIT 10

NOTICE

Focus on the NOTICE box. Read through the information as a class. Point at the use of *this is* for singular and *these are* for plural nouns. Students look at the dialogue in Exercise 3 and circle all the instances of *this is* and *these are*.

4 🔊 10.14 Write: *This is / These are my new scarf.* on the board. Point at the word *scarf* and ask: *How many?* (one). Elicit which option is correct for this singular noun (This is). Circle the correct answer.

Students work individually, read the sentences in the book and underline the correct options. Play the audio for students to listen and check. Go through answers as a class. Students then trace the correct options.

Answers

2 This is 3 This is 4 These are
5 These are 6 These are

SOUND AND SPELLING Review

5 🔊 10.15 Focus on the photographs and words. Use the photographs to check meaning. Play the audio for students to listen and read, then let them trace the letters. Play the audio again for students to listen and repeat. Students read each group of words aloud focusing on producing the sounds correctly.

6 🔊 10.16 Focus on the sentences. Say: *Listen and read.* Play the audio for students to listen and read the sentences. Tell them not to write anything yet. Say: *Listen and write.* Play the audio again for students to listen and write the missing letters. Go through answers as a class. Students read the sentences aloud.

Answers

1 The trousers are from France. The dress and glasses are from Greece.
2 They live near the shops and the airport. I live near the park, bank and the station.
3 He watches TV and plays video games. He doesn't take photographs.

Literacy tip

Mastering the sounds of consonant clusters such as *fr*, *ph*, *tch*, *rk*, etc., will help students to be more easily understood, with less strain for the listener. It also helps students build an awareness of the patterns of English spelling.

SPELLING CHALLENGE

7 🔊 10.17 Focus on the words with spelling mistakes. Say: *Look and correct.* Students work individually and correct the spelling mistakes. Play the audio for students to listen and check. Students compare their answers in pairs. Go through answers as a class.

Answers

2 student 3 drink 4 lunch

LANGUAGE FOCUS

Learning objectives

- Read and write colours – *red, blue, yellow, green, black, white*
- Review sound and spelling relationships with colours
- Read and understand sentences with possessive *'s* – *This is Hassan's jacket.*
- Review joining sentences with *and*, *but* and *also*

See p. 19 for suggestions on how to use these Learning objectives in your lessons.

Lead-in

Revise all the words for clothes taught in the previous lesson. Write on the board the words with letters out of order as below. Students work in pairs and guess what the words are. Ask them not to write anything. Elicit all the words and write them on the board.

toac (coat)

jateck (jacket)

ssred (dress)

shrit (shirt)

acsrf (scarf)

aht (hat)

Vocabulary Pre-teaching / Review

You will need printable flashcards with colours (Flashcards 10.4), which can be printed at esource.cambridge.org.

Follow the procedure on p. 15.

Elicit different colours of items around the classroom: board pens, clothes, etc. Students find things in a particular colour.

1 🔊 10.18 Focus on the pictures of colours and the words. Play the audio for students to listen and read. Students work individually and trace the words. Monitor and check students' handwriting.

2 🔊 **10.19** 👤 Students cover Exercise 1. Focus on the photographs and sentences. Students work individually, look at the photographs and match the sentences. Play the audio for students to listen and check. Go through answers as a class.

> **Answers**
> a 5 b 4 c 3 d 2 e 6 f 1

> **Optional activity**
> This is a quick and fun psychology-based activity. Say colours which are written in a different colour on the board, e.g. *green* in a blue pen, *red* in a black pen, etc. Point at the words rapidly and get students to try to say them. If they can do it easily, it suggests that they have not yet internalized the meanings – native speakers do this much more slowly than when they are written in the same colour.

SOUND AND SPELLING Review

3 🔊 **10.20** 👤 Write: *three* on the board. Underline the double *ee*. Students think of a colour that also has double *ee* in the spelling (green). Write it on the board and say both words.

Students work individually, look at the words in the box and match them to the words with the same spelling patterns. Play the audio for students to listen and check. Go through answers as a class.

> **Answers**
> 2 black 3 white 4 red, yellow

4 👤👥 Focus on the photographs, texts and the options with boxes. Students work individually, read the texts and tick the correct options to complete sentences. Students compare their answers in pairs. Go through answers as a class.

> **Answers**
> 1 blue, old 2 white, from the UK

> **NOTICE**
> Write: *My sister's shirt is white.* on the board. Read the sentence aloud. Say: *Is it my shirt?* (no). Point at my sister and say: *My sister – it is her shirt. It is my sister's shirt.* Circle the apostrophe and possessive *'s*.
>
> Focus on the NOTICE box. Read through the information as a class. Point at the use of possessive *'s*. Students look at the texts in Exercise 4 and circle all the instances of the possessive *'s*.

> 👁 **Common student errors**
>
> **Punctuation:** Arabic L1 students often miss the apostrophe whenever a possessive *'s* is required. They often confuse the plural noun form with the possessive *'s*. This is an example of the typical error: *My sisters coat is blue.*
>
> To focus students on possessive *'s*, do the exercise below.
>
> Write these sentences on the board:
> 1 *His fathers shoes are expensive.*
> 2 *His father's shoes are expensive.*
> Students work in pairs and analyze each sentence. Tell them that only one is correct (2). Students tell you which one is correct and which one has a mistake. Erase the incorrect sentence from the board.

5 🔊 **10.21** 👤 Write: *This is my sister shirt.* on the board. Write a cross next to the sentence. Elicit from students where the mistake is (possessive *'s* missing). Write the correct answer on the board (*This is my sister's shirt.*).

Students work individually, read the sentences and insert the possessive *'s*. Play the audio for students to listen and check. Go through answers as a class.

> **Answers**
> 2 These are Simon's trousers.
> 3 My father's coat is green.
> 4 Laila's scarf is yellow.

6 🔊 **10.22** 👤👥 Write: *My T-shirt is new, I do not like the colour.* on the board. Write: *and but also* next to the sentence. Elicit what is missing from the sentence (but). Write the correct answer on the board (*My T-shirt is new, but I do not like the colour.*). Indicate the two halves of the sentences and point out that one is affirmative and the other negative, so we use *but* to join them. Remind students that *and* and *also* have the same meaning, but *and* joins two sentences into one, and *also* is used for two separate sentences.

Students work individually, read the sentences and insert *and*, *but* or *also*. Students compare their answers in pairs. Play the audio for students to listen and check. Go through answers as a class.

> **Answers**
> 1 and 2 also 3 but 4 and

FREE TIME AND FASHION — **UNIT 10**

SOUND AND SPELLING Review

7 🔊 **10.23** 👤 Focus on the pictures and words and check that students understand the meanings by looking at the pictures. Play the audio for students to listen and read, then let them trace the letters. Play the audio again for students to listen and repeat. Students read each group of words aloud, focusing on producing the sounds correctly.

8 🔊 **10.24** 👥 Students look at the gapped sentences. Say: *Listen and read*. Play the audio for students to read and listen to the sentences. Say: *Listen and write*. Play the audio again for students to listen and write the missing letters. Students compare their answers in pairs. Write the sentences on the board.

> **Answers**
> 1 He <u>ex</u>ercises at h<u>ome</u>. He also goes sh<u>o</u>pping and ch<u>a</u>ts on the ph<u>one</u>.
> 2 She wr<u>ite</u>s a bl<u>o</u>g about her c<u>ou</u>ntry.
> 3 I l<u>ike</u> th<u>e</u>se gr<u>ee</u>n tr<u>ou</u>sers.

LISTENING FOCUS

Learning objectives
- Review key vocabulary as preparation for listening
- Listen for main ideas
- Listen for detail

See p. 19 for suggestions on how to use these Learning objectives with your students.

Lead-in
Write: *I like …* and *My favourite …* on the board. Draw a smiley face next to the word *like* and an even more smiley face next to the word *favourite*. Explain the meaning of the word *favourite*; encourage students to use a dictionary if they have any problems with the meaning.
Write these sentences on the board:
My favourite food is …
My favourite colour is …
My favourite city is …
My favourite subject is …
Students work in pairs and complete the sentences by sharing ideas about their favourite things. Monitor and help as necessary. Discuss the sentences with the whole class. Write a few ideas on the board. What is the class's favourite food/colour/city/subject?

1 🔊 **10.25** 👤 Focus on the topics and ask students to read them aloud. Say: *Listen and tick*. Play the audio for students to listen and tick what it is about. Play the audio again if required. Go through answers as a class.

> **Answer**
> 5 Mr Raman's free time

2 🔊 **10.26** 👥 Focus on the photographs. Elicit what the photographs represent (do exercise, a watch, cook, shop online, go to the park, a bag, chat, hot, have dinner). Say: *Listen and number*. Point out the completed example. Play the audio for students to listen and number the photographs in the order they hear them. Play the audio again if required. Students compare their answers in pairs. Go through answers as a class.

> **Answers**
> a 4 b 8 c 2 d 7 e 6 f 9 h 5 i 3

3 🔊 **10.26** 👥 Focus on the sentences with options. Students read them and see if they remember any answers from the audio played in Exercise 2. Say: *Listen and circle*. Play the audio again for students to listen and circle the correct options. Students compare their answers in pairs. Go through answers as a class.

> **Answers**
> 1 family 2 Saturday 3 hot 4 summer 5 always
> 6 father's 7 doesn't like 8 blue

Optional activity
Aural gap fill: Follow the procedure on p. 17 with the sentences below.
(These) shoes are new and expensive.
(There) are a lot of books in this library.
(This) is my favourite jacket.
(They) are from Japan.

👁 KEY WORDS FOR LITERACY

Learning objectives
- Read, spell and pronounce key words for literacy – *this, these, they, their*

Complete the sentences with the key words for literacy

1 🔊 10.27 👤 Write: *this* on the board. Write this sentence: *This is my coat.* Point at the first word you wrote (this) and elicit the pronunciation. Move your pen slowly across the sentence from left to right, encouraging students to shout *Stop!* when you get to *this*. Circle it in the sentence.

Focus on the words in bold and the sentences in the book. Say: *Read and circle.* Students work individually, read and circle the words. Play the audio for students to listen and check. Ask a student to read the sentences aloud.

2 👤 Write: *this* on the board. Write: *these this think these this*. Point at the first word you wrote (this) and elicit the pronunciation. Move your pen slowly across the words, encouraging students to shout *Stop!* when you get to *this*. Circle it twice.

Focus on the words in bold in the book. Say: *Read and circle.* Students work individually, read and circle the words.

3 👤 Students work individually, cover and complete the words. If necessary, prompt them to use something to cover the words on the left as they complete each one. Monitor and check that they are working from left to right. Encourage correct stroke direction and correct height and position of the individual letters.

4 🔊 10.28 👤👥 Focus on the gapped sentences. Play the audio for students to listen and complete the gaps. Students compare their answers in pairs. Play the audio again for students to listen and check. Write the sentences on the board. Ask a student to read the sentences aloud.

> **Answers**
> 1 These 2 They 3 their 4 This

READING AND WRITING

Learning objectives
- Read and understand main ideas in online forum responses
- Read for detail
- Complete and write sentences about your free time in an email – *In my free time, I like talking on the phone. I also like doing exercise at home, but I do not like watching TV.*

See p. 19 for suggestions on how to use these Learning objectives with your students.

Lead-in
Write these activities on the board:

watching TV, travelling, visiting friends and family, going online, baking cakes, cooking, going to the park, going shopping, learning new languages

Tell students what you like and do not like doing in your free time. You can tell them your real likes and dislikes or read the text below. Students listen carefully and remember the activities you like and do not like. Once you finish, elicit which activities you mentioned and whether you like them or not. Write ticks and crosses above the activities on the board (travelling ✓, visiting friends and family ✓, cooking ✓, baking cakes ✗, going to the park ✓).

In my free time, I like travelling and visiting friends and family. I sometimes like cooking, but I don't like baking cakes. I also like going to the park.

1 🔊 10.29 👤 Focus on the text, the names and the words to match. Say: *Look and match. Don't read!* Encourage students to look at the text really quickly and find information by focusing on the words to match. Students work individually, look at the text quickly and match the names to the words. Say: *Read and check.* Students read the text slowly and check that they matched the names and words correctly. Go through answers as a class. Play the audio for students to read and listen to the text.

> **Answers**
> Abdul: 2, 3, 5
> Miriam: 1, 4, 6

FREE TIME AND FASHION — UNIT 10

2 Students look again at the text in Exercise 1. Point at the sentences with boxes. Students work individually, read the text again and decide if the sentences are true (✓) or false (✗). Students compare their answers in pairs. Check the ticks and crosses as a class. Write the wrong sentences (1, 4, 6 and 7) on the board. Students then correct the false sentences in pairs. Ask them to refer back to the text if required. Write the corrected sentences on the board.

Answers
1 ✗ Abdul likes learning new languages.
2 ✓
3 ✓
4 ✗ Abdul's T-shirt is green.
5 ✓
6 ✗ Miriam's coat is from Spain.
7 ✗ Miriam does not like cooking dinner.

3 Focus on the survey and Hessa's answers. Ask a student to read them aloud. Check that students understand the meanings. Ask: *What does Hessa like doing in her free time?* Elicit the answers (talking on the phone, doing exercise). Ask: *What clothes does Hessa like wearing?* Elicit the answers (dress, scarf). Focus on the email and the gaps. Say: *Look* (pointing at the survey) *and complete the email.* Students work individually and write the answers in the gaps. Check the answers as a class.

Answers
1 phone, exercise, watching
2 scarf, sister's

4 Focus on the empty survey. Say: *Answer the questions* and point at the student survey to complete. Students work individually and complete the notes in the survey. Remind students that they can refer to the model text in Exercise 3. Students then use their notes and the model text to complete the email. Monitor students' handwriting and assist with grammar and spelling. Read out a few examples of emails as a class.

Model answer
To: freetime@university.ac.ae
Subject: Free time survey
Hi,
These are my answers to the survey.
1 In my free time, I like travelling. I also like reading books, but I do not like reading blogs.
2 I like wearing trousers and a shirt. I do not like wearing a hat.
Regards,
Luiz

⊙ Common student errors

Missing words: Arabic L1 students often miss the articles *a* and *an* before clothes. This is an example of the typical error: *I like wearing trousers and shirt.*

To practise articles in sentences, do the exercise below.

Write these sentences on the board:

I like wearing trousers and shirt / a shirt.

I do not like wearing a dress / dress and a scarf / scarf.

Students work in pairs and analyze each sentence and the options. Tell them that only one option is correct. Students tell you which one is correct. Circle the correct answers (a shirt, a dress, a scarf).

Optional activity

Draw the table below on the board. Students each read their email aloud. If appropriate in your context, ask a student to come to the board and make notes of likes and dislikes while students are reading their emails aloud. If not appropriate, make notes yourself. Once all emails are read, compare students' likes and dislikes and clothes preferences and ask them to choose one activity that all or most students like and dislike. Encourage students to compare their ideas.

Student's name	Likes	Does not like	Clothes

Objectives review

See Teaching tips on p. 19 for ideas about using the Objectives review with your students.

WORDLIST

See Teaching tips on p. 21 for ideas about using the Wordlist on p. 143 with your students.

REVIEW TEST

See esource.cambridge.org for the Review test and ideas about how and when to administer the Review test.

WORDLISTS

UNIT 1

Bahrain
book
country
dictionary
email address
family name
first name
India
Japan
library card
Mexico
mobile phone
name
notebook
pen
pencil
phone number
Portugal
Saudi Arabia
spell
student
student ID card
teacher
the UAE
the UK
Turkey

UNIT 2

bag
brother
camera
car
computer
Dr
doctor
family
father
grandfather
grandmother
mother
Mr
Mrs
sister
television

UNIT 3

Biology
boring
Business
Chemistry
day
difficult
easy
English
Friday
History
interesting
IT
Japanese
Maths
Monday
o'clock
room
Saturday
subject
Sunday
Thursday
time
Tuesday
Wednesday

UNIT 4

beautiful
big
cheap
city
clean
cold
country
dry
expensive
hot
new
old
small
warm
wet

UNIT 5

April
August
bank manager
December
dentist
exam
February
finish work / classes
first day of university
go home
go to university
go to the library
go to work
help people
January
July
June
March
May
meet friends
meet people
November
nurse
October
photographer
pilot
police officer
read emails
September
start work / classes
summer holiday
take photographs
travel to different countries
winter holiday
work in the city
write emails

UNIT 6

bread
busy
cheese
coffee
coffee with milk and sugar
drink
drive to work
eat
fine
fish
fruit
fruit and vegetables
get up
get up early
go to bed
go to bed late
great
green tea
have breakfast
have dinner
have lunch
healthy
hungry
juice
meat
not bad
not well
red meat
rice
salad
tea
tired
vegetables
walk to university
water

WORDLISTS

UNIT 7

airport
bank
beach
beautiful beaches
between
building
busy square
factory
famous stadium
hospital
hotel
house
interesting market
near
next to
office building
old streets
on the left
on the right
park
restaurant
shop
shopping centre
tall buildings
train station

UNIT 8

at the market
at the shopping centre
bank card
buy
buy clothes
buy shoes
buy things on the internet
day
dirhams
dollars
euros
go shopping
How much is … ?
hundred
laptop
million
month
newspaper
on the internet
once a day
once a week
pay by card
pay by cash
pounds
riyals
smartphone
spend money
T-shirt
tablet
thousand
twice a week
video game
watch
week
year

UNIT 9

adult
boy
buy apps
child
children
cook
fridge
girl
go online
glasses
hour
learn English online
look at websites
man
men
minute
people
person
play video games
second
send messages
smartwatch
tablet
use GPS
watch webinars
woman
women
write a blog

UNIT 10

bake cakes
black
blue
chat online
coat
do exercise
draw
dress
favourite
go for a walk
go to the park
green
hat
have a picnic
jacket
red
scarf
shirt
sleep
talk on the phone
trousers
visit friends and family
wait
wear
white
yellow

ACKNOWLEDGEMENTS

Publisher acknowledgements

The publishers are extremely grateful to the following people for reviewing this course during its development. The course had benefited hugely from your insightful comments and feedback.

Ashwaq Al-Jahlan, Princess Noura University, Saudi Arabia; Peggy Alptekin; Dr. Wafa Aws, Dar Al Uloom, Saudi Arabia; Anil Bayir, Izmir University, Turkey; Patrick Boylan, King Abdulaziz University, Saudi Arabia; Pauline Chahine, Qatar Armed Forces, Qatar; Esengul Hasdemir, Atilim University, Turkey; Dr Anwar Jamal, Kuwait University, Kuwait; Megan Putney, Dhofar University, Oman; Tracy Quayat, Princess Noura Univeristy, Saudi Arabia; Katherine Rick, Lincoln College, Saudi Arabia; Hussein Saeed, Jubail Industrial College, Saudi Arabia

The authors and publishers acknowledge the following sources of copyright material and are grateful for the permissions granted. While every effort has been made, it has not always been possible to identify the sources of all the material used, or to trace all copyright holders. If any omissions are brought to our notice, we will be happy to include the appropriate acknowledgements on reprinting and in the next update to the digital edition, as applicable.

p. 10 (phone): rasslava/iStock/Getty Images Plus/Getty Images; p. 10 (bone): Dave King/Dorling Kindersley/Getty Images; p. 10 (rope): gokhanilgaz/E+/Getty Images; p. 10 (computer): deliormanli/E+/Getty Images; p. 10 (kitten): Jane Burton/Dorling Kindersley/Getty Images; p. 10 (tube): AndreaAstes/iStock/Getty Images Plus/Getty Images; p. 10 (desert): JayKay57/E+/Getty Images; p. 10 (fish): Franco Banfi/WaterFrame/Getty Images; p. 10 (lock): futureimage/iStock/Getty Images Plus/Getty Images; p. 10 (stealing): jaroon/E+/Getty Images; p. 10 (bathrobe): dmitriymoroz/iStock/Getty Images Plus/Getty Images; p. 10 (note): Martina Gruber/EyeEm/Getty Images; p. 10 (knife): leschnyhan/iStock/Getty Images Plus/Getty Images; p. 10 (house): Mlenny/iStock/Getty Images Plus/Getty Images; p. 10 (reading): Blend Images - Hill Street Studios/Brand X Pictures/Getty Images; p. 10 (perfume): kevinjeon00/E+/Getty Images; p. 10 (hole): drxy/iStock/Getty Images Plus/Getty Images; p. 10 (globe): EMPPhotography/E+/Getty Images; p. 11 (station): Marcos Ferro/Aurora/Getty Images; p. 11 (train): LeoPatrizi/iStock/Getty Images Plus/Getty Images; p. 11 (street): Pinghung Chen/EyeEm/Getty Images; p. 11 (student): Klaus Vedfelt/DigitalVision/Getty Images; p. 11 (stairs): Glow Decor/Glow/Getty Images; p. 11 (star): chaofann/iStock/Getty Images Plus/ Getty Images; p. 11 (tree): Liesel Bockl/Getty Images; p. 11 (traffic jam): Kichigin/iStock/Getty Images Plus/Getty Images; p. 11 (trolley): itsskin/E+/Getty Images; p. 11 (weight): ULU_BIRD/iStock/Getty Images Plus/Getty Images; p. 11 (string): fotyma/iStock/Getty Images Plus/Getty Images; p. 11 (arrow): LeonidKos/iStock/Getty Images Plus/Getty Images; p. 12 (Tokyo): Hal Bergman/DigitalVision/Getty Images; p. 12 (jeep): Multi-bits/Photolibrary/Getty Images; p. 12 (teacher): erkan523/iStock/Getty Images Plus/Getty Images; p. 21: Katarina Premfors/arabianEye/Getty Images; p. 25 (BL): DUEL/Cultura/Getty Images; p. 25 (BR): Jon Feingersh/Blend Images/Getty Images.

Cover Photography by David Kirkland/Perspectives/Getty Images; (woman): Jenny Acheson/Stockbyte/Getty Images; (whiteboard): Nemida/iStock/Getty Images Plus/Getty Images.

Corpus

Development of this publication has made use of the Cambridge English Corpus (CEC). The CEC is a multi-billion word computer database of contemporary spoken and written English. It includes British English, American English, and other varieties of English. It also includes the Cambridge Learner Corpus, developed in collaboration with the University of Cambridge ESOL Examinations. Cambridge University Press has built up the CEC to provide evidence about language use that helps to produce better language teaching materials.

Typeset by emc design ltd.

CODE FOR TESTS

The code for the *Unlock Basic Literacy* tests is:

UBLtests-7201

Instructions for e-Source and the code for the course audio, Presentation Plus, and additional printable material are on the inside of the front cover.